The Student's Guide to Doing Research on the Internet

Dave and Mary Campbell

Addison-Wesley Publishing Company

Reading, Massachusetts • Menlo Park, California • New York
Don Mills, Ontario • Wokingham, England • Amsterdam
Bonn • Sydney • Singapore • Tokyo • Madrid • San Juan
Paris • Seoul • Milan • Mexico City • Taipei

Many of the designations used by manufacturers and sellers to distinguish their products are claimed as trademarks. Where those designations appear in this book, and Addison-Wesley was aware of a trademark claim, the designations have been printed in initial capital letters or all capital letters.

The authors and publishers have taken care in preparation of this book, but make no expressed or implied warranty of any kind and assume no responsibility for errors or omissions. No liability is assumed for incidental or consequential damages in connection with or arising out of the use of the information or programs contained herein.

Library of Congress Cataloging-in-Publication Data

Campbell, David R.
     The student's guide to doing research on the Internet /
Dave and Mary Campbell
        p.   cm
     Includes index.
     ISBN 0-201-48916-3 (pbk.)
     1. Report writing—Data processing. 2. Research—Data processing.
    3. Internet (Computer network) I. Campbell, Mary V. II. Title
    LB2369.C28 1996
    808'.02—dc20   95-13498
                                                   CIP

Sponsoring Editor: Kim Fryer
Project Manager: Sarah Weaver
Production Coordinator: Erin Sweeney
Cover design: Jean Seal
Text design: Andrew T. Wilson
Set in 11 point Palatino by Carpenter Graphics

 3 4 5 6 7 8 9-MA-99989796
Second printing, December 1995

Addison-Wesley books are available for bulk purchases by corporations, institutions, and other organizations. For more information please contact the Corporate, Government, and Special Sales Department at (800) 238-9682.

Acknowledgments

W<small>E WOULD LIKE TO THANK</small> the following individuals who offered so much of their time and creative energy in reviewing portions of the manuscript:

Dr. Charlene A. Dykman, University of Houston, Downtown

Professor Hilbert Levitz, Florida State University, Department of
   Computer Science

Professor Mike Nelson, University of Western Ontario, Department of
   Library Information Systems

Dr. Phillip Wirtz, George Washington University, Department of
   Management Science

We realize the significant demands on their time for teaching and other academic responsibilities and want them to know that we feel the manuscript offers much more to students because of their diligent efforts during the review process.

We would also like to thank the many individuals at Addison-Wesley for all of their efforts. Kim Fryer, our acquisitions editor, was a delight to work with, as she has been on all prior book projects. We struggled together to include as much as possible yet still keep this an affordable book for students. Sarah Weaver, project manager, kept the book on a tight production schedule, with the able assistance of production assistant Erin Sweeney and type and design manager John Webber. Susan Riley, our copy editor, did a superb job in dotting i's and crossing t's for us as we all raced against the clock to ensure that this book was available for the fall semester. We would also like to thank John Clelland in the Canadian division. His initial ideas for the scope of the book and his assistance in setting up the review process were a great aid.

Contents

Contents

Introduction

IN THE PAST, COLLEGE STUDENTS had to rely almost exclusively on the resources that were physically on their campus to enhance their program of study. Their learning sphere was dictated by the knowledge of their instructor, the participation of the students in their classes, and the holdings of their campus library. Today, the Internet extends any student's learning resources to schools and organizations around the globe. Students can read articles and text stored on computers in Europe or Australia as easily as they can access materials in their campus library. They can collaborate with students in Norway or Russia or just chat about the ways of campus life in different locations. Although the technology and resources to do all of this are available on many college campuses today, it is primarily the graduate engineering and science students who are tapping into this resource potential. Undergraduate students in all disciplines can reap the benefits offered by the Internet by learning a little about the rules of using it and identifying rich sources of information in specific disciplines that interest them. This book is designed to provide both a basic skill set in using Internet tools and a set of resources in each of the major disciplines to meet the needs of students in any program of study.

ORGANIZATION OF THIS BOOK

This book is organized into two parts. The first discusses the tools that you will use to access Internet resources. You will learn how to establish a Telnet session to tap into a database at a particular site or to participate in a virtual reality session called a MUD. You will learn to use an FTP client on your computer to contact a host computer in a remote location for copies of files in their archives. You will also learn how to use a Gopher client or one of the currently popular Web browsers that extend the capability of the Internet beyond text to video, graphics, and sound.

The second part of the book consists of a series of chapters, each focusing on a major area of study. There are hundreds of sites listed that can be used to support all types of research efforts in these disciplines. You can connect to a site for SEC filings or current stock prices if you are studying business. If you are an English major, you will appreciate some of the online book projects that allow you to tap a vast online source of books. Other professional disciplines such as medicine and law are covered, as are subjects in the arts and humanities. Finally, at the end you will find an appendix of sites that can help you land your first job when you complete your program of study.

EXAMPLES IN THE BOOK

Most of the screens in this book were captured using the Netscape browser to access the various sites of interest. Since the Web is the fastest growing segment of the Internet with a growth rate of over 15 percent a month, we felt it was important to show examples of a browser for the Web for those students who do not have current access to one on their campus. We have provided instructions for using all of the Internet tools directly for those students who are either restricted to a UNIX command entry or those who prefer this more direct approach. You can choose the method you prefer to connect to sites listed in the book.

CONVENTIONS USED

There are instructions in some of the first eight chapters that direct user input to perform a specific task. This user input is shown in a monospace font, Courier, to distinguish it from surrounding text.

Unless an entire site is important, the specific document or directory is often included in the address for the site. The possibility exists that the school or organization responsible for the data may reorganize their site between the time we checked its location and you attempt to locate it. If you get a message indicating that a particular document or directory cannot be located, you should specify only the site location and look through the top level menu to locate it. In all likelihood, the data has not been deleted but was simply moved to another directory. As the amount of material at a site grows, it can become necessary to split many directories into two to better categorize the data stored there. If you are having difficulty locating the data, many sites will have a search feature for the site, but you can always fall back on the various search tools that you learned about in the first part of this book.

KEEPING IN TOUCH

As you work with the Internet you are certain to discover some gem sites on your own. If you would like to make any suggestions for future versions of this book, please contact us at drc3@po.cwru.edu. Also, we will be providing you with some new site ideas on a monthly basis at the Addison-Wesley Web site: http://www.aw.com/devpress/campbell. We hope you will find these additions useful as you add to your knowledge about the Internet's vast resources.

Chapter 1

What the Internet Offers the Researcher

THE INTERNET OFFERS THE RESEARCHER access to a vast source of information scattered at locations around the world. It also offers the tools to put these information resources to work for you. The Internet can assist your research efforts whether your research is connected with a college course assignment, a job search, new product development, or self-study efforts to further your learning. If this makes the Internet sound like some magic elixir, good for whatever you need to do, in a sense that is correct. The Internet offers vast stores of text, databases of information, electronic journals, bibliographies, software programs, and forums for information. There are search engines and indexes to locate the information that you need, utilities to transfer data to your system, and browsers to make it easy to view data at many locations. Once you connect to the Internet, everything is offered for a very reasonable monthly rate. For most college students, the connection cost is already built into your tuition and fees; once you are enrolled, the Internet is free. If, however, you're working on research without the benefit of university access to the Internet, there are some low-cost alternatives to tapping into the Internet's power that you'll learn about in Chapter 2.

WHAT IS THE INTERNET?

The most important aspect of the Internet is the information it contains, made possible by an unbelievably large interconnected network of thousands of networks around the world. Although there are critical backbone networks that form its framework and utilize satellite technology and fiber optics to move data at extremely high rates of speeds, thousands of smaller networks are also an integral part of it. The software at these sites make it possible to access the huge repositories of data at various sites on the Internet.

But the Internet is more than machines and software. In a sense, it is actually the millions of people who use it. Many of these individuals have contributed to the information that is available to everyone. Whether you participate in a discussion group, send e-mail, or post a research paper for others to browse, it is really you, your thoughts and creative energies, and the talents of the millions of individuals like you that make the Internet such a worthwhile resource for the researcher. At first, you may use the Internet to glean answers, find resources, and complete your research. However, as you learn more about how to use the tools it provides, you will use the Internet to share your work with others.

NEW RESEARCH DIRECTIONS WITH THE INTERNET

The Internet holds the potential for revolutionizing the way research is done. A quick look at how it eliminates some of the constraints of the past paints a picture of the changes that are just beginning to affect what is possible for students doing research:

- The Internet levels the playing field, making it possible for students at schools with limited resources to access the same material as students in schools with large endowments and well-stocked libraries.

- The Internet is available 24 hours a day, making it possible for the student who leaves work at midnight to be able to work into the wee hours of the morning.

- Its electronic information can be scanned more quickly and thoroughly via the computer than is possible with the human eye. Topics of potential interest can then be read in more detail.

- Students can share ideas with others on the Internet via chat or e-mail. This opportunity to bounce ideas off others often adds creativity to the final efforts.

- Staleness of information is not a problem since current information can be placed there immediately—publishing, shipping, and shelving delays are eliminated.

- Global cross-cultural exchange is facilitated.

Information Source for All Disciplines

There are thousands of sites connected to the Internet. Many of these are large universities with a diverse information base that you can tap from afar. Others are more specialized information sources offered by a specific department within the university or a government agency.

Companies are also quickly establishing sites on the Internet. Although their main objective may be to garner new customers or increase customer loyalty, many have realized that they have to offer something of real value if consumers are going to visit online. For this reason, you'll begin to see more company sites offering something besides their merchandise. For example, a company that provides online stock prices might allow you to get five quotes a day at no charge. Although this isn't sufficient to manage a large portfolio, it might be just what you need for a finance project.

As you will see as you explore the subject areas at the back of this book, the Internet contains resources for all disciplines. Although the sciences may have had a head start in making materials available, other areas are quickly catching up as new Web and Gopher sites are added each day. Since you will also be learning the skills needed to explore Gopher and Web sites on your own in Chapters 5 and 7, you will have the skills needed to chase after new sources of information that are added daily. Here are a few of the Gopher and Web sites that will link you to a variety of resources:

- Uncover's Index to 17,000 periodicals
- The Journal of Statistics Information Service
- The University of Michigan's College of Engineering Technology Transfer Site
- Online Job Listings
- InterNic Internet Directory of Directories

Downloadable Text and Software

Millions of files are stored at Internet sites worldwide. You can find research papers to stimulate your thinking, software tools to save time, graphics to spiff up a presentation, and electronic books and other sources to aid your research efforts. See Chapter 4 for ways to tap the power of FTP to access these files and how to use Archie to locate resources you need. Here are some of the resources available to an Internet user:

- Gopher clients for the PC, Mac, and UNIX environments
- Molecular biology software
- Document collection on UFOs
- Microsoft Systems Journal source files

- Recipes

- Aviation information

Once you've downloaded data that might be able to assist your research efforts, you can use a text editor to scan for entries of particular significance to your work.

Databases of Information

The Internet has huge databases of information. Fortunately, you can use excellent search tools to locate information. For example, Wide Area Information Service (WAIS) can search hundreds of Internet databases. The techniques covered in Chapter 6 give you more searching power than you would have with your own personal research librarian at your side. The following list of a few WAIS sources beginning with the letter "a" suggests how many sources are available:

- Ancient DNA Studies

- Asian Computing

- Aboriginal Studies

- Agricultural Market News

- Ask ERIC Infoguides (Education)

Course Syllabi and Bibliographies

Faculty members at various schools have made course syllabi and bibliographies available on Gopher and Web servers worldwide. Since each faculty member has a different slant on the same course, you may find some research ideas and bibliographic entries that will help with your research projects.

Electronic Journals

Costs of printing and mailing have caused many libraries to scale back their subscriptions to printed journals, and this may limit the resources available in your local libraries. Electronic journals available through the Internet can supplement the resources available to you. Academic journals published through university departments are increasingly moving to an electronic format as it stretches their limited budget and eliminates some of the time lag in making materials available to the academic community. As these journals are more commonly accepted as refereed research outlets for faculty publishing, their numbers will continue to grow. As you learn to use the Internet tools throughout this book, you'll discover how easy it is to work with the electronic form of a journal when you want to search for specific information. Many of the electronic journals are small, specialized publications that may not be available in your library. For example:

- Academe This Week

- Sky and Telescope Weekly News Bulletin

- Air Force News

- GAO Day Sheets

- Malaysia News

- Mathematical and Physical Science Letters

- Physics News Update

Global Collaborators

In the past it was difficult to collaborate with others who shared your research interests. There was no easy way to identify those with similar interests until completed research was published. Print, distribution, and shelving delays meant that the latest studies were not available until your research was completed. The instant availability of online versions of material can cut this lag time and make you aware of the latest developments as you are working. This is more important than ever with technological developments occurring at such a rapid pace that information that is even a few months old can be quite dated in certain fields.

Even if you are aware of others with similar research interests, the long-distance charges for talking with them on a regular basis are too high unless, of course, they live in your dorm or at least the same town. For the average student, participation in national and regional conferences where the latest research results are discussed is also not an option, because registration fees, travel, and hotel charges can quickly exceed almost any student's budget. The Internet changes all this by making it possible to converse with students living on the opposite coast as easily as you converse with a student in the next dorm room. See Chapter 3 for ideas about how e-mail and IRC can put you in touch with the world; see Chapter 8 for ways in which news and discussion groups can connect you with others having similar research interests.

BENEFITS EXTEND BEYOND THE CURRENT PROJECT

Although this book focuses on helping you develop the research skills to get the grades you are looking for in college courses, the skills you will learn extend well beyond your classroom efforts. Businesses are just beginning to think about using the Internet on a large-scale basis, and they will be looking for individuals who are knowledgeable about the Internet and what it offers. In a competitive business environment that faces rapid global change, the need for ongoing research efforts to stay ahead of the competition will increase.

Chapter 2

Getting Connected

IN ORDER TO HAVE ACCESS to the Internet, your computer must be connected to a network that is part of the Internet. Many colleges have already taken care of the connection details for you. It's likely that the computers in your campus computer lab are connected to the Internet. However, colleges with older PCs might not be connected.

In this chapter you'll learn about Internet connections and a few topics that will be applicable to all the Internet tools discussed in Chapters 3 through 8:

- Elements of an Internet connection

- Different types of Internet connections

- Community resources such as freenets that may allow you to connect with the Internet over breaks and vacations

- A connection through a commercial provider

- How Internet addresses uniquely identify each site

- Establishing a command-line connection to another site

TYPES OF CONNECTIONS

There are several ways to connect your computer with the network of Internet sites:

- A direct wire connection from your computer to your campus local area network (LAN)

- A dial-up connection to campus or a local freenet provider that offers Internet access

- A contract with a commercial provider such as Prodigy, Netcom, or Delphi

The easiest connection for you is a hard-wired connection from a computer on campus to a network that is part of the Internet. Response time is much faster when you make a request, and there's no need to deal with the technical details and frustrations of getting software up and running on your system. If you are not so lucky, you can use dial-up connections to either your campus or a third-party provider.

Campus Network

If your PC or workstation is directly connected to your campus network and the network is connected to the Internet, you have full access to everything the Internet offers. You may have a menu for all systems on your network that provides access to a Gopher, the Web, or FTP. You may be able to choose one of these options or work with command-line entries through one of the UNIX servers.

The difference between using the menu to select various tools and working at the command line is similar to the difference between working with DOS through the DOS shell or making command-line entries at the DOS prompt. Some people insist that menus are the only approach that is efficient, while others feel you don't really understand what's happening unless you are typing on the command line. Also, some prefer command-line entries because this approach provides complete flexibility in the services they can access. Others are willing to let the structure of a menu-based system dictate some decisions if the result is less typing. A quick look at menu options for Case Western Reserve University's Weatherhead School of Management shows that students and faculty are fortunate to have both approaches available to them—they can either select Gopher or Web access, or choose to work with the Sun Workstations and connect via command-line entries with options like these:

```
WSOM Sun Workstations
Gopher
World Wide Web
```

Dial-Up Links

If your university supports dorm access to the Internet, it may be from a hard-wired connection to its network. It can also be from a dial-up connection that may also serve students and faculty working from home. A dial-up connection to the university may be from a community freenet or it may be through an Internet Protocol (IP) link. The IP connection provides a much wider array of services, including graphics and sound. Most freenet connections are limited to text access, and some freenets only provide access to Internet's mail capability.

If your connection is hard-wired, you will have access to the same menus that you do from other areas of campus.

Dial-up connection requires a modem to connect your computer to the phone lines. A 14,400-speed modem is currently the best choice to provide satisfactory response times, although you will still find graphical interfaces slow at this speed. You'll also need a communications program that will make your personal computer impersonate a terminal. This process is actually called **emulation** and is required because your campus Internet host is unlikely to be able to communicate with anything other than terminals. A VT-100 terminal is the standard that is emulated. Check with your computer lab on campus to see what communications program they recommend.

You cannot dial up your local Internet host unless your school agreed to act as a dial-up connection point to the Internet and you have installed additional software on your system. The software you install allows for Serial Line Internet Protocol (SLIP) or Point-to-Point Protocol (PPP). Installation can be a tricky process since it requires entering specific information about your Internet host. If this capability is supported at your university, you will be able to get all the specifics from files online in your computer lab. Once this software is installed, your system will have Transmission Control Protocol/Internet Protocol (TCP/IP) capabilities. (Telnet and FTP are just two of the protocols supported when your system has this capability.) You will then be able to obtain freeware and shareware programs to allow you to install Web browsers and other client software on your system.

New software programs such as SlipKnot and the Internet Adapter allow your system to simulate SLIP and PPP protocols with having them implemented on the host system. Hopefully your school has worked out a standard mechanism for all students, and you will be able to follow clear printed instructions that work perfectly the first time you try them.

Freenets

Although freenets are frequently affiliated with a university, their services are available to the community at large. The Cleveland Freenet is one example of a viable freenet and it is affiliated with Case Western Reserve University. It is the oldest freenet and has been a model for systems all over the United States.

Freenets do not provide full access to the Internet as a rule. For example, you will generally not have access to the Web or a Gopher. However, you will always find e-mail services and often find Usenet discussion groups on a wide-ranging list of topics. Also, although FTP may not be directly accessible, you will be able to use the FTP mail capabilities to mail yourself copies of files you need.

Commercial or Third-Party Access

If none of the free options apply in your situation, then a paying option is all that's left. Of course, if you plan to spend the summer in the Smokey Mountains working on your latest research project, paying for access may not seem too bad.

There are many different suppliers to select from. Ideally you want one with a local access number and a flat monthly fee for unlimited connect time. Having to pay a long-distance connect charge or a surcharge for the use of services such as Sprintnet or Tymnet can increase your costs significantly. Although most suppliers are moving toward full access to Internet services, be sure that your supplier provides access to everything. Delphi and NetCom are two of the larger Internet access providers. Table 2-1 lists a few of the national and local suppliers, including the Cleveland Freenet, which allows a login as a guest.

 You can get the most recent list of Internet access providers from Inter-NIC Information Services by sending an e-mail message to info@is.internic.net. Since new services are appearing monthly, you might find a local provider in your area.

Access Provider	Phone Number
Cerfnet	(800) 876-2373
Clark Internet Services	(410) 730-9764
Cleveland Free-Net	(216) 368-3888 Computer connection, login as guest
Delphi	(800) 544-4005
Global Enterprise Services	(800) 358-4437
MIDnet	(402) 472-5032
NetCom	(800) 353-6600
Prodigy	(800) Prodigy
PSI	(703) 620-6651
SURANet	(301) 982-4600

TABLE 2-1. *National and Local Providers*

COMMAND-LINE ACCESS TO A FULL RANGE OF SERVICES

If you either work from a workstation directly connected to the Internet or have SLIP or PPP access, you will most likely be on a UNIX system. You can enter commands at the UNIX prompt and run programs that will connect to remote sites for you. You will need to know a little more about site addresses because most of these commands require you to enter the address of the remote site to which you are connecting.

Although a Telnet session is shown in the example and is one of the most common types of sessions after making a connection, you can run other client programs such as Archie, FTP, or a Web browser.

ADDRESSES FOR INTERNET HOSTS

Each Internet site has a unique electronic address. These addresses are called **domains** and are different from your personal user id. The periods in the domain separate the levels with the highest level listed last. A domain that ends with com indicates a commercial site. Another common high-level site is edu, indicating an educational institution.

Domain and IP addresses identify sites, not users. See Chapter 3 for a discussion of user id's and how they are used in conjunction with a domain address to pinpoint a person's location.

As you move to the left, the next level indicates the name of the school or organization. In the entry po.cwru.edu, the cwru represents Case Western Reserve University; the po indicates the computer at this site that you want to connect to.

There can be more than three levels within the domain because some locations have a department or specific school for level three, and the computer is not identified until level four.

Actually, the names that you type for domains are used as pseudonyms for the real Internet addresses, which are numbers. These numbers are called IP addresses and are not used as frequently as names since they are more difficult for people to remember. If you know the domain address, you can use it to get the IP address and vice versa.

Domain addresses are unlikely to change. When you are looking for a specific document or menu at an address, it is possible that it has been moved or renamed. Connect directly to the site without specifying the document or menu you want and look around on your own to see if you can find it.

TELNET SESSIONS

Telnet is a program that allows you to connect to any Internet host where you have an account. It is available on UNIX and VAX as well as other operating systems. The commands shown here are based on access via a UNIX system, which is the most prevalent (you may have to make a few adjustments if you use another system). Some sites have set up special public access that allows you to access Archie and other tools without an account, even if you do not have a local client program for them.

If the Telnet program is not available on your system and you are using UNIX, check out the rlogin command, which is part of UNIX itself.

To start Telnet once you are logged onto your local system, type **Telnet** followed by the site address that you want to connect to, as in:

```
telnet culine.colorado.edu
```

You can also use the standard IP address for the site as in:

```
telnet 126.58.17.1
```

You will see this message or one like it:

```
Trying....
```

This indicates that the computer was monitoring the port on which you attempted to contact it. The default is port 23 for Telnet sessions. If the host monitors another port for your connection, you will have to specify it in the command, as in:

```
telnet culine.colorado.edu 862
```

Once connected, you will see a message to that effect and the escape character that can be used to temporarily suspend activities.

If you need to temporarily suspend operations at the remote system, press the control key in combination with the escape character shown. You might need to do this if the remote host has not responded for some time. You can then end the Telnet session by typing **close** to end your connection with the current site. It's better to logout from the remote host; however, if it isn't responding, most systems will log you off when the connection is dropped. To open a new site while Telnet is still active, you can type

```
open af.itd.com 6889
```

where af.itd.com is the site name. To quit from Telnet itself, type **quit** instead of **close.**

If you are running under UNIX, you can type **man telnet** *from the UNIX prompt to get more information on Telnet.*

Just for Fun

If you are working late at the library, you might miss your favorite sports games on TV. If you miss the late news, you can get the sports scores if you Telnet culine.colorado.edu. The port you specify determines the scores that are available:

Scores	Port
Baseball	862
Basketball	859
Football	862
Hockey	862

Chapter 3

Collaborating in Cyberspace

ONE OF THE MOST IMPORTANT things the Internet offers you is the ability to connect to others with similar research interests worldwide. When you use the Internet to handle your correspondence, you don't have to worry about the costs of long-distance phone calls or the time delays you experience when you use the post office to mail something. In seconds an e-mail message can travel around the world and be waiting in someone's mailbox.

E-mail is one of the most popular features of the Internet. In fact, prior to 1995 it was the only Internet service that some of the large commercial online suppliers offered. Many people found it worthwhile to subscribe to these services just to have access to the Internet's e-mail features. A whole month of electronic message transmissions might not cost any more than sending one envelope with an overnight carrier—and all of your messages will get to their destination much faster than overnight delivery.

Talk and Internet Relay Chat (IRC) are two other services that can help you connect with research collaborators. With Talk you can connect with another Internet user and chat back and forth in a private conversation. IRC lets you participate in a party-line conversation on a host of topics. Although many conversations sound like gossip and coffee-klatch banter, some are about serious topics. Incidentally, if you speak a language and want to keep your language skills sharp, you can participate in an IRC conducted in a foreign language.

MUDs (Multi-User Dimensions) allow users to interact with others in a virtual reality. Although most of their history has involved games, they are now moving more into the mainstream of educational interaction. They can be used as learning tools for all types of information and for the creation of various types of simulated environments.

In this chapter you will learn to do the following:

- Address and send e-mail messages

- Utilize Chat or IRC to connect with other researchers

- Describe what a MUD offers and learn how you can find out more about them

E-MAIL

The Internet e-mail feature sends messages from one place to another. It is an ideal resource for checking with students at other universities in subject areas of interest or for contacting professors doing research in an area you are studying.

There are two parts to a functioning e-mail system on your system: a transport agent to send your messages out over the Internet and a user agent that you work with to read and write messages. You don't need to worry too much about the transport agent since it is standardized and runs in the background waiting to respond to requests from you and other users. User agents vary in the interface presented for entering and reviewing your messages. The UNIX Mail system is widely available; although it is not quite as sophisticated as some of the newer options, it is adequate to handle your needs.

Although e-mail can only be used to transmit ASCII data, you can send programs, word-processing documents, and all types of other files that look nothing like a message as long as they are encoded and sent as an ASCII file. You will need to use a program similar to uuencode/decode or MIME to handle this for you. You will need to check in your computer lab to see which utilities are available for this purpose.

Addressing

In Chapter 2, you learned about the domain addresses that uniquely identify each site. To send a piece of mail to another Internet user, you will need both a domain address and a user id. Although you might find the same user id at a number of different sites, the combination of site and user id is unique. This means you might find individuals with user ids of mary at po.cwru.edu and cc.uks.edu, but you will not find more than one mary at each site. When you specify a location for a particular user, you will type the user id followed by an @ symbol, then the domain address for the site, as in:

```
drc3@po.cwru.edu
```

The domain portion of the addresses is case insensitive, thereby making an entry of drc3@PO.CWRU.EDU equivalent to the lowercase entry. Although user names are often case insensitive, there are exceptions. Since there is no immediate message that your e-mail was not delivered, you'll want to respect the case in user names.

Often a user name is the individual's first name or initials; however, there may be a number appended at the end since there can be duplicates when the domain is large. At some sites each new user is assigned a random number or letter pattern.

> *There was an old style of addressing called "bang addressing" because of the ! bang symbols (exclamation points) used in it. This style of addressing required you to list the entire path your message needed to follow to reach the recipient and might have looked something like this: machinea!machineb!machinec!drc3. Fortunately, this format is quickly losing popularity, but at least you will know what it means if you hear the term.*

If you are sending mail to another user on the same host, simply use the user name in the address. When drc3 wants to send a message to another faculty member at cwru, all that is necessary is the faculty member's initials, as in gjp.

Using the UNIX Mail Command

The UNIX Mail system is easy enough to use. Commands can be a little difficult to remember because you are typing individual letters rather than making menu selections. Fortunately, ? or ~? will display onscreen help.

Sending Mail

If you are using the UNIX Mail program, you can send mail by typing mail followed by the user name and domain as in

```
mail mary@ix.netcom.com
```

You can also string several names in the entry if you want more than one individual to receive your message. Typically, the UNIX Mail program will display

```
Subject:
```

Type a descriptive entry that is no longer than 35 to 40 characters to describe the subject of the message. This length allows the recipient to see your description, even when the mail window is smaller than full screen. Many systems will respond with Cc and allow you to enter additional destinations for the message. If you see this display and don't have an entry, press the Enter key and start typing your message. Type each line as you want it to appear. There is no word-wrap feature on most systems and you will need to press the Enter key for each line. To abort the messages, press Ctrl-C twice. If you finish typing it and want to send it, press Ctrl-D and the end of transmission (EOT) message should display indicating the message is finished. Your system might request that you enter ### or some other entry on the last line to indicate you are finished instead of using Ctrl-D.

The UNIX Mail system understands numerous commands. They start on a new line with a tilde to distinguish them from your message as you type. For a list you can type ~?. These commands will let you do things like edit the header placed at the beginning of messages, write your message to a file, or start your default text editor to make message entry easier.

Reading Mail

To look at the mail that is in the queue, just type **mail**. Short descriptions are displayed to let you choose the order in which you read messages. The user name, date, time, description, and size are part of this descriptive information. You can press the Enter key to see the first message or display other commands that you can use by typing a **?**. One important option is **R**, which replies to the sender. (An **r** responds to both the sender and recipients of the original message.) When you are ready to quit the Mail program, type **q** and press the Enter key.

Clean up your mail queue once you are finished with messages. To delete messages 2 through 10, type **d 2-10**.

Using Freenet

Most of the community freenets around the country provide access to an electronic mail capability. You should check if the freenet you use provides this access since it is easier to use than the single letter commands expected by

UNIX. Also, when you are at home during Christmas or spring break, you'll be able to stay in touch with fellow project team members or professors at almost no additional cost. Although each site is a little different, the menu-driven approach that most sites provide makes it easy to figure out the next step at each decision point. The material from the sample session shows exactly what you see when logging onto the Cleveland Freenet as a guest or registered user after the initial welcoming information is presented.

```
<<< CLEVELAND FREE-NET DIRECTORY >>>
1 The Administration Building
2 The Post Office
3 Public Square
4 The Courthouse & Government Center
5 The Arts Building
6 Science and Technology Center
7 The Medical Arts Building
8 The Schoolhouse (Academy One)
9 The Community Center & Recreation Area
10 The Business and Industrial Park
11 The Library
12 University Circle
13 The Teleport
14 The Communications Center
15 NPTN/USA TODAY HEADLINE NEWS
_____

h=Help, x=Exit Free-Net, "go help"=extended help
You have new mail. Your Choice ==> 2 for help
```

It is pretty easy to guess that the mail services might be hiding under the post office option, so this choice is selected to check it out.

```
<<< THE POST OFFICE >>>
1 About the Post Office
2 Check Mail
3 Send Mail
4 Check the size of your mailbox
5 See who your new mail is from
6 Edit your signature file
7 Mail Aliases
8 Have your mail forwarded
```

```
 9 Directory Services
10 Filter Your Mail
```

```
h=Help, x=Exit Free-Net, "go help"=extended help
```

At this point you can choose to read mail or send new messages.

Reading Your Mail with Freenet

When you request to read your mail by selecting option 2, information must be read and processed. You may experience a little delay as this processing occurs depending on how many new and undeleted messages are still in your mail file. The following entries show what happens when 2 is selected.

```
Your Choice ==> 2
getting user information...done
getting host information...done
Reading mail
file.............................................................
.................................................................
............
......done
New mail has arrived in /u/30/drc3/mbox, reading it in...done
Current message is #150 (150 is last)
   R     148. ErinBaker@oai.org (Erin Baker) (650 chars)
               Wed, 01 Feb — Intern Projects at OAI
   R     149. aacsb!PEGGIE@uustar.starnet.net () (9970 chars)
               Sat, 18 Feb —  Candidacy Connector
 *   N   150. jdc@ix.netcom.com (Jim Davis) (240 chars)
               Thu, 02 Mar — Manuscript Review
```

```
   n = Read next unread message
   d = Delete this message
   p = Back to previous screen
   h = Help, list of additional commands
```

You can see who sent the messages, message length, and the time messages were sent.

Composing and Replying

When using a menu-driven system at a freenet or a commercial Internet provider, the task of creating new e-mail messages or replying to ones you've received is quite easy. Because all the commands you need are in menus, there's no need to worry that you'll forget the letter to use to make things happen. The text that follows shows the creation of a message. The message is automatically dated and will indicate who sent it.

```
Date: Thu Mar  2 16:58:37 1995
To: marydave@ix.netcom.com
Verifying addresses...
marydave@ix.netcom.com - Not a local address - Assuming it's OK.
Is this correct? (y/n) y
Subject: Manuscript Design
Instructions:
     1. You may now enter or upload your text.
     2. Each line can be up to 65 characters and MUST end with a
RETURN.
     3. End the message by typing ### on a NEW LINE.
This is 65 characters:
_____

Design for pages in new book looks good. Thanks for sending an
early copy.
=|:-)
###
Would you now like to...
     1. Send the message
     2. Read the message over
     3. Re-write the message
     4. Append to the message
     5. Edit the message
     6. Cancel the message
     7. Check spelling for this message
     8. Append a file to the message
```

Using a Commercial Provider or a Graphic Browser to Send E-Mail

The commercial services are often the easiest to use. Many of them have slick full-screen interfaces and even maintain address books that are accessible when you click the To field in an address. NetCom's NetCruiser interface is shown in Figure 3-1.

Although graphic browsers are not discussed until Chapter 7, where the Web that they are designed to navigate is introduced, they do support other functions such as the ability to send e-mail. Like the commercial providers, they offer a full-screen graphic interface that makes the creation and sending of messages easy. At Case Western Reserve University, where Netscape is the browser of choice, students have an alternative to creating e-mail messages as shown in Figure 3-1.

E-mail is easy to use, but there are still problems. Addresses are not verified when you type them, so you might find out the next time that you sign on that mail you sent was undeliverable. Also, there is no way to request delivery confirmation.

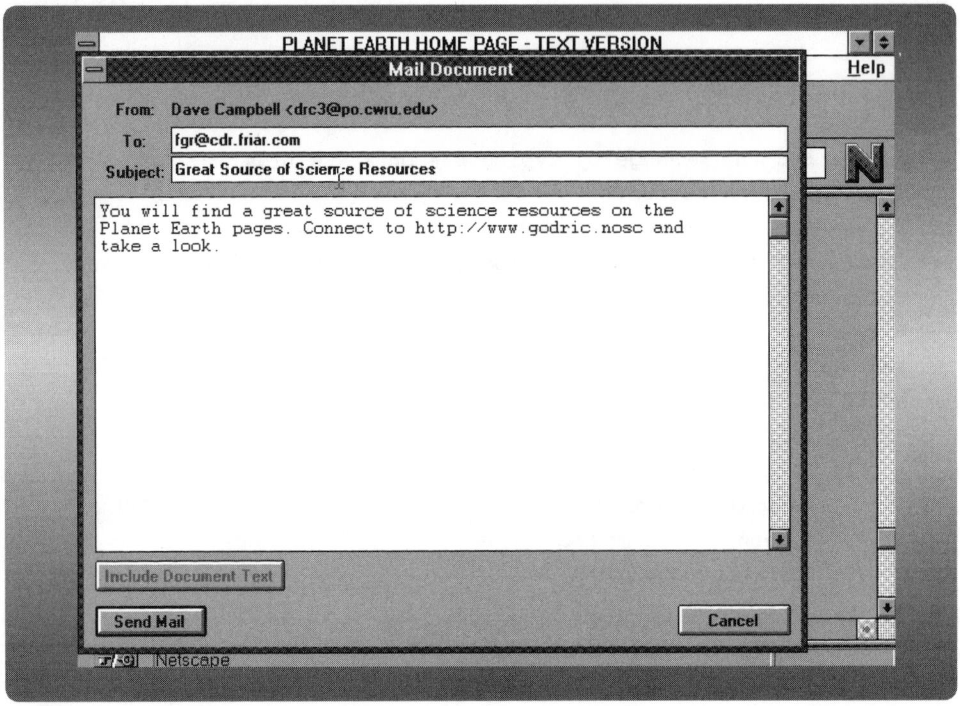

FIGURE 3-1. *The interface to Netscape's e-mail*

TALK

The Talk program provides a convenient way to share ideas with a student at another university without the expense of long-distance calls. You will have to send e-mail messages prior to your planned conversation although, unlike trading e-mail messages, your communication must be synchronized. It does offer the advantage of immediate answers to questions traded back and forth and instant comments on material sent. You might attach a manuscript to an e-mail message, allow time for it to be read, then arrange a talk session to trade ideas for revisions back and forth.

To begin the conversation you arranged with the individual at another location, you might enter something like this:

```
talk drc3@po.cwru.edu
```

Assuming both of you have access to a talk program, a message will appear on the other student's screen that looks something like this:

```
Message from Talk_Daemon@po at 9:22 ...
talk: connection requested by mvc@loyal.lcb.edu
talk: respond with:    talk mvc@loyal.lcb.edu
```

Assuming the response is entered as requested, the two parties can converse back and forth. Each time you press the Enter key, what you have typed will be transmitted. When you are finished, either of you can press Ctrl-C to end the conversation.

INTERNET RELAY CHAT (IRC)

IRC first came into prominence during the Gulf War when the *Wall Street Journal* ran a story about how thousands of Internet users were using it to obtain up-to-the-minute reports from Internet users in the Middle East. It allows users in different locations to chat back and forth. Because it follows the client/server model, you will not be able to utilize its features unless you have an IRC client installed.

Using an IRC Client

To see if IRC is available, activate your UNIX system, then type one of these lines:

```
irc
ircii
```

If an IRC screen something like this appears, you will know you have an IRC client installed locally and can proceed.

```
**  IRCII: /HELP for help  drc3  (I) 2:41 PM
**********************************
```

You will need to specify an IRC server such as irc.uiuc.edu or irc.colorado.edu with the /server command:

```
/server irc.colorado.edu
```

Once connected, you might want to get a list of available IRC channels. You'll find lots of channels with people gathered just to talk, but there are others in foreign languages and other topics that might pique your research interests. To see available channels that have at least ten people on them, type:

```
/list -min 10
```

There are many other commands that you will pick up if you get hooked on IRC. For now, the two most important are /help and /quit.

Using IRC Through a Commercial Provider

NetCom and other commercial providers have an IRC connection. Simply request it from the menu and an IRC control window will be established. You can enter commands in the bottom line. Commands for displaying the list of active channels and users work just as they do when starting a session from UNIX.

MUDS, MOOS, MUSES, AND MANY RELATED OPTIONS

Historically, MUDs (Multi-User Dungeons, Multi-User Dimensions, or Multi-User Dialogues) were a game involving a virtual reality scenario and more than one user. Over time this family has grown to involve cousins such as a MUSE (Multi-User Shared Environment), MOO (Multi-user Object Oriented), and MUSH (Multi-User Shared Hallucination). Also, educators have begun to realize their potential for involving students in a learning situation in which they can actively participate. Educational options borrow some of the same character-istics of adventure games developed for this environment. They are often elec-tronic learning rooms filled with a variety of objects. A set of rules exists for each individual offering. MediaMOO and MariMUSE are two popular educa-tional creations. If your instructor has established one for a class project, you will be given all the rules you need for full participation before beginning. If you decide to explore and participate in ones that you find as you surf the Internet, be sure to take some time to study the rules before participating. Figure 3-2 shows a serious experimental MOO called Diversity University con-nected through a Telnet session.

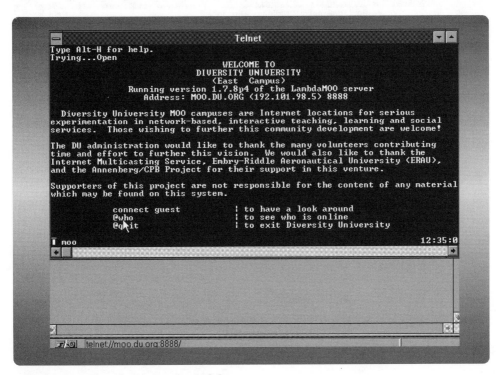

FIGURE 3-2. *Diversity University MOO*

If you want to learn more about the ins and outs of this popular game form and future educational tool, you will want to read through the material in the Frequently Asked Questions list at the University of Texas. After you learn how to use a Gopher client in Chapter 5, you will want to connect to this address:

```
gopher://home.asctlab.utexas.edu:70/11/MUD
```

You will be able to select Jack In to connect directly to a number of MOOs and MUDs through a Telnet session as shown by the options in Figure 3-3.

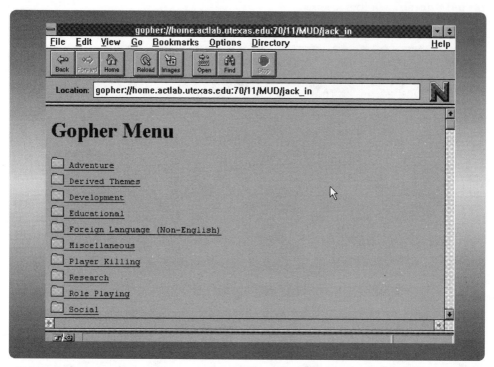

FIGURE 3-3. *Some of the MOOs and MUDS accessible through the University of Texas Gopher*

Just for Fun

There are all kinds of recreational information you can pursue with e-mail capabilities. One of the most popular is sending a mail request to ask to be included in lists that pertain to a particular topic. See Chapter 8 for more information about list groups. Join too many and your e-mail will be overflowing before long. We've listed just a few for you to consider depending on your interests:

Folk dancing newsletter request	tjw+@pitt.edu
Subscription to a list group on DisneyAfternoon programs	mail:ranger-list-request@orange.com
To subscribe to a list for novice and professional DJs	mail:bpm-request@andrew.cmu.edu
Rock Music list	mail:droneon-request@ucsd.edu

Chapter 4

FTP: Your Key to Unlimited Resources

WITH FILE TRANSFER PROTOCOL (FTP), you can transfer files between many different kinds of computers and have access to millions of files around the world. You might find software to perform just the data analysis you need, documents that provide a bibliography in your area of study, jokes to lighten up your presentation, graphics and sound files, or statistics that back up a report you are preparing.

Many files available through FTP are available to the public. In this chapter you'll learn how to:

- Run FTP locally and connect to sites that have the files you want

- Change directories at the remote site and look at the files in a directory

- Get the files you need

- Use FTP without a local FTP client

- Use Archie to locate sites that have the files you are looking for

- Use the Archie Whatis command when you don't know the names of the files you want

RUNNING FTP LOCALLY

On most campuses you can run an FTP client program locally and connect to any FTP site you want. The servers you connect to are called **anonymous FTP servers**. The word anonymous is used because in the past when asked to logon, you typed anonymous and followed with a password of guest. Although this still works on some servers, others now ask you to type **ftp** for the user name and your e-mail address for your password. (You'll know that you *don't* have a local FTP client program if you connect to your campus UNIX server, type **ftp**, and your request is rejected. Later sections of this chapter provide alternatives for accessing the storehouse of data in anonymous FTP sites.) You normally follow these steps to use a local FTP client program to get the files you need:

- Start the FTP client on your system and establish a connection to the desired site.

- Provide a user name and password.

- Change to the pub directory or other location to get the data you need.

- List the directory to verify the spelling of the desired filename.

- Change any settings you need to alter.

- Get the file that you need.

- Close the connection with the FTP site or continue to get more files.

Since most FTP sites are Unix based, you will need to learn a few Unix commands to make your way through the directories on these servers and obtain the files you want. The following sections provide a description and example of the commands you'll use most often. Table 4-1 lists the frequently used FTP commands.

<u>Command</u>	<u>Sample Entry</u>	<u>Action</u>
?	?	Display a list of all FTP commands
? command	?get	Display help on the get command
ascii	ascii	Set the file transfer type to ascii (text)
binary	binary	Set the file transfer type to binary
cd directory	cd pub	Change the current directory to the one specified
close	close	End the connection to the current host but remain in FTP

TABLE 4-1. *Frequently Used FTP Commands*

Command	Sample Entry	Action
dir	dir	Display a listing of the directory on the remote host
get local-file remote-file	get list.readme list.me	Download a file from the remote host to the local computer
lcd local directory	lcd /dc3/papers	Change the local directory
ls	ls	Display a short directory listing of the local computer (file names)
mget file1 file 2 file3	mget readme JAN FEB	Download all the files listed
open site	open stats.bls.gov	Connect to the specified site

TABLE 4-1. *Frequently Used FTP Commands (continued)*

Starting Your FTP Client

If your campus system supports FTP, you can type **ftp** followed by a space and the site you wish to obtain files from. For example, if you type

```
ftp stats.bls.gov
```

and press the Enter key, you will start the FTP client program and connect to the Bureau of Labor Statistics Public Access Server (LABSTAT).

Another option is to start your local FTP client by typing

```
ftp
```

and pressing the Enter key. When you see a prompt like ftp> or FTP>, you will know that you can begin using the FTP facility because the connection has been satisfactorily completed. You can connect to any site you want by typing **open** followed by the site, as in

```
open stats.bls.gov
```

This approach is normally used after closing a connection with one FTP site and remaining within your local FTP client to work with other sites.

Providing a User Name and Password

You will be asked to provide a user name. Unless specified otherwise, ftp or anonymous is the obvious choice. When prompted for a password, type your e-mail address. The display you see when connected with LABSTAT looks like this:

```
331 Guest login ok, send your complete e-mail address as password.
230-
230-              W E L C O M E   T O   L A B S T A T   ! ! !
230-              ===========================================
230-
230-      The Bureau of Labor Statistics' Public Access Server
230-
230-    Available through Anonymous FTP and gopher at stats.bls.gov
230-            Available through the World Wide Web at
230-                  http://stats.bls.gov/blshome.html
230-
230-
230-    All transfers from this server are logged for reference by
230-                  the LABSTAT support staff.
230-
230-
230-         Please address any comments or questions to:
230-
230-                  labstat.helpdesk@bls.gov
230-
230-
230-Please read the file README
230-it was last modified on Thu Nov  3 08:40:30 1994 - 102 days ago
230 Guest login ok, access restrictions apply.
```

Each server will display different messages. Take the time to read them since they provide some important information such as files to read for help and an e-mail address if you encounter problems.

If your FTP client has a problem processing the informational message returned by the server you connect to and loses its connection shortly after establishing it, try reconnecting and using a "-" as the first character in your password entry. This will turn off the informational messages that many servers return.

Listing Files in the Current Directory

The information that you want from FTP servers is stored in files (a file is nothing more than a collection of information). Since there can be many files at a site, the files are organized into directories. Although it may not be readily apparent when you first begin working with a site, directories organize groups of similar files. If you have a hard disk on your personal computer, you are likely to be familiar with the concept of files and directories; however, you will have to remember to use UNIX commands on most servers to work with the files and directories since most FTP servers are UNIX based. To list the files in the current directory, type the following at the FTP prompt:

```
dir
```

and press the Enter key. The response will include a directory listing and might look something like this:

```
200 PORT command successful.
150 Opening ASCII mode data connection for /bin/ls.
total 36
dr-xr-xr-x   8 0      200        512 Sep 26 12:50 .
dr-xr-xr-x   8 0      200        512 Sep 26 12:50 ..
-rw-rw-r-   1 208     200       1302 Nov  3 13:40 README
d-x-xr-x    2 0        2         512 Dec  7 1993 bin
dr-xr-xr-x   2 0        1         512 Dec  7 1993 dev
dr-xr-xr-x   2 0        1         512 Dec  7 1993 etc
drwx----    2 0        0        8192 Dec  7  1993 lost+found
dr-xrwxr-x   6 209     200        512 Feb 13 21:52 pub
dr-xr-xr-x   3 0        1         512 Dec  7 1993 usr
-rw-rw-r-   1 208     200        565 Feb  3 17:54 welcome.msg
226 Transfer complete.
```

The first column of the entry indicates whether you are looking at a directory (d) or a file (-). (Other columns display read/write authority, size, time of last update, and directory or filename.) You'll notice that the README file mentioned in the initial screen is in the directory. In a few minutes we'll explain how you can get a copy of it, but first you'll need to learn how to change directories in case what you need isn't in the first place that you look.

Changing Directories

Most servers have several levels of directories. The levels below the highest level are referred to as subdirectories. Some of the subdirectories in the current example are bin, dev, etc, and pub. Many of the files that you want will be located in the pub subdirectory or subdirectories beneath it as you work on servers around the world. Unlike some other operating systems, UNIX is case sensitive, so it's important to pay attention to capital letters that appear in directory names—otherwise, the directory change you request will not occur. The command you will use to change the directory is cd. The following entry requests a change to the pub directory and shows the response returned from LABSTAT:

```
FTP> cd pub
250 CWD command successful.
```

You can continue to list the contents of the current directory by using the dir command as you move around in the directory structure.

You can back up one level (the parent directory) by typing:

```
cd..
```

To change directories on your local computer you will need to use the lcd command.

Changing the Mode

Files stored on the servers you access can be transferred in two ways depending on the type of information they contain. An ASCII transfer is appropriate for files that contain text (that is, ordinary letters and other characters). Binary files contain information that is not stored as text, including program files, graphics, and sound files. These files require a binary transfer mode. You can check the filename extensions for some clues as to the type of data in a file. Table 4-2 provides the transfer mode setting appropriate for some common file types. Often directories contain a README file that contains information about the files stored there.

The FTP program assumes files that you transfer are ASCII or text unless you tell it otherwise. To change the setting for FTP to binary, type the following and press the Enter key:

`binary`

To change the setting back to ASCII, type the following and press the Enter key:

`ascii`

In both cases the response indicates that the type has been changed.

Although an ASCII setting will not work for transferring a binary file, a BINARY setting will handle ASCII files just fine even if it does slow down the transfer a bit.

Extension	Contents	Appropriate Mode Setting
.doc	Word processing files with special codes added to text	Binary
.exe	Executable program	Binary
.ps	Postscript file	ASCII
.txt or blank	Text	ASCII
.uue	Uuencoded file which is binary data specially coded in an ASCII format; it must be decoded before use	ASCII
.Z, .tar, .zip	Compressed and archive files	Binary

TABLE 4-2. *Filename Extensions Can Help Determine the Correct Mode Setting*

Getting the Desired File

Once you locate the file(s) you want and determine the correct mode setting, you are ready to transfer a copy of them to your local system. You will want to check not only the spelling but also the capitalization with the filename, as an exact match is essential. You can use the get command to get an individual file or mget when you want to provide a list of several files. If there is a file called README in the current directory, you can transfer a copy of it to your local computer by typing the following at the FTP prompt and pressing the Enter key:

```
FTP>get README
```

The response might look something like this:

```
200 PORT command successful
150 Opening ASCII mode data connection for README (1302 bytes)
226 Transfer complete
```

The file is transferred to your local computer (on most campuses this will be the UNIX server from which you are running the FTP client). You might want to transfer this file to your PC's hard drive after completing your FTP session, if this is appropriate. Your local lab consultant can provide information on how to do this using FTP or another option.

To store the file under a different name on your local computer, you can specify it after the name of the file that you are transferring, as in:

```
get readme labsread.me
```

This is useful when the server has a filename extension that is longer than what you will ultimately be able to use, or you already have a file of the specified name on your local computer.

There's a tendency to get carried away with downloading files at first. You can quickly fill up your allocation of space on the server or your hard disk if you are not careful. With text files you might want to take a look at shorter files onscreen by placing a "-" after the filename as in get readme -.

After transferring files to your workspace, just close the connection to your current site and open a new site or quit from the FTP client altogether. To close the connection with the current site, type the following and press the Enter key:

```
close
```

To both close the current connection and quit the FTP client program, type:

```
quit
```

To get acquainted with new FTP sites as quickly as possible, look for the pub directory and any files with a name of README.

Dealing with Special Types of Files

Although you might expect all files you download to be text or binary files, you will encounter some other special file types at FTP sites. These files may contain the files you are actually looking for in a compressed or archive format. These files have either .Z or .tar as their extension. Learn how to handle both special types of files.

Z Files

Z files are compressed to allow storage in less space. You will find either the uncompressed or gzip utility on most UNIX systems. You can obtain documentation after quitting your FTP client by typing either

```
man uncompress
```

```
man gzip
```

If you use gunzip to expand the file, enter the following:

```
gunzip books.Z
```

Tar Files

Tar files are archive files created when many files are combined into one file to make backup easier. You can use uncompress to split the file into its original component files. You might want to make a new directory (mkdir) and move your .tar file to it before using the tar command to expand it into its components. The original file is not deleted when it is expanded. You can use rm to eliminate it if you no longer want the original file.

Other File Types

Although there are numerous file types you might encounter, another common type is a .tar.Z file. This file is a tar file that has been compressed. You need to uncompress the compressed tar file, then unpack its components.

If you use e-mail to access FTP sites, any binary files you request will have to be specially coded before transmission to you because only ASCII files can be attached to mail messages. You will need to use the uudecode program to decode these files before use. Although it is not a required extension, you can often identify these files as ones with a .uue extension.

Establishing a Remote FTP Connection

If you do not have FTP client software on your system, don't give up on using FTP's vast storehouse of information. There are some other options that you can explore depending on the resources available to you on campus. Although all the details are not included here due to space limitations, you'll know there are some alternative routes that may be available to you.

Using Delphi or Netcom to Get Files

If you subscribe to a third-party access provider, you can use the services of their system to access FTP sites. The only important difference is that your files may be stored in a workspace on the access provider's system and will need to be transferred to your system for permanent storage. For example, when you use Delphi to get FTP files, you quit FTP, then transfer the files from your workspace to your personal computer. You can use the wo command to tell Delphi you want to work with the files in your workspace, then download the file to your local system using a file transfer protocol supported by your communication package. Look at the transcript of this Delphi session to see how the transfer was made with this provider. (User entries are underscored.)

```
Internet SIG>Enter your selection: wo
Your prompt mode has been temporarily set to brief.  Enter ? at the
WS> prompt for a list of commnds.


WS> download


Download Method Menu:


XMODEM (128 byte blocks)      RT Buffer Capture
Kermit                        YB (YMODEM batch)
WXMODEM (Windowed XMODEM)      ZMODEM
YMODEM (1024 byte blocks)     Help
Buffer Capture                Exit


DOWNLOAD> (Xm,Kermit,WXm,Ym,Buff,RT,YB) z
Name of file 1 for ZMODEM download to you ? overview.doc
```

```
(Batch contains 1 file:  4060 bytes = 5 YMODEM blocks, 33 XMODEM
blocks)
   You may now enter additional filenames to download.
   Press RETURN to begin downloading.
   Press Control-Z to review the list of filenames.
Name of file 2 for ZMODEM download to you ?
Type five consecutive <Control-X>'s to cancel.
ZMODEM mode
Ok, receive! (1 file:  4060 bytes = 5 YMODEM blocks, 33 XMODEM
blocks)
**B00000000000000
File Received: c:\scwinle\rcv\overview.doc (4021 bytes, 1:16.4 sec-
onds, 52 CPS)
OO
FINAL STATUS = Transfer successful.
FINAL STATUS = 1 file successfully transferred.
```

You can use a Web browser such as Mosaic or Netscape to utilize FTP if you specify ftp:// followed by the site location. Your interface will have a graphic look.

Netcom's NetCruiser FTP graphic interface in Figure 4-1 is very different from the text interface shown in Figure 4-2. You can type the name of an FTP site or click on a map to locate known sites.

Using E-Mail

If you have only e-mail access to the Internet, you can utilize it to obtain the benefits of FTP. A number of Internet sites support an FTP Mail capability, including: ftpmail@cs.uow.edu.au and ftpmail@decwr1.dec.com.

   You can place FTP commands in the body of the e-mail message sent to these sites. You need to begin with a connect command and place the full path or location of the desired file location in one cd command as in

```
cd pub/stats/labor
```

Automatic Binary mode to ASCII encoding will take place if you set Binary mode for the transfer.

FIGURE 4-1. *Netcom's graphical interface for FTP with NetCruiser*

USING ARCHIE TO FIND A FILE

Perhaps you have heard of a particular shareware program that you'd like to try or you already know the name of a file that answers lots of questions about a specific Internet tool. Although the name of the file is part of what you need, you also need to know the server and path to search for the filename. Archie servers located around the Internet can help you find the exact location of the files you are looking for. These servers keep track of all the anonymous FTP public files on the Internet by searching the public directories of the FTP hosts on a regular basis. Archie can search for either an FTP directory or filename.

FTP sites with FTP in the name of the site normally indicate dedicated FTP sites that might allow a larger number of concurrent users than sites without FTP in the name.

```
                                    FTP
ftp> open acfcluster.nyu.edu
Trying...<128.122.128.16>
Connection to acfcluster.nyu.edu open
220 acf6.acf.nyu.edu MultiNet FTP Server Process 3.3<14> at Sun 30-Apr-95 1:11
-EDT
Connected to acfcluster.nyu.edu.
Login: anonymous
331 anonymous user ok. Send real ident as password.
Password:
230-Guest User DRC3@PO.CWRU.EDU logged into DISK$ANON:[ANONYMOUS] at Sun 30-Ap
95 1:12PM-EDT, job 8329c7.
230 Directory and access restrictions apply
ftp> ?
Commands may be abbreviated.  Commands are:

!                form          mdelete       quit          struct
append           form          mget          quote         tenex
ascii            get           mkdir         recv          type
bell             hash          mode          remotehelp    user
binary           help          mput          remotestat    verbose
bye              lcd           open          rename        wildcard
cd               lpwd          prompt        rmdir         ?
close            ls            put           send
delete           lscol         pwd           status
ftp> .
```

```
  Ann
  Art
  Clients
  FTP Sites
```

```
  Document Done
```

FIGURE 4-2. *The text look of a screen with an FTP session*

If there is an Archie client on your local system, it can automatically connect to Archie server sites for you. If not, you can Telnet to one at a remote site.

 Although it will take a little longer to get a response, you can e-mail an Archie server with your request and get a response back in the mail.

Getting Connected

If you are using a UNIX terminal on campus, Archie client software may be installed on your system. You can check to see if this is the case by typing **archie** and pressing the Enter key. If "Command not found" displays, you will know that it is not installed. You can check with your lab manager to see if xarchie or other Archie client software is installed. Although the Telnet procedure works just fine, you'll get your results a lot quicker with a local Archie client and you'll avoid any limitations that Archie servers have on the number

41

of concurrent Telnet sessions. If you are lucky enough to have an Archie client installed, type **archie** followed by the name of the file you want to search for, as in

```
archie rfc1201
```

It is possible that the syntax of the entry for your client might be a little different than this example, but it is likely to be similar. If you don't have a local Archie client, you can Telnet to one of the Archie servers in Table 4-3. To connect with the server archie.ans.net, type

```
telnet archie.ans.net
```

After the connection messages are displayed, you will be prompted for a login to which you respond like this:

```
login: archie
```

On most Archie servers, you are not prompted for a password. When the archie prompt appears, you can enter settings or a find command to locate a specific file. The following session transcript shows how to make a setting change where a maximum of ten sites will be returned, followed by a find command that requests that a file named rfc1201 be located. Once the sites are located, you might want to quit Archie and utilize your FTP client to get a copy of the file.

```
archie> set maxhits 10
archie> find rfc1201
find rfc1201
# Search type: exact.
# Your queue position: 8
# Estimated time for completion: 01:53
working... /

Host ftp.ucdavis.edu    (128.120.8.149)
Last updated 08:13  9 Jan 1995

    Location: /rfc
        FILE   -r-r-r-   16565 bytes  00:00  7 Feb 1991  rfc1201
Host nisca.acs.ohio-state.edu    (128.146.1.7)
Last updated 08:02  9 Dec 1994

    Location: /pub/rfc
```

```
        FILE    -rw-r-r-   16565 bytes  01:00 23 Aug 1991  rfc1201
archie> quit
quit
# Bye.
```

There are other settings you might want to change for the search. For example, you can change the search variable to perform a substring search. It will then look for your entry within the filename and you won't have to type the full file-name. Check the help features of your Archie client or the Archie site to get more information on settings changes.

Server Location	IP Address	Geographic Location
archie.univie.ac.at	131.130.1.23	Austria
archie.cs.mcgill.ca	132.206.51.250	Canada
archie.uqam.ca	132.208.250.10	Canada
archie.funet.fi	128.214.6.102	Finland
archie.univ-rennes1.fr	129.20.128.38	France
archie.th-darmstadt.de	130.83.128.118	Germany
archie.unipi.it	131.114.21.10	Italy
archie.wide.ad.jp	133..4.3.6	Japan
archie.kornet.nm.kr	168.126.63.10	Korea
archie.sogang.ac.kr	163.239.1.11	Korea
archie.uninett.no	128.39.2.20	Norway
archie.rediris.es	130.206.1.2	Spain
archie.luth.se	130.240.12.30	Sweden
archie.switch.ch	130.59.1.40	Switzerland
archie.twnic.net	192.83.166.10	Taiwan
archie.ncu.edu.tw	192.83.166.12	Taiwan
archie.doc.ic.ac.uk	146.169.11.3	United Kingdom

TABLE 4-3. *Archie Servers*

Server Location	IP Address	Geographic Location
archie.hensa.ac.uk	129.12.21.25	United Kingdom
archie.unl.edu	129.93.1.14	USA (NE)
archie.internic.net	198.49.45.10	USA (NJ)
archie.rutgers.edu	128.6.18.15	USA (NJ)
archie.ans.net	147.225.1.10	USA (NY)
archie.sura.net	128.167.254.179	USA (MD)

TABLE 4-3. *Archie Servers (continued)*

Using the Archie Whatis Command When You Don't Know the Filename

When you know the filename you are looking for, Archie does a great job of locating all the sites where you can obtain that file. If you only know that you are looking for a file that relates to microbiology, Archie's regular search capabilities won't help. However, Archie does have a whatis command that will look for files relating to the word you enter. The whatis command searches a Software Description Database, which contains only a subset of files in anonymous FTP sites. The database is not updated as frequently as the Archie Archives database and is dependent on individuals who place files in anonymous FTP sites to provide descriptions of the information in the files. Since the whatis command looks only at descriptor information, files that lack descriptions will never show up in a list provided by the whatis command. As a result, only a small percentage of the files accessed show up when you use whatis to search by topic.

Entering Whatis

To use the whatis command, type **whatis** followed by a word at the Archie prompt. For example, if you are working on a computer project related to ARCnet and want a listing of related files, type

```
whatis ARCnet
```

The following is returned:

```
RFC          1051         Prindeville, P.A. Standard for the
transmission of IP datagrams and ARP packets over ARCNET networks.
1988 March; 4 p. (Obsoleted by RFC 1201)
```

```
RFC          1201          Provan, D. Transmitting IP traffic over
ARCNET networks. 1991 February; 7 p. (Obsoletes RFC 1051)
```

Since the whatis command accepts only a single word after it, whatis adventure games would be rejected. If you need to search for more than one word, enclose your entry in quotes. The following is acceptable:

```
whatis "molecular biology"
```

 As you traverse the Internet, check for the mention of FTP sites of interest as you browse Gopherspace and the Web. Since the sources referenced in these locations may not show up if you do a whatis search, you will want to maintain your own list of sources that interest you.

Using the Results of Whatis to Locate the Files

Once you get output from the whatis command, you will have to ask Archie to locate the sites where you can find the file. You'll use the standard Archie search technique discussed earlier in the chapter. For example, to locate sites for the file rfc1201, type **rfc1201** at the archie prompt. The response will list the sites shown earlier.

Just for Fun

We hope by now you're convinced that the Internet has the resources you need to get a competitive edge in your research activities. To learn a bit more about it and have fun at the same time, you might want to play the Internet Hunt, a competitive effort that will pit you against some of the best Internet surfers out there. This game is written by Rick Gates each month and consists of a list of questions whose answers can be found somewhere on the Internet. Look at FTP site ftp.cic.net in the /pub/hunt directory. Although there has been a brief hiatus from new Hunts, just looking at the answers for earlier Internet Hunts will teach you a lot about how the experts find the information they need on the Internet.

Chapter 5

Gophers, Veronica, and Jughead

I F YOU WANT A TOOL that can help access all the Internet's features with a minimum of effort, you'll want to look at Gopher. Gopher organizes a vast number of options and lets you travel through Gopherspace to the worldwide resources you need. After you select the desired option from a Gopher menu, Gopher takes the necessary steps to display a lower-level menu or make a connection with another site.

"Gopher" may remind you of the furry creature that burrows under lawns and golf course greens, but it is actually named after the athletic teams (Golden Gophers) of the University of Minnesota where it was developed. In a sense, the Gopher does burrow through the Internet for you; as you make selections from menus, it connects to other computers and may retrieve files. Gopher follows a client/server model (Gopher refers to both ends of the connection).

Most universities have a campus-wide Gopher, and some even have different Gopher servers for the various departments to organize access to information on the Internet for their faculty and students. Don't get concerned if your machine doesn't have a Gopher client—you can Telnet to public-access Gophers.

In this chapter you'll learn how to:

- Use a local Gopher to connect to Gopher servers and other resources

- Use Telnet to connect to a public Gopher site

- Use Veronica to search Gopher menus

- Use Jughead to search one specific Gopher site

ACCESSING A GOPHER

You have a number of options for using Gopher. The most common method is accessing a local client from a UNIX terminal. Other options include accessing it through a Telnet session or a third-party access provider such as Delphi.

Using a Local Gopher Client

The two most popular Gopher clients are gopher and xgopher. On a text-based UNIX terminal you type:

```
gopher
```

and press the Enter key. The menu that appears will depend on the setup for your local system.

You can also direct your local Gopher client to connect to a specific Gopher site. If you type **the Gopher site** immediately after gopher, the menu of the remote Gopher Server will display. The initial Gopher menu at Michigan State University looks like this:

```
-->   1.  Gopher at Michigan State University.
      2.  Help Using Gopher (More About Gopher)/
      3.  Keyword Search of Titles in MSU's Gopher <?>
      4.  About Michigan State University/
      5.  MSU Campus Events & Calendars/
      6.  News & Weather/
      7.  Phone Books & Other Directories/
      8.  Information for the MSU Community/
      9.  Computing & Technology/
     10.  Libraries/
     11.  MSU Services &Facilities/
     12.  Outreach / Extension / Community Affairs/
   Press ? for Help, q to Quit, u to go up a menu
```

The current selection is marked with "-->" and can be selected with the right arrow key. You can move down selection by selection with the down arrow key. You can access help for a look at the full set of options for moving to different menu options.

 If you are running X Window under UNIX, start Gopher by typing `xgopher`.

Establishing a Remote Connection

You can Telnet to a public Gopher server to establish a session. Your entry might look something like this:

```
telnet
```

When prompted for a user name, most public sites will accept gopher, although some utilize a different entry. For example, if you Telnet to gopher.ohiolink.edu, you will need to enter ohiolink for the user name. Although a Telnet connection is better than no access, there are a few drawbacks including these:

- You cannot utilize menu selections that initiate another Telnet session since you connected to the Gopher from one.

- You cannot save or print the text files displayed on your screen.

Using a Third-Party Access Provider

All the third-party Internet access providers such as Delphi and NetCom have some type of Gopher tool. With Delphi, a full Gopher menu is located within Internet SIG. Once you select Gopher from Delphi's Internet SIG, you'll see options similar to those shown next.

```
Internet SIG Gopher
Page 1 of 1


1    PERSONAL FAVORITES                                      Menu
2    "ABOUT DELPHI'S GOPHER SERVICE"                         Text
3    >>> FAQ: FREQUENTLY ASKED QUESTIONS <<< (REVISED 11/4)  Menu
4    ALL THE WORLD'S GOPHERS                                 Menu
5    BUSINESS AND ECONOMICS                                  Menu
6    COMPUTERS                                               Menu
7    FTP: DOWNLOADABLE PROGRAMS, IMAGES, SOUNDS              Menu
8    GAMES AND MUDS, MUSHES, MUSES, AND MOOS                 Menu
9    GOVERNMENT AND POLITICS                                 Menu
10   HEALTH AND MEDICINE                                     Menu
11   INTERNET INFORMATION                                    Menu
12   LAW                                                     Menu
13   LIBRARIES AND RESEARCH GUIDES                           Menu
14   SCHOOLS, COMMUNITY RESOURCES, AND FREE-NETS             Menu
15   SEARCH UTILITIES                                        Menu
16   SUBJECT MATTER MENUS                                    Menu
17   THE GRAB BAG (WITH WHAT'S NEW)                          Menu
18   WORLD WIDE WEB                                          Menu


Enter Item Number, ?, or EXIT: 14
```

You'll notice that the Delphi Gopher client looks a little different from the display shown earlier. Options are numbered and the item type is indicated by a word at the far right of the menu option. But, just as before, selecting an option causes Delphi to go through Gopherspace looking to locate a Gopher hole and connect to the site you requested.

NetCom's Gopher Browser provides a graphic interface to Gopher. You can use the point-and-click method to make menu selections and choose other options from icons and menus onscreen.

Using a Web Browser to Access a Gopher Site

Web browsers are covered in Chapter 7. If you happen to be using one already, there is no reason to use anything else to access Gopher sites. Your Web browser will provide a graphic interface to the information in any Gopher site you link to. You will be able to tell by the icons on the screen which entries are folders and which are documents. All you have to do is indicate by your location entry that you want to point at a Gopher. For example, to connect to the site gopher.unr.edu, you would enter the following for the desired location:

```
gopher://gopher.unr.edu
```

You would see the Gopher menu shown in Figure 5-1.

Gopher Menus and Other Options

You've already seen two different looks that a Gopher client can present. The Gopher client you use will determine how you select the desired menu option and other subtleties of the display. Here are the most popular methods for making menu selections:

- Type the number appearing to the left of the desired selection and press the Enter key.

- Use the up and down arrow keys to move the pointer to the desired item and press the right arrow key to select it.

- Type enough of the option for a unique entry and press the Enter key.

Gopher menus are hierarchical. When you make a selection from one, you may see the next level of the menu or a different type of resource. Check your display to see if there are special symbols at the end of the menu options. Some UNIX Gopher clients display a symbol to indicate the type of resource that the menu selection represents. Check this list if you see symbols at the end of your menu options:

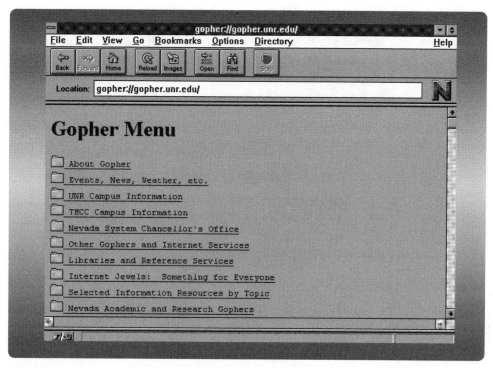

FIGURE 5-1. *Netscape browser displaying the University of Nevada, Reno, Gopher*

Symbol	Meaning
/	Lower-level menu displays.
.	Text file displays.
<?>	Database will be searched with your criteria.
<Picture>	A JPEG or GIF image file will be displayed if a compatible viewer is available.
<TEL>	Telnet connection will be established.

You may find an entry in a Gopher menu for UPI News, then wonder why you can't seem to connect. In all likelihood, your campus has a license only to make the information available to users on site.

Setting Bookmarks

Bookmarks are essential to using Gopher effectively; without them you are constantly burrowing your way through Gopherspace to the desired level in menus at remote sites. You can set a bookmark at any level and return to that location at any point in the future by selecting the bookmark. On the typical Gopher client, you can add a bookmark by typing an **a** and filling in the requested information. You can view existing bookmarks by typing a **v**. If your Gopher client provides menu options for command selection, you can set and view bookmarks with menu selections.

To keep your bookmarks in a personal file rather than using the default bookmark list, start your Gopher client by typing **gopher -b**.

Other Gopher Commands

Since there are a number of Gopher clients, commands may vary. Those shown here are used at many Gopher sites:

Command	Action
=	Displays information about the link or other technical aspects of the current selection.
?	Displays help information.
a	Adds the current item to the bookmark list.
b	Displays the previous menu page.
m	Displays the Main Menu.
O	Displays Gopher options.
Q	Quits Gopher.

Check help for your Gopher as a first step since the commands may be different; for example, TurboGopher uses command-i instead of the = symbol to display link information.

USING VERONICA TO SEARCH GOPHERSPACE

Veronica is a tool you can use to search Gopherspace. The results of your search are placed into a Gopher-type menu. Since you've already worked with Gopher, you'll feel instantly comfortable with the output presented by Veronica.

You can search for either item or directory matches. You can also create simple searches that look for a single entry or get more complicated combining multiple criteria with AND and OR.

The Veronica Harvester at the University of Minnesota searches all of Gopherspace to update its index about once a month. If you are working on a project that will last longer than a month, you should repeat your search periodically since new entries are constantly added.

Creating a Basic Search

If your Gopher server doesn't have a link to Veronica, you can connect to the Gopher at gopher.unr.edu. In Figure 5-1, you saw the main Gopher menu viewed with Netscape's Gopher browser. Since Veronica does not conduct a case-sensitive search, you can enter your criteria lowercase if you like. The following entry will search for Mozart:

```
mozart
```

You can add an asterisk (*) after your query entry to have Veronica look for entries that begin with the characters you specified. For example, if you entered turkey for your criteria, Turkey, turkey dressing, turkey sandwich, and turkey bologna could all be returned.

Adding Sophistication

There are several changes you can make when entering search criteria that will give you greater flexibility in the search process. First, you can use switches to determine search options such as the number of matches that are returned; second, you can use Boolean operators to combine search criteria.

Using Special Switches to Affect Search Outcomes

You can make several changes when completing search specifications. The most important options are those that change the number of matches returned and the types of Gopher items queried.

The default for the number of matches returned is 200. You can increase it to 500 by typing -m500 to your query expression. If you want unlimited matches, just type -m without a specification for the number of matches after it.

Since Gopher menus have several different types of items—files, directories, phonebook servers, images, and sound—you might want Veronica to restrict your search to a certain type of item. If you add -t to your query followed by one of the codes in Table 5-1, Veronica will return matches only if the item type is correct.

Item Code	Item Type
0	File
1	Directory
2	Phonebook server (CSO)
7	Index-Search server
8	Telnet session
9	Binary file
I	Image file
s	Sound file

TABLE 5-1. *Some Common Gopher Item Types*

Boolean Operators Add Flexibility

Veronica supports the Boolean operators AND, OR, and NOT, as well as parentheses that allow you to change the priority in which operators are evaluated. As in mathematical operations, any expression in parentheses is evaluated first.

To look for all entries containing Bach, type this in the query:

```
bach
```

To see anything on Bach or Mozart, type

```
bach OR mozart
```

To get Bach and Mozart items, type

```
bach AND mozart
```

To see only the first fifty Bach and Mozart items, type

```
bach AND mozart -m50
```

 Since searches aren't case sensitive, type your search criteria in lower-case and type the Boolean operators in uppercase. This will make your query entries easier to check.

SEARCH A SINGLE GOPHER SERVER WITH JUGHEAD

Jughead supports the same options as Veronica, except its search is limited to one Gopher server. If you are aware that a certain Gopher server specializes in information pertinent to your research efforts, this can be a quicker approach. To use the features of Jughead to look for Gopher menu items like these, follow these suggestions:

- Search the University of Minnesota Gopher Using Jughead.
- Item Search for the University of Virginia Gopher Server.

Since system administrators can create any name for the menu items, you'll find some variation.

Just for Fun

Put your newly learned Veronica search strategies to work. You'll find lots of opportunities for goof-off activities when you search Gopherspace with the query "fun." Everything from random dot stereograms to games and entertainment entries will be in your match list. Although you might not make any immediate progress on your research project, you can always justify the time as a needed break. If you are feeling especially guilty, you can convince yourself that you were practicing with Veronica to develop search strategies to speed up your research.

Chapter 6

WAIS

WIDE AREA INFORMATION SERVER (WAIS) was designed as a joint venture between Apple Computer, Dow Jones, and Thinking Machines. The initial idea was to develop a prototype system able to process large quantities of textual data and to extract just the information of interest to the reader. The companies involved hoped that WAIS would be so successful that they could charge for its use and turn this prototype into a profit-generating venture. The initial premise behind its development was that people were dealing with an overload of text and would be willing to pay for something that would simplify matters. The plan was to make daily newspapers and other data sources available through WAIS. Although this potential has not been realized by the companies involved in its development, it does explain why you see a cost column when the sources display. As you use this tool on the Internet at this time, the only cost entries are Free or $0.00/minute.

WAIS's contribution as an Internet tool is that it provides a text-searching capability between systems with hardware and software differences. WAIS allows you to search hundreds of text databases or sources containing information on a wide variety of topics, from aeronautics and Australia to information about Archie and FTP sites. WAIS is different from the Archie and Veronica search tools you discovered in earlier chapters because it actually searches the text in documents rather than file and directory names or Gopher menus. You can perform a keyword search of one or more databases very quickly.

Using WAIS is not complicated, although you do have to map out a strategy to get what you are looking for. Usually it is a good idea to search the directory of servers. This source is available on most WAIS servers and provides an overview of what each of the sources contains. You can specify subject keywords to locate the sources that will be most effective for your search. Even if you are aware of a source or two, checking the directory of servers can alert you to possibilities you didn't think about and may uncover newly added sources. You can look over the list of sources returned and decide which ones to search for the actual document keywords.

In this chapter you will learn how to

- Search the list of WAIS sources

- Search for specific keywords

- Obtain a search report and any of the documents that interest you

USING WAIS

You may have a WAIS client on your machine, or you can Telnet to a WAIS server to perform your search. Since not all of the source files are available from each server, the results you get when performing a search on different servers may not be identical. If you have a choice between using a local client or Telnet, you should choose the former. When you run WAIS locally, you can save the output of a search to disk and reprocess the search output for words with which to do additional searches. You can also utilize WAIS through menu options in many Gophers. You might connect to your local Gopher client and look around, or you can use a third-party provider such as Delphi or NetCom to travel through Gopherspace in search of a path that lets you access WAIS sources.

If your computer has a TCP/IP Internet connection, you might consider downloading WAIS client software. If you are not certain, review the information in Chapter 2. The Simple Wide Area Information Server (SWAIS) program is a popular UNIX version of WAIS, but there are also versions available for other platforms including X Windows, DOS, and the Macintosh. You might use FTP to access Thinking Machines at quake.think.com or use the Archie whatis command to search for relevant filenames.

If you want to try WAIS to see if it offers what you are looking for, a Telnet connection or Gopher link will work just fine. See Table 6-1 for a few sites that support public WAIS sessions or let you use it through their public Gopher. The example in this chapter uses SWAIS at quake.think.com. If you use a local client, your first step should be to look for help on the command your client uses if it is different than SWAIS. To connect to the remote WAIS server, type **telnet** followed by the location of the site, as in:

```
telnet quake.think.com
```

At the time of the connection, there were 529 source files available at this Thinking Machines site containing tens of thousands of documents on a wide variety of topics.

All sites do not have the same number of sources available. You may need to look around as you surf the net to see which ones best suit your needs.

Site	Connection
www.wais.com	Point your Web browser at this location and select the hypertext for search.
swais.cwis.uci.edu	Telnet connection; login as swais.
chicagokent.kentlaw.edu	Point your Gopher at this location and look under Internet Resources for Search Tools.
gopher.micro.umn.edu	Point your Gopher to this location and look under Other Gopher and Information Servers; then select WAIS-Based Information.

TABLE 6-1. *Sites for Using WAIS*

Selecting a Source

Once you are connected to a site, the first screen you see shows a list of the source files available as shown in Figure 6-1. You can begin to select the source files you want to search by moving to the line containing the filename and pressing the spacebar. The source will be marked at the left side of the line. Pressing the spacebar a second time removes the selection. You can also press "=" to remove the selection from all files.

Never work with all the source files. Your searches will take too long and will return many extraneous entries of no interest in the search results.

```
─                          NETCOM NetCruiser                      ▼ ▲
 File   Edit   View   Internet   Settings   Window   Help
 [icons toolbar]

 ─                    Telnet To: quake.think.com              ▼       ▲
 SWAIS                        Source Selection          Sources: 549 ▲
 001:   [ wais.access.gpo.gov]  103 cong bills                    Free
 001:   [ wais.access.gpo.gov]  103_cong_bills                    Free
 002:   [ wais.access.gpo.gov]  104_cong_bills                    Free
 004:   [ wais.access.gpo.gov]  1993_cri                          Free
 005:   [ wais.access.gpo.gov]  1994_cri                          Free
 006:   [ wais.access.gpo.gov]  1994_hob                          Free
 007:   [ wais.access.gpo.gov]  1994_record                       Free
 008:   [ wais.access.gpo.gov]  1994_register                     Free
 009:   [ wais.access.gpo.gov]  1994_unified_agenda               Free
 010:   [ wais.access.gpo.gov]  1995_cri                          Free
 011:   [ wais.access.gpo.gov]  1995_hob                          Free
 012:   [ wais.access.gpo.gov]  1995_record                       Free
 013:   [ wais.access.gpo.gov]  1995_register                     Free
 014:   [ wais.access.gpo.gov]  1995_unified_agenda               Free
 015:   [          archie.au]   aarnet-resource-guide             Free
 016:   [ndadsb.gsfc.nasa.gov]  AAS_jobs                          Free
 017:   [ndadsb.gsfc.nasa.gov]  AAS_meeting                       Free
 018:   [     munin.ub2.lu.se]  academic_email_conf               Free

 Keywords:
```

FIGURE 6-1. *A list of source files for a WAIS search*

If you are not certain which keys to use to move down in the list, try the up and down arrow keys. Depending on the WAIS program, you may be able to move a screen at a time with keys such as the J and K that SWAIS supports. The following keys are also supported in SWAIS:

Entry	Effect
##	Position on the source document number indicated by ##. (If you type **122**, source file 122 will be highlighted in the list of sources.)
/sss	Position on the source item beginning with the letters sss. (If you type **/dir**, the first source document beginning with the letters dir will be highlighted.)

Entry	Effect
Spacebar	Display the current item.
Enter	Display the current item.
j or ^N	Move down a line.
k or ^P	Move up a line.
J	Move down one screen.
K	Move up one screen.
S	Save current item in a file. (This option is not available in a Telnet session.)
m	Mail current item to the e-mail address specified.
v	View technical details about the current item.
s	Specify new sources for a search.
w	Enter keywords.
h	Display help.
q	Quit WAIS.
Ctrl+U	Clear the command line for a new entry.

 Key presses are automatically processed when the source list is active in SWAIS. There is no need to press the Enter key after pressing a key such as J or K.

What to Do When You Are Not Sure What Source File to Search

If you are not certain which source files are likely to contain the information you need, you can conduct a subject level search against the source file called directory of sources. Some servers might use a different name, but it is likely to be similar.

In the following example, we were trying to help a student doing a project on soybeans for a finance class. When searching the list of sources, we recommended using agriculture and commodities. When the list of sources was returned, we recommended searching the agriculture-market-news source for soybeans. The student was able to locate a Weekly Feed report that included current information on soybeans. You might follow these steps if you are trying to see if there are any sources providing information on agriculture and commodities:

1. With the source list onscreen, type **/directory** and press the Enter key to move to the location in the list that begins with directory.
At the quake.think.com WAIS site, this action highlighted the source directory of servers.

2. Mark this source with the spacebar. An asterisk marks the selected source.

3. Press the Enter key or type **w** to move to the keyword area at the bottom of the screen.

4. If keywords were entered earlier, press Ctrl-u to erase the current entries.

5. Type **agriculture commodities** and press the Enter key.

WAIS checks each word in the source directory of servers looking for either word in any entry. The result of the search is a list of sources that includes these titles:

Source	Score
sustainable-agriculture	1000
agriculture-market-news	783
usdacris	409
USDARCIS	407
epafutures	279

The source deemed most likely to meet your needs is at the top of the list with a score of 1000. Relative point values are assigned to the other search results. You can press the Enter key to see more detail about the source but will need to return to the original source list by typing **q** to quit the pager displaying the search results. You can look at each entry in the list of search results or evaluate your chances of finding what you are looking for by the names of each of the files. In this example, it seemed that the second source, which provided agriculture market reports, might provide the information the student needed; this would be the recommended first stop. We'll use that source with a keyword of "soybeans."

 You can also download a file that provides a description of many of the WAIS sources from FTP site archive.orst.edu. Look for the file src.list.txt in pub/doc/wais.

Specifying a Keyword Search

If you searched the directory of servers to identify the best sources for your subject area, you will need to quit the pager that is displaying the Search Results, then return to the source list by typing **s**. Next type **=** to unselect the directory of servers before selecting the sources you want to use to locate specific documents. Once you've marked the sources, you are ready to specify the keywords. WAIS keywords are easy to enter; unfortunately, there is no depth to their capabilities. No Boolean operators are supported to use the keywords in AND/OR combinations, and there is no way to prioritize the keywords. Every word in the documents (except articles and prepositions, which are considered common words) is compared to the keywords for which you are searching. For example, if you type **crop** for a keyword, WAIS will find documents that discuss an agricultural crop—but it will also find a match if the source contains an article on how to crop a pet's hair in the summer. WAIS does not consider content or context, but does a thorough job of searching for any keywords you specify.

To search for the keyword "soybean," follow these steps:

1. Type **w** when you are ready to make your entries.

2. Press Ctrl-U to erase the current keyword entries.

3. Type the new keywords and press the Enter key.

To look for documents containing the word soybeans, type **soybeans**. The search results are returned as shown in Figure 6-2. You can highlight the one you think most closely meets your needs, and press the Enter key. In the soybean example, a Weekly Feed report with a current date was selected. The first

```
┌─────────────────────────────────────────────────────────────┐
│ -                    NETCOM NetCruiser                  │ │ │
│  File  Edit  View  Internet  Settings  Window  Help          │
│ ┌───┬────┬────┬───┬─────┬─────┬─────┬───┬─────┬───┬─────┐     │
│ │ ? │ ⬎ │ 🚗 │   │ 🔄 │ ▦ │ ▨ │   │TEL│ 🕸 │ ▦ │      │
│ │   │    │    │   │     │     │     │   │NET│     │   │      │
│ └───┴────┴────┴───┴─────┴─────┴─────┴───┴─────┴───┴─────┘     │
│ ┌───────────────────────────────────────────────────────┐   │
│ │ -              Telnet To: quake.think.com              │   │
│ │ SWAIS              Search Results            Items: 32 │ │ │
│ │   #   Score   Source            Title           Lines │   │
│ │ 001: [1000] (agricultural-ma) Re:   JO GR211,WEEKLFEED   169 │
│ │ 002: [1000] (agricultural-ma)   LS.MN.YY.Re:   WH LS130  156 │
│ │ 003: [ 910] (agricultural-ma) Re:   JO GR210,WEEKLYFEED  148 │
│ │ 004: [ 910] (agricultural-ma) Re:   MS GR215 MPLS FEEDSTUFFS  61 │
│ │ 005: [ 910] (agricultural-ma) Re:   PA GR110             34 │
│ │ 006: [ 819] (agricultural-ma) Re:   GX GR211             53 │
│ │ 007: [ 728] (agricultural-ma) Re:   RH GR110            112 │
│ │ 008: [ 728] (agricultural-ma) Re:   WA FV199            346 │
│ │ 009: [ 637] (agricultural-ma) Re:   JO GR115  WEEKLY GRAIN  90 │
│ │ 010: [ 637] (agricultural-ma) Re:   LR GR210             43 │
│ │ 011: [ 637] (agricultural-ma) Re:   SJ GR210 KC FEED     36 │
│ │ 012: [ 637] (agricultural-ma) Re:   SJ GR851 CORRECTION NAT GRAIN SUM  92 │
│ │ 013: [ 546] (agricultural-ma) Re:   GX GR210 ST. LOUIS FEEDSTUFFS  47 │
│ │ 014: [ 546] (agricultural-ma) Re:   MD GR111 WISC GRAIN  51 │
│ │ 015: [ 546] (agricultural-ma) Re:   MS GR111 CBT         54 │
│ │ 016: [ 546] (agricultural-ma) Re:   MS GR210 WKLYFDSTF$  34 │
│ │ 017: [ 546] (agricultural-ma) Re:   MS GR711 CBOT SETTLEMENT  54 │
│ │ 018: [ 546] (agricultural-ma) Re:   RH GR111            54 │
│ └───────────────────────────────────────────────────────┘   │
└─────────────────────────────────────────────────────────────┘
```

FIGURE 6-2. *Documents in the search results for soybeans*

part of the document is displayed on the screen as shown in Figure 6-3. If you are using a local WAIS client, you can save the file to disk. Otherwise, if you need a copy, use the mail option to e-mail yourself a copy. You can browse the document on screen, using Space to see more of it, then type **q** when you are ready to quit the pager.

The pager supports only limited commands such as q for quit and the spacebar or arrow keys to move through the document.

Looking for WAIS in Unexpected Places

Many Web and Gopher sites provide access to WAIS capabilities. You'll just have to do a little checking. For example, the liberty.uc.wlu.edu Gopher menu offers a look at new Internet resources. After selecting this option, you can

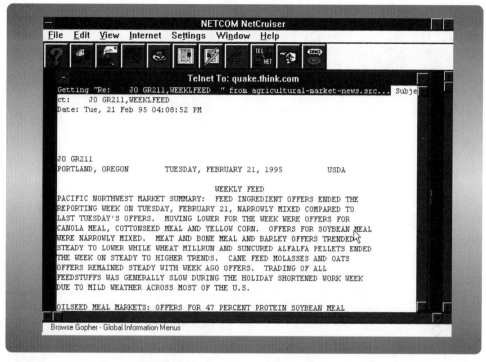

FIGURE 6-3. *WAIS actually displays the source documents it finds with a pager*

choose the type of new Internet resource in which you are interested. After selecting new WAIS sources, a list of new WAIS server databases appears. You can click on any option and the Gopher will provide a text box and let you enter your keywords. In Figure 6-4, the Gingrich entry is used to check the U.S. Congress information.

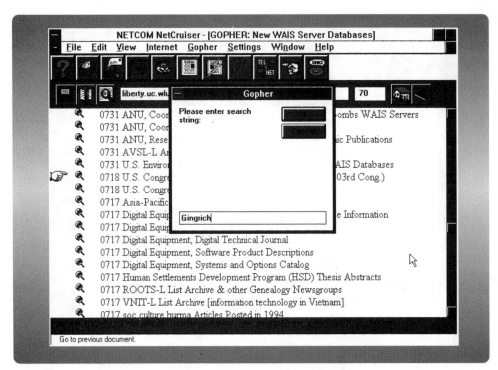

FIGURE 6-4. *Using NetCom's Gopher interface to perform a WAIS search*

Just for Fun

Most WAIS resources are pretty serious stuff. There are a few sources you might find interesting when you are in the mood for goofing off. You'll find recipes, Aesop's Fables, and science fiction review source files to play with when you have some spare time.

Aesop-Fables.src

recipes.src

sf-reviews.src

Chapter 7

The World-Wide Web

THE WORLD-WIDE WEB (better known as the Web or WWW) is a gateway to all of the Internet's resources. It was developed for the scientists involved in the CERN project in Switzerland and is designed to provide a much friendlier interface than the command-line entries required when using each of the other Internet services directly.

Documents developed for the Web follow the hypertext model, which allows the selection of highlighted text to transport you to either a new section of the text or a brand-new document. Hypertext itself is not new. It was first touted as a solution for the information explosion in the 1960s and was later popularized in the Macintosh environment with the introduction of a software program known as HyperCard, which allowed users to construct their own hypertext applications easily. The Web introduces these hypertext features for text data stored on Web servers. In fact, the Web goes beyond hypertext and could more appropriately be called a hypermedia tool since it supports video, graphics, and audio. The exact capabilities available to you when you use the Web depend on the browser or viewer you use to access Web documents.

You can perform all of your Internet tasks from the Web if you want because it allows you to access Gopher data transfer files, locate newsgroup data, and carry out many other functions. All of these tasks can be performed in a full-screen graphical environment.

Since 1992 the WWW has grown increasingly in popularity. Its use has grown much faster than other Internet tools because it provides these features:

- Access to all types of Internet resources without command-line entries

- Utilization of graphics, sound, and video information along with text

- Links to related material without the need to predefine menus

- Use of one interface for all Internet tasks

After reading this chapter you should be able to do the following:

- Describe the features offered by the Web that are not available with other Internet tools

- Name several popular browsers

- Define a URL and describe its components

- Specify various file transfer formats

- Enter URL's with correct syntax

- Describe typical browser features

- Describe the basic steps needed to define a home page

- Define HTML codes and what they offer

- Create a document with basic HTML codes

WEB BROWSERS

Web browsers are viewers that are designed to display data coded for the Web as well as information from other Internet resources. The browser that you use determines how the Web information is displayed. Some browsers provide a text-only capability and cannot display the richer content of Web files that may include graphics, video, or audio clips. Some browsers even support access to auxiliary programs such as Excel to display an external spreadsheet file. No matter which browser you choose, you will be able to access thousands of research sources. The only thing you might miss are the effects of a multimedia presentation.

Mosaic

Mosaic is one of the best-known browsers for the Web. It requires a TCP/IP connection. It may be available as part of your campus network or, if you have a connection to the Internet, you may be able to install it locally. There are versions for PC Windows, X Window (UNIX), and the Macintosh. Since the current Windows version is a 32-bit application, it uses the Win32 add-on libraries and requires that you run 386-enhanced mode Windows with a swap file. You would also need a program such as the shareware Trumpet Winsock to let Windows utilize TCP/IP.

If your computer is connected to your campus network or if you have SLIP access, you might consider downloading copies of the files needed to run Mosaic from your machine. If you decide to use the program Trumpet Winsock, you'll find that the nominal shareware fee is quite reasonable. You can use FTP to get Trumpet Winsock from the site ftp.utas.edu.au in the /pc/trumpet/wintrump directory (wtwsk???.zip) and the Windows 32-bit libraries from the site ftp.ncsa.uiuc.edu in the PC/Mosaic directory (win32s.zip). Mosaic is at the same site in the same directory (wmos???.zip). Note the ?s represent the numbers shown in these positions in the filename.

Netscape

Netscape is another browser, used at Case Western Reserve University. It is the most popular browser at the Weatherhead School of Management. When it is loaded from any Weatherhead faculty or student workstation, the Weatherhead School of Management home page shown in Figure 7-1 displays. A home page like this serves two purposes: it allows you to present an image of what you or your institution is about, and it lets you establish links to other sites of interest. In the CWRU home page the highlighted entries point to other Web or Gopher servers on campus as well as at other sites around the world. If you have a Web browser available through your campus system, your home page will provide a completely different set of links since each site's home page defines the links it feels are most appropriate. At some campuses students are given the ability to create their own home page. This allows them to share research interests with other students and to define a custom set of links for sites frequently visited.

Like Mosaic, Netscape is a very popular browser. It is inexpensive; single copies of the Netscape Navigator license are available for as little as $39, including 90 days of support. There are versions that run on the Windows, Windows NT, Mac, DEC, and Sun platforms. You can get more information on the various platforms supported and the current cost of individual and network copies by sending e-mail to info@netscape.com or by cruising their electronic store located at http://home.mcom.com/netstore/index.html. Or, you can reach them by phone at (415) 528-2555.

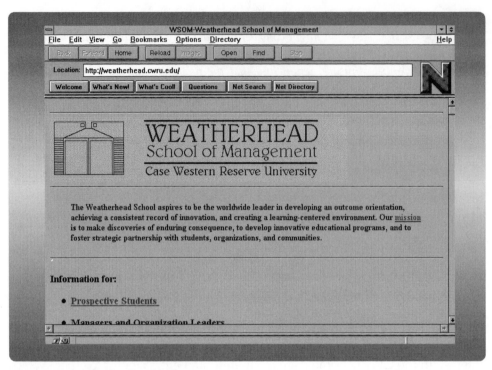

FIGURE 7-1. *Weatherhead home page*

Other Popular Campus Browsers

There are numerous browsers that access the Web. Cello, which is a Windows-based browser developed at Cornell University, is available through anonymous FTP at this location:

```
file://fatty.law.cornell.edu (in directory /pub/LII/cello)
```

To run Cello on your machine, you need a configuration identical to what was discussed for Mosaic and Netscape.

Lynx is a full-screen text browser that you can access with a Telnet session. Because it is full-screen, it requires that you emulate a VT100 terminal. You might Telnet to Lynx at this location to give it a try using www as your login:

```
telnet://lynx.cc.ukans.edu
```

Other text-based browsers accessible through Telnet are line oriented. You can Telnet to one in Hungary if your terminal does not support full-screen.

You'll learn lots of interesting facts about Hungary. You can use www as your login at this site:

```
telnet://fserv.kfki.hu
```

Third-Party Web Access

Campus access to the Internet is the preferred access method. In most cases, the cost of this resource use is built into your tuition and fees and you will not incur any direct charges. If your school bills separately for computer usage, these charges are normally quite reasonable for what you are getting. If you want to access the Web from home, ask if your institution provides dial-up SLIP access, or an alternative, for students. If it does not, you can contract with a third-party supplier of Internet access. The cost and sophistication of these services vary widely. Two of the most popular third-party suppliers are NetCom and Delphi. Both have a number of plans that provide a fixed number of hours during the month and a relatively low hourly fee for additional time. Figure 7-2 shows the Web browser available through NetCom's NetCruiser.

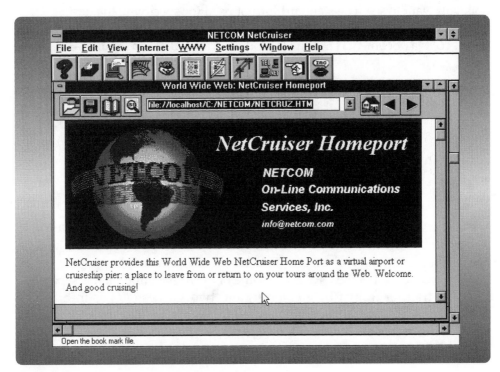

FIGURE 7-2. *NetCruiser's Web browser*

Check to see if the supplier you are considering has a local access number. If it does not, you will either have additional charges for a long-distance connection or a Tymnet or SprintNet surcharge.

ACCESSING RESOURCES

Once you are running a Web browser, you can access all types of Internet resources. Although a big advantage of the Web is being able to use the hypermedia links in Web documents to thread your way through all types of related information without the need for a menu, you can access any document you want directly by entering its location through a URL. In this section you will learn a little bit about constructing URLs as well as what it is like to look at resources you've been accessing with command-line entries.

The Simplicity of a URL

A Uniform Resource Locator (URL) is a pointer that tells your browser which data you want to see. The standard format used for specifying the desired URL is composed of four simple components that identify the critical elements needed to access a document. The four components are labeled in Figure 7-3.

Transfer Format	Host Computer	Directory Path	Filename

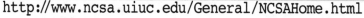

`http://www.ncsa.uiuc.edu/General/NCSAHome.html`

FIGURE 7-3. *URL components*

The first part of the URL is the transfer format, which indicates the type of server the document is located on and specifies the transfer format that will be needed. Some common transfer formats are shown in Table 7-1.

The second part of the URL is the name of the host computer. It is separated from the transfer format by a colon (:) and two slashes (//) as in http://-www.cwru.edu. Standard Internet naming standards are used by each institution that is a part of the Internet.

Transfer Format Specification	Server Accessed
http	World Wide Web
gopher	Gopher
file	FTP
news	USENET

TABLE 7-1. *Common Transfer Formats*

The third part of the URL is the directory path on the host computer where the data is stored. Again, standard Internet and UNIX naming standards apply. Note that components of the directory location are separated from each other with a slash (/), not the backslash (\) that some other operating systems expect.

The last part of the URL is the filename itself. Web documents are usually given the extension .html or .htm. It is important that your entry in the File Open dialog box or the link that you establish from a home page matches exactly. This is also true for the capitalization present in any component. Since UNIX is case-sensitive, you need to match capitalization and spelling carefully.

Other Web Sites

You can cruise through the hyperspace of other Web servers with direct links to documents on these servers. Typically you will have the address of a home page of an organization located through this book, online news services and bulletin boards, or organizations of which you are a member. Using the capabilities of your browser, you will request that it open the site at the remote location by specifying the URL, which begins with http:// if it is a Web server.

Other Resources

You can access more than Web pages if you specify the proper transfer format and location. Gophers, FTP servers, and newsgroups can be accessed. Since many campuses are also served by Gophers, this is another type of connection you will frequently make. In fact, some schools have added a bit of extra overhead and have servers that function in dual capacity functioning as both a Web and a Gopher server. Because Gopher servers typically provide a hierarchical menu structure to access the resources available, you may prefer this approach when you want an overview of what is available and it is not provided from the Web home page you accessed initially. The Gopher server at the University of Minnesota is accessed with this URL:

```
gopher://gopher.tc.umn.edu
```

It looks like Figure 7-4 when accessed using Netscape's Web browser.

You can use FTP to go to a site to download software or data that provides downloading capabilities. For example, to access information on network law, you would contact this site using anonymous for your login and your e-mail address for your password:

```
ftp://ftp.sura.net
```

You will have to provide the directory /pub/nic and the filename network.law.info. Most browsers will display the directory structure for you. This is much easier than using FTP through command-line entries to locate what you want.

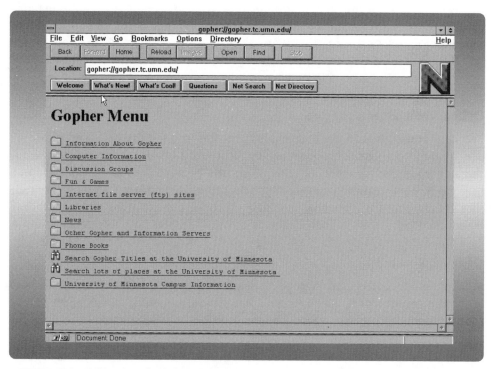

FIGURE 7-4. *University of Minnesota Gopher accessed with the Netscape browser*

You can establish a Telnet connection from the Web as long as your Web session was not established via Telnet with a remote host. Also, some of the third-party providers provide a special menu option for Telnet and do not support this type of connection from their Web browser.

TYPICAL BROWSER FEATURES

There are many browsers (quite a few of which are available in several versions), yet most share some common features. Watch for options providing the basic capabilities mentioned here as you look through the menu options your browser provides. These are the features that you will use again and again.

Access to Local and Remote URLs

As noted previously, URLs point to the names of the documents that you want to view with your Web browser. The File menu of most browsers provides commands for opening a remote or local URL.

History

Many browsers provide a way to go back to your most recently accessed documents without using the File Open menu again. These options might be located under a Navigate menu or may be available through a toolbar with a button that allows you to look back at previous documents.

Bookmarks and Hot Lists

As you work with the Internet sites, you are going to identify favorite places that you will want to revisit frequently. Rather than type the long address each time you need to access the site, you will want to define a bookmark or hot-list entry. Your browser will provide a way to go directly to these documents without retyping a URL. With Netscape's browser you establish bookmarks that can have unique names. You can activate the list by clicking the Bookmark option in the menu and selecting an established bookmark.

Figure 7-5 shows a bookmark list. You can add a new one for the current location by selecting the Bookmark option and Add Bookmark. With Mosaic you can use a Navigate menu option to add the current document to the hot list. When you open the File Open URL dialog box, you can click the drop-down list arrow to look at a hot list of documents as shown in Figure 7-5.

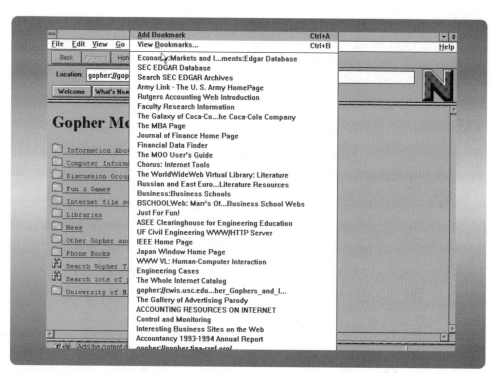

FIGURE 7-5. *Netscape bookmark list*

CREATING HTML DOCUMENTS

Hypertext Markup Language (HTML) documents have special codes that allow you to format pages for viewing with a Web browser. You can facilitate your research in two ways if you learn to create these documents by:

- Setting up your own home page with links to frequently accessed sites
- Creating a Web page to be read by other researchers in your area of interest

Defining Your Own Web Pages

Although you can add bookmarks to return to Web documents that you will want to use again, you might find that creating your own home page is the best approach for the data you want to access on a regular basis. This capability is available for most browsers if you store your home page on your local hard disk drive. Essentially you create your own custom menu of http links to access the resources you want. As soon as you start your Web session, the home page will display and allow you to pick the site you want to access.

Creating a Page to Share Research Interests with Others

Putting your page out on a Web server is a good way to collaborate with others doing research in your area. Although this is not appropriate for a weekly report you need to write for a course, it is a good alternative for a semester-long or postgraduate project. Without incurring the cost of attending a conference to hear about the latest research in your area, you can often connect with others working in the same area. It may be possible to share good sources and preliminary results from efforts already undertaken to either expand your perspective or hone your focus. When creating pages for this purpose, you will want to provide an overview of your activities and interests on the first page. This will allow the readers to decide whether they want to explore information in more detail. You can create links to other documents that might present papers you have written, preliminary findings, or a bibliography composed to date. Figure 7-6 displays a page developed to share departmental activities. It is viewed locally with NetCruiser before putting the final page on the Web server for the university.

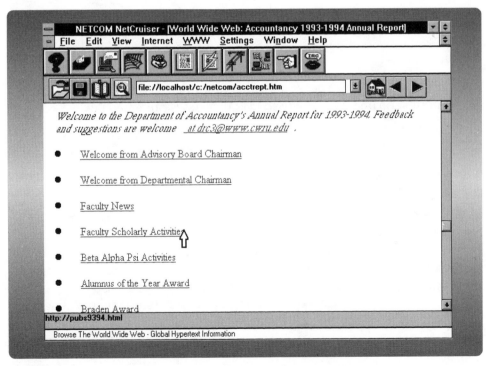

FIGURE 7-6. *Page viewed locally while under development*

Many schools, including the University of Notre Dame, are encouraging their students to put a personal home page out on the Web. Some schools are encouraging students to make their resumes available to recruiters using this resource. At most schools you will not be able to copy your HTML files directly to the Web server but will need to provide a copy on diskette to computer center staff for uploading to the Web server. Check with your computer center staff for the procedures at your institution.

An Overview of the Steps Needed to Create a Web Page

Although the specific codes needed to code your document are of obvious concern, there are some other important steps in the process. Many of these will vary slightly depending on your campus, but the following overview will guide you through the process:

1. Determine whether your school supports the creation of a Web page that is publicly accessible. If not, you can still create a local home page to access your favorite sites if your browser supports opening local URLs.

2. Determine what information you want to present and how you want to structure it. The ability to use hypertext links lets you provide a brief summary or outline with links to more information or related topics on other pages.

3. Enter the text for the pages and add appropriate HTML codes. More information on frequently used HTML codes is presented next.

4. Test the page by opening it locally if this feature is supported on your browser, and make any necessary coding corrections.

5. Copy the files to your Web server or have the appropriate computer center staff perform this function for you.

6. Determine the exact location for your pages. Test the access by opening your document directly as well as by opening it through any higher-level document that links to it. For example, if you are a graduate student in the chemistry department, your home page may have a link from the page that lists graduate research projects in chemistry at your institution. This step is necessary, since most universities will place student home pages somewhere within the campus-wide Web information.

Adding HTML Codes

Just a few codes are needed in an HTML document. We'll look at a few of them here so you will know the basics. You will also want to be able to go to a source document that contains the latest and greatest list of codes. There is a good source of online information that covers both Mosaic and HTML codes:

```
http://www.ncsa.uiuc.edu/SDG/Software/Mosaic/Docs/mosaic-docs.html
```

This document is updated as new coding options are added and is a good source if you want to impress fellow students with your expertise.

 Some browsers allow you to look at the codes in Web documents from other locations by selecting a command from the View menu that displays the source file.

Creating the Basic Document

The easiest way to create your document is with the word-processing package you use all the time. After adding the text and the codes, just remember to save the file as ASCII text. Normally this is a dialog box option for File Type once you have requested Save from the File menu. This change in file type is very important since the codes in a word-processing document would not be recognizable by a Web browser. The following is part of a set of Web pages developed for a university department and corresponds to the sample shown in Figure 7-6.

```
<HTML><HEAD><TITLE>Accountancy 1993-1994 Annual Report</TITLE></HEAD>

<BODY>

<IMG SRC="casepic.gif"><P>

<I>Welcome to the Department of Accountancy's Annual Report for 1993-
1994. Feedback and suggestions are welcome <A
HREF="mailto:drc3@www.cwru"> at drc3@www.cwru.edu</A>.</I><P>

<UL><LI><A HREF="http://guido94.html">Welcome from Advisory Board
Chairman</A><P>

<LI> <A HREF="http://annrep94.html">Welcome from Departmental Chair-
man</A><P>

<LI> <A HREF="http://faculty.html">Faculty News</A><P>

<LI> <A HREF="http://pubs9394.html">Faculty Scholarly Activities</A><P>
```

```
<LI> <A HREF="http://bap.html">Beta Alpha Psi Activities</A><P>

<LI> <A HREF="http://aofyear.html">Alumnus of the Year Award</A><P>

<LI> <A HREF="http://braden.html">Braden Award</A><P>

<LI> <A HREF="http://departme.html">Department News</A><P>

<LI> <A HREF="http://alumni.html">Alumni News</A><P>

<LI> <A HREF="http://honoroll.html">Honor Roll of Giving</A><P>

</UL>

</BODY></HTML>
```

 If you are creating a file on your PC that will later be placed on your UNIX server, you will not be able to use the full .HTML extensions when you save the file on your PC. Instead, you will need to change the filename extension to UNIX when you copy it. If you are copying it to a UNIX server, remember that UNIX is case-sensitive.

Housekeeping Activities

At first glance, some codes that you will add to an HTML document don't seem to buy anything. The codes indicate to the Web browser that it is working with an HTML document and separate the sections of your document into a header and a body. Although most Web browsers will process your file correctly without these codes, it is a good idea to include them to ensure that browsers used by others will display your documents correctly. These codes are needed only once in each document, so it will not take too long to add them and you'll be playing it safe.

- Start each document with <HTML> to indicate the document type to the browser. The ended code in the pair is </HTML>, which should come at the end of your document.

- Use <HEAD> at the top of the document. Include a <TITLE> code as the first entry to title your page. End the title with a </TITLE> code followed by a </HEAD> code to end the header.

- Use <BODY> following the header. At the end of the page right before the </HTML> code, end the body with </BODY>.

Paragraph Marks

Paragraph codes insert a line feed at the end of a line. They make your Web pages much more readable. At the end of the line where you want a line feed to follow, enter <P>.

> *Even if you are an unsophisticated computer user, you can save some time by copying the coding from place to place. Select the code that you want to use in another location, then choose Copy from the Edit menu. Move to the location where you want the code, then choose Paste from the Edit menu.*

Headings

You can use six levels of headings in Web documents. The levels correspond to different font selections in most browsers. Begin a level 1 heading with <H1> and end it with </H1>. Replace the number 1 with a number between 2 and 6 for the other levels.

Special Font Styles

You might want to emphasize key elements of text in your Web documents. You can underline book titles, show a quote in italics, or boldface a time deadline with appropriate codes around the text to be affected. You can combine text style codes for additional effects.

You can add boldface to text by placing <B> immediately preceding the text to be shown in boldface. A </B> code should be placed at the end of the text shown in boldface. You might want to highlight the date for signing up for a seminar. The text **June 1, 1995** could be shown in boldface to call attention to the deadline. The entry for this text in the document looks like this: <B>June 1, 1995</B>.

The code to begin underlining is a <U> and to end it </U>. To underline a book title your entry might look like this: <U>Little Women</U>. The code for italics is I. <I>Call Ext 6870 for all UNIX support questions</I>. displays the entire phrase in italics like this: *Call Ext 6870 for all UNIX support questions.*

You can combine two or more of the codes by using both beginning and ending codes for each attribute you add: <B><U>We will be camping in Utah this summer while researching geologic formations. We would be interested in identifying other students with similar interests who may want to join us and share expenses.</B></U> These sentences display like this: **<u>We will be camping in Utah this summer while researching geologic formations. We would be interested in identifying other students with similar interests who may want to join us and share expenses.</u>**

 Be careful not to overdo the use of special formatting since any links to other documents will be shown highlighted. This is especially true for the use of boldface—many users will try to execute hypertext links for them with unsuccessful clicks.

Graphics

Many Web browsers can display graphics with a Web page. Although graphics can be stored in many formats, including JPEG, GIF, and TIFF, you may want to utilize the GIF format since it is almost universally supported on all browsers with graphics capabilities. To insert the graphic students.gif at the current location on a Web page, type

```
<IMG SRC = "students.gif">
```

To prevent the display of an error message in a browser without graphics support, add an extra parameter that specifies an alternative message to display.

```
<IMG SRC = "students.gif" ALT="A picture of students at the
accounting banquet">
```

Since a location is not specified for the graphic file, it must be stored in the same location as the text for the current Web page.

Links

You can link to another Internet resource or to another location in the current Web page. You can use either text or an icon as the area to be clicked. Text will be highlighted to make it easy for the user to identify all the hypertext links presented on the screen at a glance. To link to another resource, use the <A> command. Although the command supports a number of parameters, the ones that are most widely used are

- The HREF parameter to specify the Internet resource that you want to access

- The text to be clicked to activate the link

- A mandatory </A> to indicate the end of the anchor command

The HREF parameter may include the type of link, the host computer, path, and filename or may be limited to the type of link and filename if you are using the same host and path as the current document.

For example, to have the user see the text "Click here to see a bibliography" stored as a Web page in the same location as the current page, type

```
<A HREF="http://bibliography.html">Click here to see a bibliog-
raphy</A>
```

If the bibliography is on a different Web server, specify the server and path as in

```
<A HREF="http://www.cwru.edu/students/research/chemistry/bibliog-
raphy.html">Click here to see a bibliography</A>
```

You can link to resources other than Web pages. Just use the proper type with your URL. To access a Gopher, start your HREF location with gopher:// rather than http://.

To establish an anchor to another location on the current Web page, you must use the anchor command to first name this location. The anchor command that establishes "start over" as the label for the current location uses the NAME parameter as shown here:

```
<A Name=start over>Here are all your options</A>
```

At the location where you want to provide an option for returning to the start over location if the user clicks "Begin Again," you would type

```
<A HREF="#start over">Begin Again</A>
```

The # indicates that the location is in the current document. If you want to display an icon and have the user click the icon image to link to another location, use <IMG SRC> code within the anchor command. For example:

```
<A HREF="http://details.html"><IMG DRC="icon1.gif">Click the icon
for more info</A>
```

Lists

You can create ordered lists, unordered lists, horizontal lists, and menu lists with special HTML coding. Each item within the list is marked with an <LI> code at the beginning regardless of the list type. Special codes that precede the first list item and follow the last one determine the type of list. For an unordered list the codes are <UL> and </UL>. The other list type codes are provided in Table 7-2.

List Type	Beginning Code	Ending Code
Ordered List	<OL>	</OL>
Horizontal List	<DIR>	</DIR>
Menu List	<MENU>	</MENU>

TABLE 7-2. *Other Types of List Codes*

Shortcuts to Adding the Codes

You can create a few macros for your word processor, use a special HTML editor, or obtain a special add-in to your favorite word processor (available for WordPerfect and Word). If you are going to code documents on a regular basis, you will find that these alternatives represent a considerable time saving over manually entering each code.

 Once your .HTML file is on the Web server, you may be able to use emacs or another UNIX editor to make minor changes. If you can access the server where your data is stored, this approach will allow you to make minor modifications much faster than uploading a whole new copy of the file to make a small change.

Just for Fun

Although the Web can provide your transportation to research sites around the world, you can also find leisure activities among its vast resources. If you happen to be a Trekkie and want to see all the Star Trek resources on the Internet, take a look at this Web page:

```
http://www.COSY.sbg.ac.at/rec/startrek/index.html
```

You'll find information on Internet role-playing games, books, episodes, quotes, pictures, sounds, and newsgroups. The Web offers more opportunities for leisure activities than you will be able to take advantage of, assuming grades are an important component of your school experience. Check out these major Web indexes for all types of information that interests you:

```
http://www.yahoo.com or http://akebono.stanford.edu
```

```
http://www.einet.net
```

```
http://www.gnn.com
```

You will find categories for topics such as Art Exhibits, Entertainment, Leisure and Recreation, Crafts, and Cooking.

Chapter 8

Other Internet Resources

ALTHOUGH YOU ALREADY HAVE a powerful group of Internet tools in your arsenal for winning the research battle, there are many more tools available through the Internet. You don't need to learn to use them all at once, but you will want to know a little bit about them to be aware of everything at your fingertips. Some of the things you will be able to do after reading this chapter are:

- Describe what a newsgroup is

- State what is needed to use a newsgroup

- Describe a mailing list

- Understand the difference between sending a message to the administrator versus the entire list readership

- Locate individuals on a given host computer

- Locate an individual with only his/her name

USENET NEWSGROUPS

Usenet consists of thousands of discussion groups called **newsgroups**. The topics discussed range from academic topics of interest to researchers to local news, recipes, etiquette, and investments. It seems as though there is at least one newsgroup for almost any topic. There are also news services such as Clarinet to which your site may subscribe. Unlike Usenet, which is actually many discussion groups, Clarinet provides current news but charges a site fee. (Whether or not these supplemental services are available may depend on the budget at your site.)

Newsreaders

You will need to use a newsreader to access the newsgroups that you decide to join. Popular readers on UNIX are tin, nn, and rn. You may have one or more and can ask around campus to see which ones fellow students prefer. If you subscribe to a commercial service such as NetCom, a newsreader is available.

*You can use the UNIX man command to get more information about the newsreaders available on your system. Type **man tin** to get a little more technical information about the tin newsreader.*

Although most of the newsreaders are started by typing in their name, some may require setup steps to create a .newsrc file for you to keep track of which of the available newsgroups you subscribe to. Since the newsreader commands on UNIX systems vary so much, let's take a quick look at the output of a Usenet session in NetCruiser instead.

If you are inexperienced with newsgroups, first read the news.announce.newusers and news.answers newsgroups. They provide valuable information for fledgling newsgroup users (newbies).

Using NetCom to Read the News

When you first start using the Usenet features on NetCom, you can select the groups you are interested in from a menu. The first part of the newsgroup name tells you something about the group. Use the following list to guide your initial selections:

Prefix	Subject Area
Alt	Alternative newsgroup typically with little censorship and at times some liberal topics
bionet	Biology
biz	Business
comp	Computers
news	Usenet related
rec	Hobbies and recreational topics
sci	Science

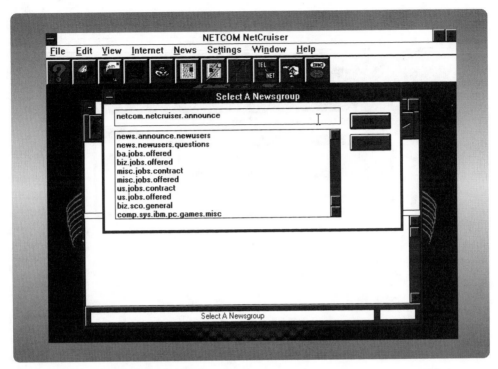

FIGURE 8-1. *Newsgroup subscriptions*

NetCom will monitor the lists for you. When you tell it you want to read Usenet articles, it supplies a list of the groups you've selected, as shown in Figure 8-1. When you choose a group, NetCruiser's newsreader looks to see which articles are awaiting your review. If it is an active group or it's been a while since you last looked at it, there may be more entries than you expected. Figure 8-2 shows that there are 400 entries in biz.jobs.offered that have not been reviewed. You can choose to review later entries by making selections in the dialog box. The headers from the selected articles are read in. You can select any header to read the article. Figure 8-3 shows part of the list at the top of the screen along with the first part of a selected article at the bottom of the screen. Easy-to-use icons let you either move to the next article or newsgroup or reply to any submission.

SUBSCRIBING TO MAILING LISTS

Like the discussion groups that you can participate in through Usenet, mailing lists also have a topic or interest. There are thousands of lists, and you can find

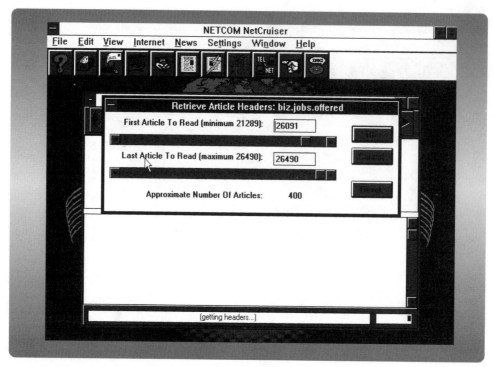

FIGURE 8-2. *Accessing biz.jobs.offered*

everything from serious academic disciplines such as quantum physics to jokes and erotic literature. Since everyone with Internet access has an e-mail address, your ability to participate is not dependent on client software installed at your institution. Lists offer an advantage over the Internet Relay Chat (IRC) groups because they are not time dependent; you can sign on at any time and check your e-mail for messages that may have been added to the list since you last read your mail. With IRC, you see only messages that appear while you are connected. Although IRC offers the advantage of an immediate response to a question, you are less likely to acquire pertinent information unless you have many hours to monitor the conversations. Another advantage of mailing lists is that they're less chatty than IRC groups.

Joining a Mailing List

You need to subscribe to a mailing list to start receiving the messages that make up a mailing list. Unlike magazine subscriptions to printed media such as

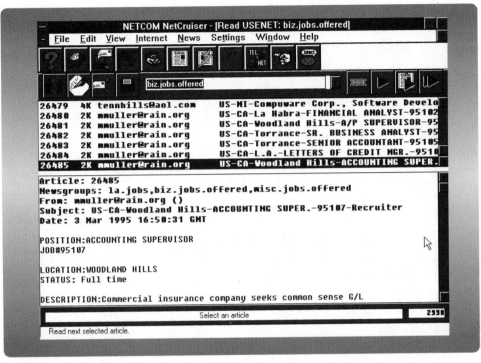

FIGURE 8-3. *Selecting a header to read an article*

Sports Illustrated or *Business Week,* there is no charge for subscribing to a mailing list—just send an e-mail message to the individual or computer program that administers the list. There are several places you can look for information on mailing lists that might be of interest:

- Check the WAIS database named mailing lists. The keyword search capability that WAIS supports makes it easy to focus on lists of potential interest.

- Use FTP to connect with Kent State ksuvxa.kent.edu. Get the acadlist.readme in the library directory.

- Use FTP to connect to Dartmouth at dartcms1.dartmouth.edu. Get the READ.ME file in the siglists directory for directions.

- If you have access to Usenet, check its news.lists.

Mailing lists are popular on other worldwide networks such as Bitnet. Although these networks are a little different from the Internet, the subscription process is similar if you have access to these networks.

There may be a special format required for subscriptions to lists administered by a computer, since the programs that process your request scan for specific information. You will need to provide information in the exact format requested. Some requests will have listserv in the domain and can be sent as shown:

```
mail listserv.harvarda.harvard.edu
Subject: Subscription request
SUB taxacom ffffff llllllll
```

The ffffff and llllllll are replaced by your first and last name, respectively. Following your request, you will begin receiving discussion list information of interest to biologists. To post information for members of the discussion group, use the address taxacom.harvarda.harvard.edu.

For other requests you might be asked to append -request after the first word, as in:

```
soundtracks-request@ifi.unizh.ch
```

Sending your request to soundtracks@ifi.unizh.ch posts your subscription request to the entire group. Other groups may request that you send a message to the system administrator.

Posting Messages

As you begin subscribing to lists that interest you, the volume of your electronic mail will increase substantially, and you will begin to make your own contributions to the lists when you post your messages to everyone on the list. Of course, you always have the option of e-mailing just the writer. You might decide to do so if the writer has asked for help with an obscure problem, or if the writer is a new member who might not have seen a past posting with which other readers are already familiar.

FINGER

Finger can help you locate individuals if you know their host computer. You can search this host by the individual's userid or name. Assuming the finger program is installed at your site, type

```
finger drc3@po.cwru.edu
```

The resulting display shows the individual's name, as in:

```
David R. Campbell
```

The finger server may also display information about the person's mail, phone number, and last login. If the individual you are trying to locate has a .plan and a .project file in his or her home directory, some of the information in these files also displays.

If you don't know the host system an individual uses, read the next section to learn how you can locate them with Netfind.

NETFIND

Netfind can help you locate a person if you supply his or her name. Let's say you are trying to locate Gary Previts at Case Western Reserve University in Cleveland, Ohio. You can search by name combined with city, state, or university as in these entries:

```
netfind previts cleveland ohio
netfind previts case western
netfind previts case western reserve university
```

Unfortunately, you often get more matches than you were bargaining for and will have to select domains to search further. The domains must have a white pages directory for your search to work. Although this is not a fail-safe method for locating an individual, it is worth a try.

There are a number of public servers you can use if Netfind isn't available. Try one that's listed in Table 8-1. You need to Telnet to the site specified and use the user name netfind.

Site	User Name
Alabama	redmont.cis.uab.edu
Minnesota	mudhoney.micro.umn.edu
Virginia	ds.internic.net

TABLE 8-1. *Publicly Accessible Netfind Servers*

When you first login, you will need to choose item 2 from this menu to begin your search:

```
Top level choices:

        1. Help

        2. Search

        3. Seed database lookup

        4. Options

        5. Quit (exit server)

Enter person and keys (blank to exit) --> previts cwru edu cleve-
land ohio

previts cwru edu cleveland ohio
```

The list returned has 71 different domains connected with Case Western Reserve University and must be stopped with your system's Pause key combination if you want to read it. You are limited to three selections.

```
Please select at most 3 of the following domains to search:

        68. student.cwru.edu (case western reserve university,
cleveland, ohio)

        69. ucom.cwru.edu (case western reserve university, cleve-
land, ohio)

        70. uh.cwru.edu (case western reserve university, cleve-
land, ohio)
```

```
        71. ul.cwru.edu (case western reserve university, cleve-
land, ohio)

Enter selection (e.g., 2 0 1) --> 0 33 68


  0 33 68
```

The results returned this time will indicate if an entry is found that matches the name you entered.

Just for Fun

There are hundreds of Usenet groups that begin with rec, indicating that they contain information on recreation, the arts, and all types of hobbies. Although your main interest might be in subscribing to groups for your research effort, allow yourself to subscribe to at least one group that is purely for entertainment. Here are just a few:

rec.arts.movies	rec.arts.poems	rec.games.pinball
rec.games.video.arcade	rec.boats	rec.food.recipes
rec.games.chess	rec.pets.dogs	rec.sport.golf
rec.travel	rec.video	rec.woodworking

Chapter 9

The Humanities

SINCE THE HUMANITIES REFER to any area of study that emphasizes the importance of man, the list of potential courses that would come under this umbrella is quite lengthy. Art, architecture, anthropology, history, journalism, literature, language, psychology, religion, and many others qualify for inclusion. History and literature sites are covered in Chapters 15 and 17, respectively. Some of the best humanities sites for the remaining disciplines are classified by topic within this chapter. Most of these sites provide information for other humanities disciplines.

ART/ARCHITECTURE

The entries in this section focus on architecture and fine arts. You will find additional sites for other art-related areas as you browse these items. You can check a resource like the World-Wide Web Worm or use WAIS to help you locate additional resources for your area of study.

ArchiGopher

gopher://libra.arch.umich.edu

Greek architecture, Tunisian architecture, and image archives are just a few other options at this gopher site. Figure 9-1 shows some of the options in this site's gopher menu.

Architecture Index

http://www.clr.toronto.edu.1080/VIRTUALLIB/arch.html

This site provides announcements of interest to architects. It also contains other resources with access to older listings.

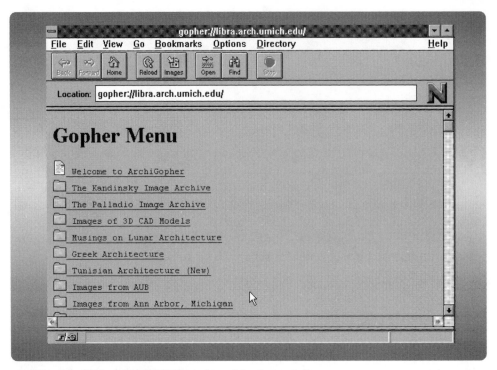

FIGURE 9-1. *University of Michigan's architecture gopher*

Architecture Resources

http://indycad.archlab.tuwien.ac.at

There are links to gophers, WWW servers, FTP sites, and electronic journals from this Vienna site. You will also find information on architecture news-groups and list servers.

ArtServe Australian National University

http://rubens.anu.edu.au

This server has many resources related to art history and architecture. There are over 10,000 images. Some of the menu options include

- Prints A–Z
- Hong Kong images
- Classical Turkish architecture

- Islamic architecture
- Leni Rieffenstahl images
- Classical architecture

FineArt Forum–Mississippi State University

`http://www.msstate.edu/Fineart_Online/index.html`

This Web site can keep you busy all day checking out its many links. A few of the main areas covered are

- Galleries and electronic journals
- Museums
- Electronic art
- General and academic resources

Index Art Source

`http://www.uky.edu/Artsource/artsourcehome.html`

You will find links to gopher sites, museum information, art/architecture lectures, and art journals online at this location.

New York Art Line

`gopher://gopher.panix.com:70/11/nyart`

This is a great art resource with an emphasis on visual arts. Some of the main menu items are

- Arts wire
- Art magazines online
- Design—architecture, interior fashion, and more
- Galleries online
- Images and imaging software
- Museums and schools
- Technology and art
- Other art gophers

JOURNALISM AND DRAMA

This section lists journalism and drama resources.

English Server–Carnegie-Mellon University

```
gopher://english-server.hss.cmu.edu/
```

This well-known English server has some great resources for drama, film, TV, and fiction including Alex, which catalogs electronic texts on the Internet. You will also find resources here in these diverse areas: cultural theory, feminism, literacy, language, music, philosophy, poetry, and rhetoric.

Journalism Periodicals

```
http://www.rsl.ox.ac.uk/bardhtml/bardmenu.html
```

The Bodleian Library of Oxford University hosts this server that lets you search over fifty journalism periodicals containing thousands of citations. Choose selected Internet Resources, then Journalism.

Journalism Resources

```
gopher://gopher.tamu.edu:70/11/.dir/journalism.dir
```

This is a list of sites that caters to journalists. It includes FTP, gopher sites, newsgroups, and discussion lists.

Screenwriters and Playwrights Home Page

```
http://www.teleport.com/~cdeemer/scrwriter.html
```

This site includes a frequently asked questions list, reviews, scripts, and tips from the pros. Figure 9-2 shows some of the options from this site.

LANGUAGE AND LINGUISTICS

The Internet offers resources that will assist in the study of any language. You can also connect to foreign sites to practice reading in a foreign language.

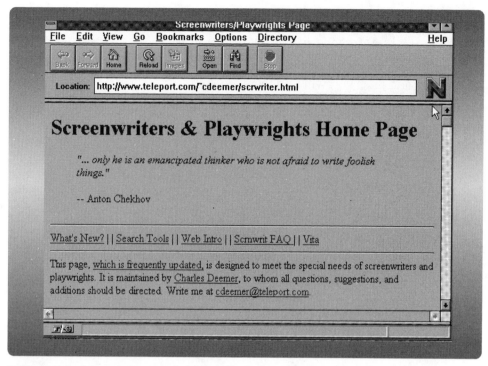

FIGURE 9-2. *Screenwriters and playwrights home page*

CELIA: Computer-Enhanced Language Instruction Archives

```
gopher://gopher.archive.merit.edu:7055/1/celia-gopher
```

Here are just a few of the languages you will find resources for at this gopher:

- Thai
- Spanish
- Welsh
- Russian
- Italian
- German
- Japanese

General Language–Rice University

```
gopher://riceinfo.rice.edu/11/Subject/Language
```

There are resources for many different languages at this gopher. Some of the information and links you will find there are

- Italian–Humanities
- LING Linguistics (University of Oregon)
- Nordic Linguistics Bulletin
- Small Urdu dictionary
- Spanish gophers
- Voice of America News in many languages with sound files
- Welsh language and culture archive

Human Language

```
http://www.willamette.edu/~tjones/Language-Page.html
```

You will find dictionaries, tutorials, and spoken language samples at this site.

Linguistics

```
http://www.sil.org/linguistics/linguistics.html
```

For an incredible list of worldwide resources, check this site. Some of the links you will find are

- World-Wide Web Virtual Library Index for Linguistics
- Conferences, workshops, and meetings
- LINGUIST List Web Sources
- University of Rochester Linguistics home page
- Association for Computational Linguistics
- Centre for Computing in the Humanities
- University of Michigan Linguistics Server
- The American Dialect Society
- Center for Advanced Research on Language Acquisition

- Natural Language Software Registry

- Department of Linguistics at Stockholm

- Universal Survey of Languages Proposal

Ohio University CALL Lab

`http://www.tcom.ohiou.edu/OU_Language/OU_Language.html`

You will find language resources, projects, information tools, and news at this site. Figure 9-3 shows the screen after making the connection to this site.

MISCELLANEOUS

If you want to browse for information on a given area, these sites are great places to start your cruising.

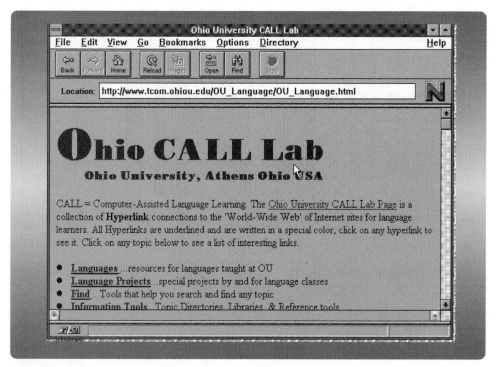

FIGURE 9-3. *Ohio University CALL Lab initial screen*

Art and Humanities Index

`http://lib-www.ucr.edu/rivera`

The listings here are diverse. The following sampling shows several entries beginning with the letter A. The numeral in parentheses indicates the number of entries available in each category:

- Anthropology (5)
- Archeology (7)
- Architecture (6)
- Art (15)
- Asian studies (3)

Photography Index

`http://www.ksu.edu/~camk/photography.html`

You will find listings of newsgroups and links to other photography resources and galleries at this site. Figure 9-4 shows a small portion of the information you can access from this site.

Oxford University's HUMBOL Humanities Home Page

`http://sable.ox.ac.uk/departments/humanities/international.html`

Some of the subject-specific resources at this site are

- Anthropology
- Archeology
- Classics
- Electronic text centers
- Film and media studies
- History
- Hypermedia and multimedia
- Language and linguistics
- Medieval studies
- Music

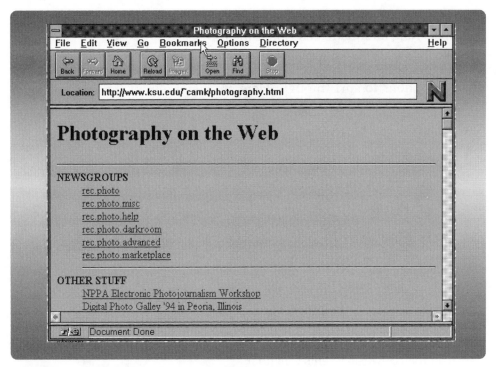

FIGURE 9-4. *Kent State's photography links*

- Philosophy
- Religious studies
- Visual arts

MUSIC

Whether you are looking for classical music or rock-and-roll, you can find a wealth of information at the following sites.

Indiana University–Music Resources

```
http://www.music.indiana.edu/misc/music_resources.html
```

This site has links to all types of music resources on the Internet. Academic links include other schools, electronic magazines, FTP sites, and newsgroups.

Non-academic site links include record company home pages, a hitlist, a MIDI home page, and information on Gothic music.

This gopher contains information maintained by the Indiana University Music Library. If you explore each branch of the main menu, there are hundreds of options to surf through. Here are just a few of the non-academic Web sites:

- Adam Curry's Metaverse
- Artist and band photos
- The Atlanta Symphony Orchestra
- Allegro Records
- The American Music Center
- American recordings
- AMM/Lipstick and Jazzline
- Patrick Godfrey/Apparition Music
- ASCAP: Live from South by Southwest
- Automatrix Music Events Calendar
- Axiom Records: The Music of Bill Laswell
- Bad Habits Music
- Ballet Austin
- Banjo Collection
- The Big Backyard
- Big Dummy's Guide to the Internet—Music
- Big Dummy's Guide to the Internet—Gopher Music
- Big Marble Foot Records
- Black Boot Records
- The Blue Highway
- Blue Jay Recording Studios
- BMG Australia

- BMG Music Club / Columbia House Catalogs
- BMG Classical Music World
- Bogus Records
- BOMP! Records Internet Cabal
- BPM Music Express
- Breakfast Records
- Canadian Internet Music Resources
- Caroline Records
- Christmas Music
- Musical CD database search

Web Wide World of Music

`http://american.recordings.com/wwwofmusic/`

This site provides over 3,000 links to bands with 1,000 Web pages. There are also numerous music links, a trivia quiz, and music charts and polls.

Classical Music

`http://akebono.stanford.edu/yahoo/Entertainment/Music/Classical_Music`

This Stanford Yahoo index is great to consult on any topic. Some of the entries for classical music are

- Bach
- Classical MIDI archives
- Classical music reviews
- Early music
- Opera
- Promoters
- Symphony orchestras
- WWW classical music resources
- Sony Music's classical artists

Musical Newsgroups

`http://www.leeds.ac.uk/music/NetInfo/MNews.html`

This document provides a list of sites such as rec.music.reviews where you can read reviews of singles and albums.

Jazz Web–WNUR-FM

`http:www.acns.nwu.edu/jazz`

This radio station provides all types of jazz information. Some of the options are

- Jazz artists
- Wolverine Antique Music Society
- Jazz improvisation
- Jazz education
- Other jazz resources on the Web

Country and Western Music

`http://www.nol.com/nol/NOL_Home.html`

If you are researching the craze that seems to be taking today's aging boomer generation by storm, you will want to visit this site. Nashville Online, will let you sample the lyrics from a different group of songs each month. After looking at the songs, you can check other resources such as record labels, recording studios, and independent artists.

University of Illinois at Urbana–Champaign–Music Education

`http://www.ed.uiuc.edu/EdPsy-387/Tina-Scott/project/home.html`

This site lists the major research journals in music education and provides links to all types of music education resources.

PHILOSOPHY

Whether you want to study about French philosophers like Sartre and Voltaire or the ancient Greek philosophers Plato and Socrates, the Internet has resources that can help you.

Department of Philosophy–Utrecht University, The Netherlands

`gopher://gopher.phil.ruu.nl/`

This department's gopher has the following options:

- Electronic texts
- Frequently asked questions
- Journals
- Bibliographies
- Conferences
- Mailing lists

University of California, Irvine

`http://philosophy.cwis.uci.edu`

After selecting UCI Libraries, you can explore information on philosophy and other humanities by selecting Humanities. There is also a fine arts listing you might want to explore.

University of Chicago

`http://csmaclab-www.uchicago.edu/philosophy/Project/philos.html`

This project provides an electronically mediated discussion forum for philosophical works. At the current time these discussions include

- A criticism of Nelson Goodman's theory of metaphor
- A proposal of a new theory of pictorial representation
- The Language of Thought Hypotheses
- Kripke's Naming and Necessity
- A discussion of counterfactuals

- Philosophy and genetics
- Philosophical approaches to the work of Noam Chomsky

The Electronic Journal of Analytic Philosophy

```
http://www.phil.indiana.edu/ejap/ejap.html
```

This page provides access to the articles in current and back issues of the journal. Figure 9-5 shows this journal's home page.

American Philosophical Association Gopher

```
gopher://gate.oxy.edu:70/1
```

Some of the information in the main menu includes:

- Grants, fellowships, and academic positions
- Bibliographies
- Software for philosophers
- Internet resources
- Philosophical images

Philosophy Newsgroups

Here are two newsgroups you may want to look at if you have access to a newsreader.

Group	Topic
comp.ai.philosophy	Philosophical issues
sci.logic	Formal logic and philosophy

PSYCHOLOGY AND SOCIOLOGY

If you are interested in Sigmund Freud or Carl Jung, you can start at the following sites.

Demography and Population Studies

```
http://coombs.anu.edu.au/ResFacilities/DemographyPage.html
```

This site provides over 100 links to worldwide demographic information.

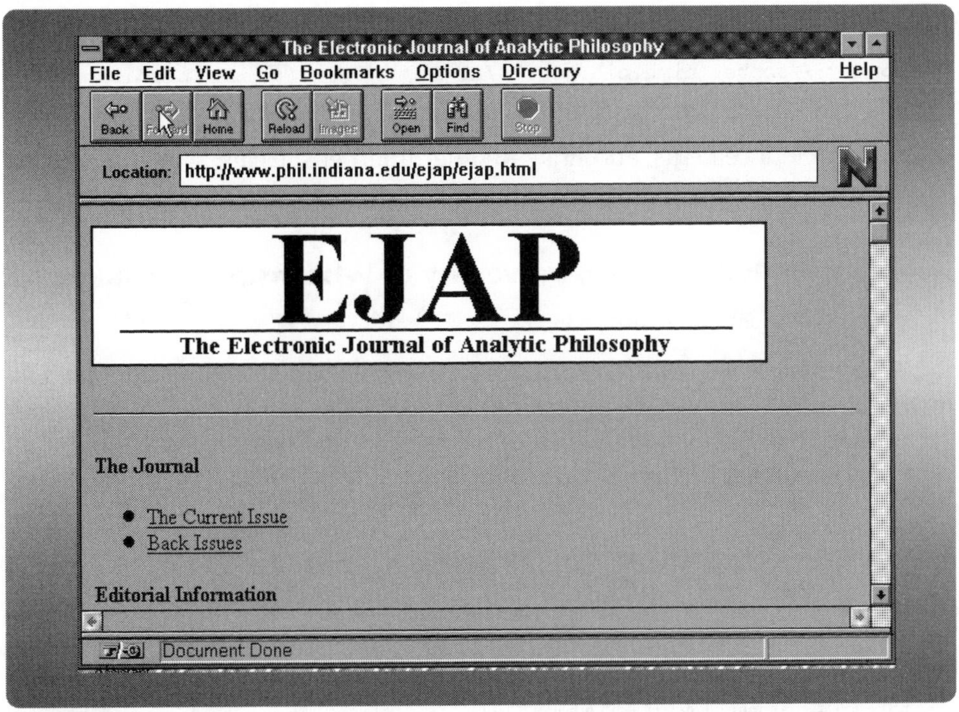

FIGURE 9-5. *The Electronic Journal of Analytic Philosophy home page*

Human Rights Organization

```
gopher://gopher.humanrights.org
```

A number of groups, including Amnesty International, have contributed to this site. You will find information with regional, national, and international focuses.

American Psychological Society

```
gopher://gopher.hanover.edu:70/11/Public/APS
```

This site includes general and subscription information about the American Psychological Society as well as other resources. Selected articles from the organization's *Observer* publication are available along with posters from recent conferences and software for PC and Mac users. There are links to other resources including the student caucus sponsored by the group.

National Institutes of Mental Health

`gopher://gopher.nimh.nih.gov:70/11`

General information about the organization, an FTP archive, documents, program announcements, and links to other Internet sites are available. Figure 9-6 shows some of the gopher menu options.

Behavior Analysis Archive, University of Wisconsin, Milwaukee

`gopher://alpha1.csd.uwm.edu`

After connecting, select University of Wisconsin Milwaukee (academic) followed by UWM information/Psychology/Behavior Analysis. You will find papers and manuscripts, lecture and lab materials, and other resources of interest to the researcher in this field.

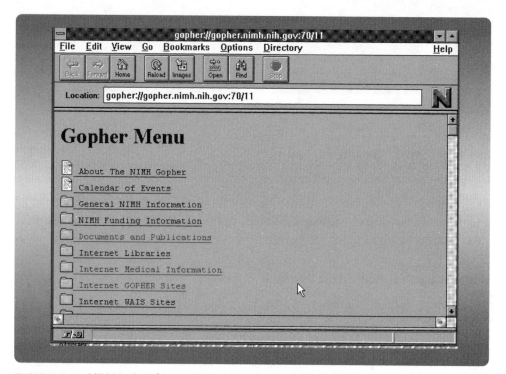

FIGURE 9-6. *NIH National Institutes of Mental Health gopher menu options*

RELIGION

There are Web and gopher sites that allow you to learn more about any of the world's religions.

Islam

`gopher://ucsbuxa.ucsb.edu:3001/11/.Social/.Phil/.Islam`

This gopher has fifteen different papers on Islam including

- Islamic Newsgroups
- God & Worship
- Islam, Qurad, and Mohammed
- Marriage Laws in Islam
- Women in Islam
- Islamic Resources on the Internet
- Halal Foods

Judaism

`gopher://riceinfo.rice.edu:70/11/CampusLife/Orgs/Hillel/OtherGophers`

This gopher will link you to numerous Jewish resources including

- Union for traditional Judaism
- Jewish travel
- Jewish Online White Pages
- Israeli Foreign Ministry Information Service

Catholic

`gopher://wiretap.spies.com:70/11/Library/Religion/Catholic`

This gopher includes information about Catholic rituals and the writings of Pope Boniface VIII, Pope John Paul II, Pope John XXIII, Pope Leo XIII, Pope Paul VI, Pope Pius XI, and Pope Pius XII.

Mormon

`gopher://wiretap.spies.com:70/11/Library/Religion/Mormon`

From this site you can look at the following:

- Book of Mormon
- Mormon doctrine and covenants
- Pearl of Great Price

  —Articles of faith

  —Book of Abraham

  —Book of Moses

  —Extract of the Holy Bible from Matthew

  —Extracts from the history of Joseph Smith, the Prophet

Rice University Religion and Philosophy Menu

`gopher://chico.rice.edu:70/11/Subject/RelPhil`

This site provides a variety of links like these:

- America and Christianity (paper)
- American Philosophical Association gopher
- Anglican
- Bible
- Billy Graham Center archives
- Coptic
- Gasso (Electronic Buddhist journal)
- Jainism
- Koran
- Moorish Orthodox Church in the U.S. (paper)
- Quran
- Taoism bibliography

Just for Fun

Walt Disney has a site on the Internet that can provide access to information about their movies. Although they may not be art classics yet, the movies are lots of fun. If your system can support QuickTime video, you can even view a series of clips from movies such as *The Lion King* and *A Goofy Movie*. Even without QuickTime, you will want to connect to http://www.disney.com where you can take the movie quiz and look at some great graphics.

Chapter 10

Management School Resources

WHETHER YOU ARE COMPLETING an undergraduate degree in finance or accounting or working on a program of studies for an MBA, the Internet is a valuable resource that you shouldn't overlook. You will have online access to data without making a trip to the library and in many cases the data will be more up-to-date than your library's printed material. Every discipline in your program of study is covered by sites at business schools, professional organizations, and companies with Web or gopher sites. You will even find software programs in shareware libraries at FTP sites around the world that might help with statistical computations or provide the data needed for a thorough analysis in the area you are studying.

ACCOUNTING

If you are taking an accounting principles course, you can use the resources on the Internet to examine the financial reports of companies such as Coca Cola or General Mills. If you are getting closer to finishing your accounting degree, you might be participating in a tax assistance program and will appreciate all the tax help and forms that are available from the Internet. Cost accounting, tax, auditing, and other disciplines within the profession are well represented in the links that you will find at several of the sites provided in this chapter. You will also find valuable references in Chapter 16 regarding taxation and business law.

Accounting Web (Rutgers)

`http://www.rutgers.edu/Accounting/raw.htm`

This site provides access to an accounting information retrieval system. There are links to the other university sites included in The International Accounting Network: The Summa Project and ANet. Other sites accessible from here include

- American Accounting Association
- American Institute of Certified Public Accountants

- Institute of Management Accountants
- Accounting Resources on the Internet

Accounting Resources on Internet

http://www.rutgers.edu/Accounting/raw/internet/internet.htm

This location provides extensive links to the following accounting-related sites:

- Accounting associations
- Accounting journals
- Financial markets
- Government agencies
- Taxation
- Corporate SEC filings
- International accounting network
- Financial Accounting Standards Board
- University's Accounting Pages
- Info from accounting professors
- Accounting professional info
- Accounting articles

American Institute of Certified Public Accountants (AICPA)

http://www.rutgers.edu/Accounting/raw/aicpa/home.htm

This site is under construction; it currently includes special committee reports, teaching materials, and professional newsnotes.

American Accounting Association (AAA)

http://www.rutgers.edu/Accounting/raw/aaa/aaa.htm

This site provides access to research papers and databases; classroom case materials and the Iowa Electronic Markets; practice links; information about the Association and its strategic framework; and newsletters distributed by the Association.

ANet–The Accounting Network–Southern Cross University

`http://anet.scu.edu.au/anet`

This page is part of the International Accounting Network. The other links are at the University of Exeter (Summa Project) and the Rutgers Accounting Web (RAW). This site has thirty different accounting mailing lists, a complete list of accounting organizations and journals, a 6.5K accounting bibliography, accounting software, and other resources.

AuditNet Resources List

`http://www.unf.edu/misc/jmayer/arl.html`

This site contains numerous audit-related links of interest to auditors in all types of organizations. Some of the links you will find include

- Audit discussion list
- Internal audit resource pages
- Auditor General of Canada's office
- Computer operations
- Audit and Security Technology Project
- Computer Security Resource Clearinghouse

Contact Points in Accounting

`http://darkwing.uoregon.edu:80/~nfargher/acts/list.html`

Some of the links you will find here are

- Price Waterhouse Technology Center
- KPMG Online Canada
- Rutgers Accounting Web
- Academic Courses on the Web

Control and Monitoring

`http://www.euro.net/innovation/Management_Base/Man_Guide_Rel_1.0B1/Controland Monitoring.html`

This is part of an extensive management educational resource that presents accounting's role as a control mechanism in the management of an organization.

Accounting is covered in "An Introduction to Classical Accounting and Accounting and Control" section. The major areas covered are

- An introduction to classical accounting
- Accounting and control
- Non-financial measurement
- Quantitative techniques
- Additional resources

Department of the Treasury Tax Forms and Instructions

`http://www.kiosk.net/irs/taxforms.html`

At this site you will find a list and illustrations of all federal tax forms, which you can search by keyword.

Internal Auditing

`http://WW01.DHMC.Dartmouth.EDU`

You can access the various sites through a map or a menu. A voice introduction is available if your system has sound capabilities. These options are among the selections:

- News report
- Professional interest groups and associated networking resources
- Conferences
- Audit subject index
- Industry-specific topics
- State-by-state resources under construction
- Country- and industry-specific topics

SEC EDGAR Database

`http://www.town.hall.org/edgar/edgar.html`

At this site you can retrieve recent filings to the Securities and Exchange Commission that are publicly available. You can access daily, full, and archival indices of corporate SEC filings. This location also provides links to other centers such as the Center for Corporate Law. The initial screen at this site is shown in Figure 10-1.

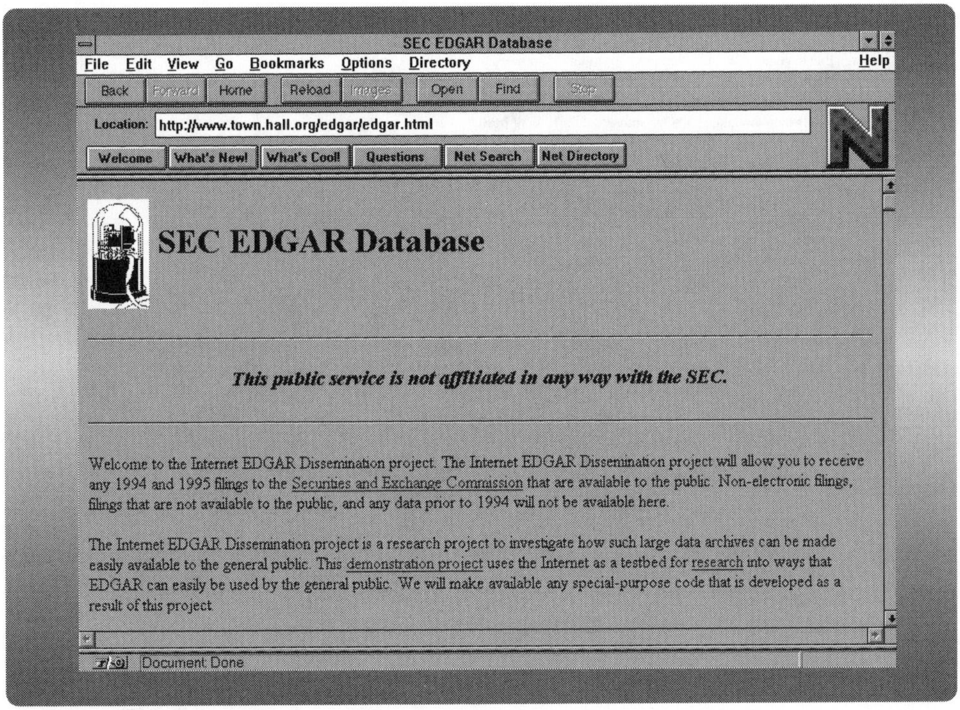

FIGURE 10-1. *SEC EDGAR database initial screen*

Summa Project–Chartered Accountants of England

`http://www.ex.ac.uk/~BJSpaul/ICAEW/ICAEW.html`

This site is the home page for the Institute of Chartered Accountants in England and Wales as shown in Figure 10-2. From this location you can link to the Summa Project. The Summa Project mirrors the information found in the ANET site in Australia, including some additional information such as UK company information, the Institute for Fiscal Studies, the Cost Accounting home page, UK government servers, and UK educational links.

Tax Information on the Internet

`http://www.best.com/~ftmexpat/html/taxsites.html`

This site is an index of tax resources on the Internet. It includes tax FAQs, tax articles, the tax code, tax treaty information, tax shareware, and numerous links to other sites.

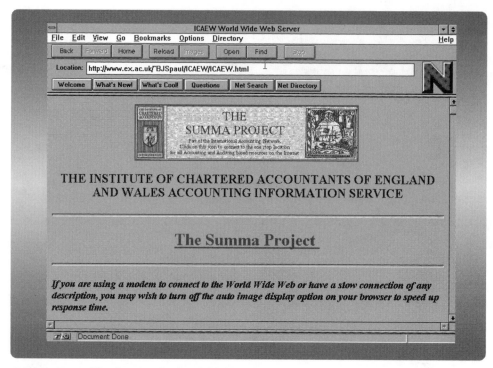

FIGURE 10-2. *The Summa Project initial screen*

Tax World

http://omer.cba.neu.edu/home

This site was developed by Professor Omer at Northeastern University. The page includes information about tax information sites, a tax policy exercise, a history of taxation, and teaching resources information.

U.S. Tax Code Online

http://www.fourmilab.ch/ustax/ustax.html

Go right to the source and access what you need. There are lots of helps to make your search easy:

- A hierarchical table of contents
- A comprehensive flat table of contents
- 6,000 pages of text to search
- Development details about the database

FINANCE

There is a wealth of information and data available for students and faculty interested in researching finance-related topics. You can find up-to-date and historical stock price data for firms listed on the major stock exchanges. In addition, you will find investment newsletters and abstracts of articles from many of the finance-related periodicals. Many of the sites listed in this section provide important links to financial data and reports on a global basis. You should find cruising the Net in this area most rewarding.

Chicago Mercantile Exchange

http://www.cme.com/market/quote.html

You will find current daily prices for futures and options for agricultural commodities, foreign currencies, interest rates, stock indices, and special options offerings. What's New at the Merc and Background on the Merc are also available.

Experimental Stock Market Data from MIT

http://www.ai.mit.edu/stocks.html

This data is updated at night for the previous close. A directory of databases, stock and mutual fund charts, a directory of data files, and other finance information are available here.

Finance Index

http://www.cob.ohio-state.edu/dept/fin/overview.htm

This is an excellent site to visit. In addition to serving as the home page for the *Journal of Finance,* this location lets you link to numerous other finance resources.

- Popular sites

- Sites of interest to institutional and personnel investors

- Financial services corporations

- Sites of interest to financial researchers

- Sites of interest to finance students

- Sites of interest to finance executives

- Sites of interest to investment bankers

- Sites of interest to financial educators

- Financial data

- The Detective's Guide to Financial Information

FINWeb Financial Economics

`http://riskweb.bus.utexas.edu/finweb.html`

Some of the resources you can access here are

- *Journal of Financial Abstracts* (sample journals)

- ECONbase journal articles

- Data archive of the *Journal of Applied Econometrics*

- Data archive of the *Journal of Business and Economics*

- *Financial Executive Journal* in hypertext format

- Access to UnCover (a database of 17,000 periodicals)

Historical Stock Prices

`ftp://ftp.ai.mit.edu/pub/stocks/results/`

You can access stock prices by their ticker symbol at this site.

International Financial Encyclopedia

`http://www.euro.net/innovation/Finance_Base/Encyclopaedia/`

This site contains an exhaustive list of definitions of financial terms. It uses icons to help distinguish between the different types of information presented.

Investment Newsletters

`http://www.yahoo.com/Business/Corporations/Financial_Services/`
`Investment_Services/Newsletters/`

This page links you to another set of investment newsletters. Some of the options are Global Gold Investors Digest, Hot Stocks Review, Insider Information, and Investing Online.

Personal Finance Center

`http://gnn.com/meta/finance`

When using this index of Internet resources, you can browse by topic or type of resource. There is also a "What Is New" section.

Personal Finance Resources

`http://networth.galt.com/www/home/info/insider`

This site provides a variety of information on personal financial topics such as:

- Currency and exchange rates

- International trade data

- Government economic data

- Loan and credit data

- Insurance data

- Investment information

Publicly Held Companies

`http://networth.galt.com/www/home/insider/publicco.htm`

This site provides access to publicly held companies with home pages on the Web. You can also access information on products and services, press releases, financial filings, and the exchange on which stocks are traded.

Quote Com

`http://www.quote.com/quot.html`

Although you won't have access to a sufficient number of quotes to manage a large portfolio, you can get up to five free quotes a day through this site.

Wells Fargo Bank

`http://www.wellsfargo.com/`

Here you'll find well-designed access to a wide range of services. Through their "Commerce on the Net" section, you can link to other resources.

ECONOMICS

The Internet has resources to help you study and research microeconomic issues such as prices, the cost of production, and influencing factors from both the government and private sectors. You will also find resources relating to the broader macroeconomics issues like employment, Gross National Product, and inflation. You will want to check the section on International Resources for additional sites that can support research needs for International Economics.

American Economic Association (Directory Search)

`gopher://gopher.eco.utexas.edu/11/aea`

One of the things you can find at this site is the results of a survey of the research interest of the organization's members.

Economics Departments by Country

`http://sol.uvic.ca/econ/depts.html`

Although the largest number of links are in the United States, many additional departments are represented in countries such as Australia, Austria, and Belgium.

Economics Index

`gopher://una.hh.lib.umich.edu/11/ebb`

Some of the resources you can link to from here are

- U.S Treasury auction results
- USDA agriculture leads
- State-by-export resources
- Regional economics statistics

Economics WWW Page at Helsinki

`http://www.helsinki.fi:80/~lsaarine/econ.html`

This site provides an extensive list of economics resources. Some of the link categories are international trade, newsgroups, software, libraries, and lists of economics journals, publications, and publishers.

The Economist Home Page

```
http://www.rand.org/misc/rje/bookmarks.html

http://econwpa.wustl.edu/EconFAQ/EconFAQ.html
```

You will find various resources for economists at these sites. There are links to other Web sites and the home page for the Resources for the Future group.

FDIC Gopher

```
gopher://fdic.sura.ner:71/
```

The Federal Deposit Insurance Corporation will share these resources with you:

- Historical statistics on banking dating back to 1934
- Links to economics and statistics resources
- Survey of real estate trends
- Recent banking statistics

Federal Reserve Board Data

```
gopher://town.hall.org/1/other/fed
```

You will find a number of databases at this location, including

- Flow-of-funds tables
- Industrial production and capacity utilization
- Reserves of depository institutions
- Money stock measures
- Selected interest rates

List of Economic Resources

```
http://csclub.uwaterloo.ca/u/nckwan/fin/econ.html
```

This site provides links to various economic resources at locations around the globe.

London Business School

`http://www.lbs.lon.ac.uk/cef/cef.htm`

You can find a number of resources here, including forecasting and macro-economics models, links for economists, and papers.

National Bureau of Economic Research

`gopher://nber.harvard.edu/`

When you connect to this site, you can search working papers and reprints by keyword.

NetEc Archive

`http://netec.mcc.ac.ufk/NetEc.html`

This site provides access to 35,000 working papers in finance and economics. Figure 10-3 shows the initial screen that appears when you connect to this page.

Resources for Economists

`gopher://gopher.econ.lsa.umich.edu/EconFAQ/EconFAQ.html`

You can access any of these resources from this site:

- World data
- Financial market data
- Working papers
- Online journals
- Economic societies
- Useful books

University of Michigan Economic Bulletin Board

`gopher://una.hh.lib.umich.edu/11/ebb`

This is a great economics resource. You can access the following links from here:

- Best Market Reports
- Current business statistics

- Economic indicators
- Foreign trade
- Industry statistics
- U.S. Treasury auction results
- State-by-state export listings
- Regional economic statistics
- Price and productivity statistics

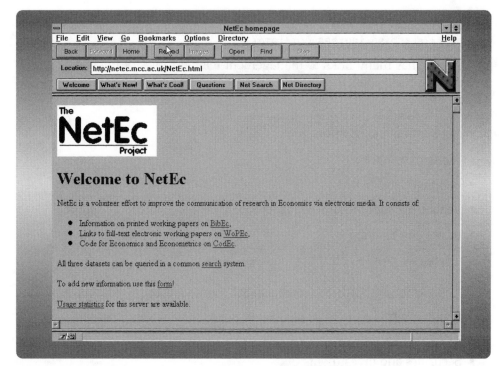

FIGURE 10-3. *The NetEc Archive for Economics and Finance initial page*

MANAGEMENT AND HUMAN RESOURCES

The Internet provides resources that allow you to look at major events that might affect labor relations or management policy. Although the number of sites available currently lag behind disciplines such as accounting and finance, the resources available are growing quickly. In addition to sites for professional organizations and business schools with graduate programs in this area, you will also find consulting firms with a presence on the net. Most consultant sites provide value-added information as a way of sharing some of their expertise with potential customers.

Institute of Management and Administration (I.O.M.A.)

`http://starbase.ingress.com/ioma/`

This site has many links to management-related topics of interest. Some of the main areas included are

- News
- Accounting and taxation
- Human resources
- Insurance and risk
- Legal/regulatory issues and corporate law
- Banks and banking
- Corporate profiles, filings, and information
- Economic indicators
- Mutual funds
- International
- Securities and investments
- Competitive intelligence and strategy
- Information systems
- Inventory and supplier management
- Sales and marketing for domestic, international, and Internet-related products
- Usenet newsgroups

The Management Archive

```
gopher://ursus.jun.alaska.edu:70/1
```

You can search the Management Archive globally or link to resources like these:

- Management teaching archive

- Health care corner archive

- Internet tools archive

- Gopher gateway services

Methods of Equity-Based Compensation

```
http://baccus.itl.saic.com:80/fed/methods/
```

This site provides information on equity-based compensation and the types of plans available. Stock option, stock bonus and purchase, and employee stock ownership plans are discussed.

MARKETING

If you need demographic data for a marketing project, you will find that everything you need is readily available. There are even studies on the demographics of Internet users that are publicly available in case you decide to write your paper on the potential (and pitfalls) of product marketing through this relatively new channel. You can also stay attuned to everything happening in the industry through newsgroups and professional organizations on the Net.

1990 Census Lookup

```
http://www.census.gov/cdrom/lookup
```

You can use numerous census databases from the 1990 census when researching demographic issues.

American Marketing Association

```
http://nsns.com:80/Mix/
```

You will find information about the association, a doctoral student special interest group, collegiate chapters, local professional chapters, and the organization's journals and publications.

Census Data from 1980 and Earlier from the Lawrence Berkeley Lab

`http://cedr.lbl.gov/mdocs/LBL_census.html`

This site has the Internet's most complete collection of census data.

Dun & Bradstreet Information Services

`http://www.dbisna.com`

Although you are not going to get free access to all the D&B data here, there are some resources that are worth exploring:

- Marketing your business globally
- Strategic business planning
- Predicting slow payers
- Tactical marketing
- Finding a job
- How to manage vendors
- Research effectively

Internet Advertising and Marketing Guidelines

`http://www.img.om.com/img/hp020000.html`

Advertising and marketing present new challenges on the Internet. Not only is the medium different—the Internet has its own culture and rules that you will need to observe for a successful advertising campaign. Ogilvy & Mather Direct Interactive Marketing Group developed the practical suggestions shown here.

Internet Demographics

`http://www.tig.com/IBC/Statistics.html`

You may be surprised at some of the statistics from this year's survey:

- 51% indicate that they are affiliated with an educational institution.
- 26% list their occupation as student.

There is also data on market segments and Internet size and growth.

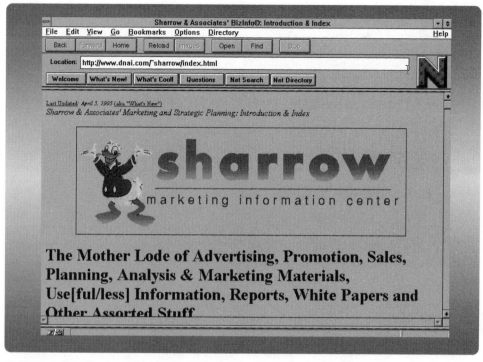

FIGURE 10-4. *Sharrow Marketing Information Center initial page*

Marketing and Advertising

http://www.dnai.com/~sharrow/index.html

There are a few unique marketing links that you can access after connecting to the Sharrow site shown in Figure 10-4:

- An organizational design for marketing departments

- A sample marketing audit

- A paper on effective sales management

- A discussion of what database marketing is

Marketing Cases

http://garnet.acns.fsu.edu/~chofack/homework.html

This site includes five market cases that provide a good example of a short case if you need to write one for a class assignment.

Marketing Research

`http://nsns.com/MouseTracks/academic.html`

This site provides links to a number of academic publications and projects. Here are some examples of what you will find:

- A server dedicated to computer-mediated markets
- *Computer-Mediated Communications Magazine*
- The Hermes Project

Marketing Listservs

`http://nsns.com/MouseTracks/tloml.html`

This site allows you to join list servers from marketing communications, marketing research, and direct marketing.

Net Demographics

`http://www.gatech.edu/pitkow/survey/survey-1-1994/`

Results of the Graphics Visualization and Usability Center's "First World-Wide Web User Survey" are provided at this site. Figure 10-5 shows the initial screen for the site. Tabular and graphics data highlights the demographics of Web users.

White Paper on Internet Marketing

`http://www.tig.com/IBC/White/Paper.html`

This paper focuses on the Internet culture and its impact on business.

INTERNATIONAL BUSINESS

Even if you are not enrolled in an International Business course, global events and policies affect every business discipline today. Multinational companies are an important part of the corporate picture. Emerging markets will form the basis of sustained product growth in the years to come. Even the investor focusing on small domestic companies cannot ignore the global picture as weather conditions, civil uprisings, and other events in foreign lands can have a dramatic effect on the price of a company's stock. You will find on the Internet the

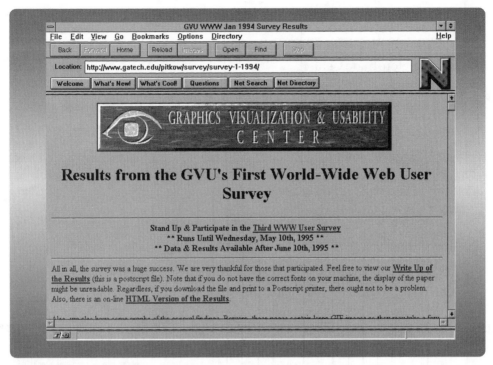

FIGURE 10-5. *Graphics Visualization and Usability Center initial screen*

materials you need to obtain a closer look at any discipline from a foreign perspective. You can also tap into information about various countries and cultures and thereby gain a better understanding of the business climate in those locations.

International Trade Resources

`http://www.helsinki.fi:80/~lsaarine/internat.html`

This site provides exhaustive links to topics and organizations relating to international trade. Some of the items you will find are

- Trade policy and global environmental change

- Resources for social and economic development

- Glossary of foreign trade jargon

- *The Journal of World Trade*

- The National Trade Data Bank (US)

- International affairs resources

- Washington Trade Center

BISNIS Federal Clearinghouse for Business in the Former Soviet Union

`http://www.itaiep.doc.gov/bisnis/bisnis.html`

The U.S. government's one-stop shop for doing business in Russia and other states of the former Soviet Union is shown in Figure 10-6. Some of the information you will find includes

- Market information and business leads

- Reports and publications

- Searchable access to the U.S. embassy cables

- Other sources of information on the newly independent states

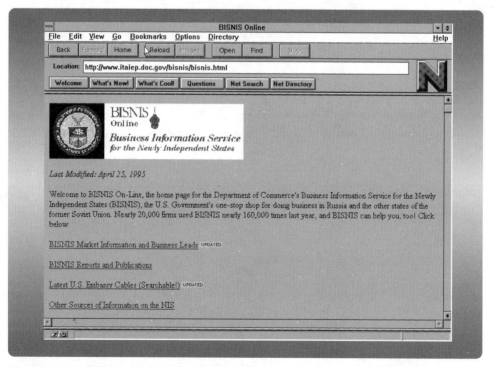

FIGURE 10-6. *BISNIS site for information on business in the newly independent states*

Business Information about Central and Eastern Europe

`http://www.itaiep.doc.gov/eebic/bicee.html`

You can gather more information in a few minutes at your computer than you could with a trip to Europe if you mine the resources at this site effectively. Some of the things you will find are

- Top 50 exports by commodity and country

- Sources of financing and government assistance

- Best prospects for trade and investment

- Economic and commercial overviews

- Trade and investment regulations and incentives

Foreign Trade Division of the U.S. Census Bureau

`http://www.census.gov:80/org/econ/foreign_trade`

The U.S. Census Bureau provides files that extend your outlook beyond domestic borders. Some of the foreign trade resources you will find at this site are

- Schedule B commodity lookup

- Links to other trade pages

- Information on ordering printed reports, CD-ROM , or tapes

Information Market—Europe

`http://www.echo.lu/home.html`

This site provides information about Europe and its electronic information market. Here's some of what you will find at this location:

- News and announcements

- Information about the European Union

- The Economic and Social Committee

- Links to other European resources, such as a map of European Web sites and government servers by country

The International Business Resources at Nijenrode University – The Netherlands

```
gopher://zeus.nijenrode.nl:70/11/Business/International
```

This gopher lists many resources, such as international business departments, international statistics, international business guide, international business and trade, the GATT agreement, and other links.

International Trade

```
http://www.eskimo.com/~bwest
```

This site connects you to the Washington State Trade Center. The resources provided include the Russian Economy Resource Center and international contacts and resources

International Trade Law Project

```
http://ananse.irv.uit.no/trade_law/nav/trade.html
```

This site includes links to information on WTO/GATT 1994, United Nations trade-related organizations, European Union information sources, NAFTA resources on the Internet, and a list of subject-related resources.

Multinational Companies with a Web Presence

```
http://www.wlv.ac.uk/~b9125478/welcome.html
```

A list compiled as part of a research project for doing business on the Internet, this list includes many large multinational firms from locations around the world.

National Trade Bank Database

```
gopher://gopher.stat-usa.gov/11/STAT-USA/NTDB
```

This location provides a basic guide to exporting, a comprehensive guide to international trade terms, the Army area handbooks, a small business guide to trade finance, Business America, international labor statistics, and state trade contacts.

Russian Economy Resource Center

```
http://mail.eskimo.com/~bwest/rerc.html
```

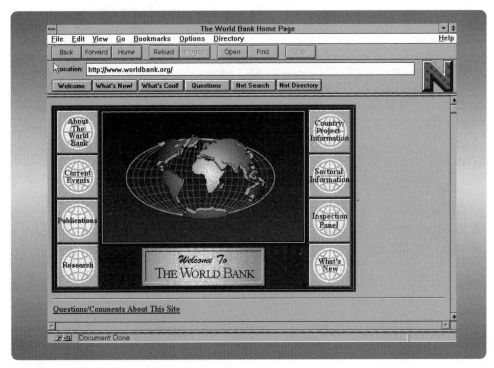

FIGURE 10-7. *The World Bank home page*

This site provides information on financial markets, telecommunications, international trade assistance, and new sources in the newly independent states.

The World Bank

`http://www.worldbank.org/`

The World Bank site shown in Figure 10-7 provides a wealth of data and reports prepared by the World Bank, including

- Publications

- Research studies

- Current events

- Country/project information

- Sectional information

- "What's New on the World Bank" WWW server

INFORMATION SYSTEMS

Although only a few information systems resources are listed in this section, you should check the Information Systems material at the Institute of Management and Administration site listed earlier in this chapter. You will also want to check Chapter 11, which provides many other alternatives relating to technology and computers.

ISWorld Net

http://www.cox.smu.edu/mis/iswnet/home.html

This site is designed to provide professors and students a single entry point to resources related to information systems. Some of the resource categories include

- Research

- Teaching and learning

- Links to professional practice

- Journals

- Research centers

MIS Quarterly

http://www.cox.smu.edu/mis/misq/archivist/home.html

At this site you will find abstracts of current and previous issues and the full text of prize-winning articles.

GENERAL BUSINESS RESOURCES

The resources listed in this section provide value across disciplines and are grouped together rather than entering each in multiple disciplines.

The Business Guide

http://www.helsinki.fi:80/~lsaarine/ssbusg.html

This book focuses on the Internet as a business resource.

Today's Newspaper

`http://www.sjmercury.com/today.htm`

This site provides up-to-date news provided by the *San Jose Mercury News*. The major areas of coverage include the front page; international, national, local, and state news; business; sports; living; and entertainment.

DowVision

`http://riskweb.bus.utexas.edu/dowvision.html`

This site provides a limited-time free access to a WAIS search of the full text for *Wall Street Journal* articles. WAIS client software is available at this site for free downloading.

Financial and Business Newsletters

`http://networth.galt.com/`

After registration, this site provides free stock quotes and access to a number of investment advisory letters such as the Mutual Fund Forecaster, Morningstar 5-Star Investor, Investment Research Reports, and Investment Horizons.

Harvard Business School Publications

`http://henry.harvard.edu:Welcome.html/`

This site presents abstracts to back issues of the *Harvard Business Review* for the past five years. This site also has links to other resources.

The Nando Times Business Report

`http://www.nando.net/newsroom/nt/biz.html`

This site provides continuously updated coverage of the major financial news of the day. You can receive a Bloomberg Business News update by selecting "Stock Report." The initial screen shown in Figure 10-8 provides an overview of some of the paper sections you can select.

Nijenrode University (The Netherlands)

`http://www.nijenrode.nl/resources/bus.html`

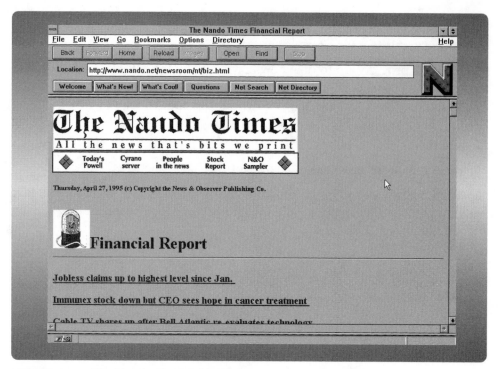

FIGURE 10-8. *The Nando Times initial screen*

This site has extensive resource links throughout all the business disciplines. In addition to the basic business disciplines, there are links to the following:

- Entrepreneurship

- International business

- Training and development resources

- Business-related collections and directories

- Business news

- Business journals, magazines, working papers, and case studies

Professional Information Services

    http://www.euro.net/innovation/

This site, shown in Figure 10-9, has a wealth of information that spans multiple management disciplines. A visit here will show the following links:

- Management Guide

- Encyclopedia of Financial Products

- Dictionary of Management and Technology

- The Hong Kong Stock Report

Small Business Administration

`http://www.sbaonline.sba.gov`

At this site you will find small business tips like these:

- Starting your business

- Financing your business

- Expanding your business

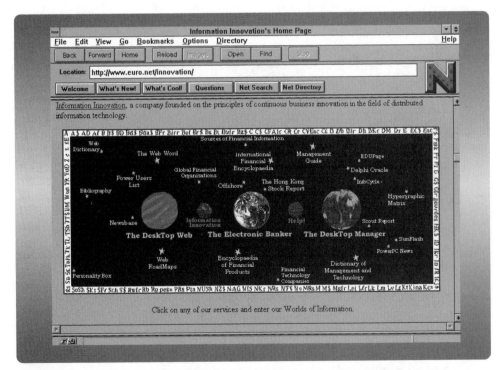

FIGURE 10-9. *Clicking on the euro.net icons activates some interesting reports*

Small Business Association—Industry Profiles

`gopher://UMSLVMA.UMSL.EDU:70/11/LIBRARY/GOVDOCS/INDPRO`

This site provides an in-depth profile of the following industries:

- Restaurant
- Subdividers and developers
- Dental services
- Advertising industry

Small Business Association—States

`gopher://UMSLVMA.UMSL.EDU:70/11/LIBRARY/GOVDOCS/STATES`

This link provides comprehensive information on small businesses in all fifty states and the District of Columbia. Data and baseline statistics on each state's small business economy include

- Business formations
- Business dissolutions
- Small business income
- Industrial composition
- Small business exports
- Detailed data on minority- and women-owned businesses

Texas A & M Business Collection

`gopher://gopher.tamu.edu:70/11/.dir/business.dir`

This is a gopher containing numerous business links. You can access the following:

- Asia Pacific business and marketing resources
- Business Information Directory from Tucson, Arizona
- Current business statistics
- East and Southeast Asia business and management

- Economic Bulletin Board via University of Michigan
- *Occupational Outlook Handbook*
- Pacific Region Forum on Business and Management
- The Management Archive
- Trade news

Web of Wonder: Business

`http://www.digimark.net/wow/business/index.html`

This site contains many categories of links, including

- Business administration
- Business management
- Business resources
- Employment
- Industry resources
- Marketing and sales
- Organizations

University of California Berkeley Library

`gopher://infolib.lib.berkeley.edu:70/11/resdbs/busi`

This gopher contains numerous business links. You can access the following types of information:

- Economics working papers
- Industry information
- Electronic journals
- International business
- Public policy reports
- Company reports and stock information

MISCELLANEOUS RESOURCES

Every possible area of the business disciplines is represented on the Internet. Although space does not permit a separate section on each discipline, a few additional areas are represented here.

Business Policy and Strategy

`http://comsp.com.latrobe.edu.au/bps.html`

This is the site for the Business Policy and Strategy Division of the U.S. Academy of Management shown in Figure 10-10. In addition to many links to other management-related sites, there is an extensive bibliography for a number of areas of study:

- Strategic decision making
- Organizational learning
- Diversification
- Resource-based strategy
- Strategy implementation
- Problems in implementation
- Seminal publications
- Strategy process
- Research methods
- Journals

J. P. Morgan's RiskMetrics

`http://www.jpmorgan.com/RiskMetrics/RiskMetrics.html`

Financial risk management methodology and data files are provided at this site.

Operations Research Gopher at Nijenrode University– The Netherlands

`gopher://zeus.nijenrode.nl:70/11/Business/Operations`

This gopher has links both to other university programs and operations research resources.

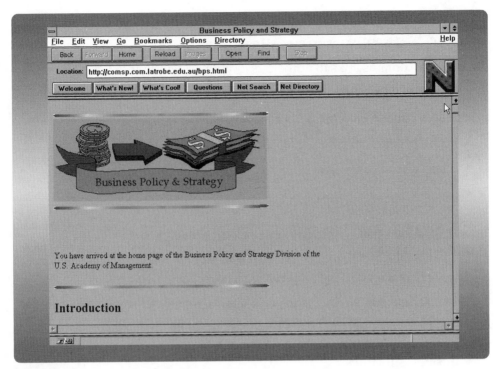

FIGURE 10-10. *Business Policy and Strategy site*

Risk Management and Insurance

http://riskweb.bus.utexas.edu

James R. Garven presents an interesting collection of resources, including the Risk Theory Society home page, access to course materials, and various working papers.

LEGAL

Whether you are interested in researching national or international legal topics, you will find a vast collection of resources available at the sites in this section. Be sure to check Chapter 16 for additional legal resources.

Center for Corporate Law

http://www.law.uc.edu/CCL

This site contains text of the Federal Securities laws and accompanying forms and rules.

Law-Related Gophers and Web Servers

`http://riskweb.bus.utexas.edu/legal.html`

This site contains links to numerous locations, including

- The Virtual Law Library Reference Desk
- Lawnet from Kent Law School
- Legal Information Institute at Cornell University
- International Trade Law Project
- The Internet Legal Research Tool

Law Talk from Indiana University—Business Law and Personal Finance

`http://www.law.indiana.edu:80/law/bizlaw.html`

This site requires audio capabilities, although you can save the files to disk for later replay on a more up-to-date system. Many legal topics are covered, including

- Business structures
- Product liability
- Environmental regulations
- Forming a corporation

Legal Information Institute at Cornell

`http://www.law.cornell.edu`

This site contains both gopher-based and WWW-based materials offered by the Institute. There are many links to other sources on the Web. Materials are organized by legal topic and by source or topic. There are links to Canada, the WWW Virtual Library–Law, and the Internet Law Library of the House of Representatives.

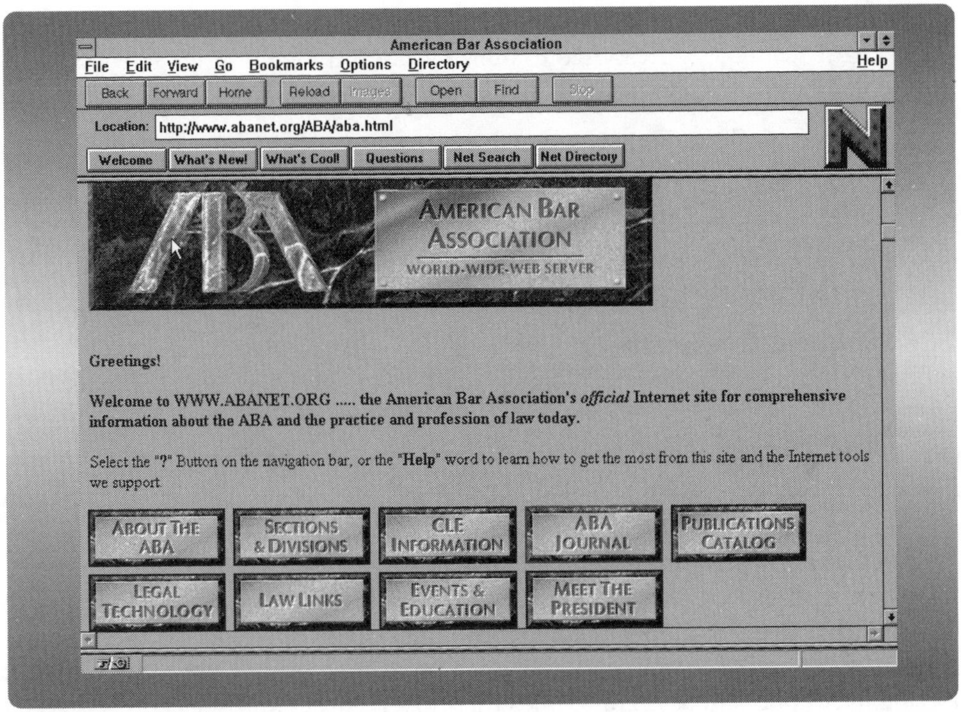

FIGURE 10-11. *The ABA site*

WWW Virtual Library–Law

http://www.law.indiana.edu/law/lawindex.html

Some of the major link categories you will find are

- Material organized by legal topic

- Chicago-Kent's Guide to Legal Resources

- Law on the Web Master Index

- Topical law index from EINet Galaxy

American Bar Association

http://www.abanet.org/ABA/aba.html

The ABA site, shown in Figure 10-11, contains general information about the ABA and provides abstracts of articles in recent issues of the ABA Journal.

The ABA provides technology services and support to its members through the ABA Legal Technology Resource Center. Through the Law Links selection you can access legal resources from the following locations:

- Selected law libraries and research centers

- General Federal Government (that is, U.S. Department of Justice)

- The Judiciary

- The Executive Branch

- The Legislative Branch

Just for Fun

Although all the sites are designed to help you maintain a competitive edge in your business classes, it doesn't mean that they can't be fun to work with. Major companies are investing significant resources in Web sites that present their image to the outside world. If you want to see some great graphics and sites that are a pleasure to visit, browse through the list of publicly held companies mentioned earlier and select ones that are dependent on consumer recognition for the sale of their products and services. Two that you are certain to enjoy are Coca Cola and Wells Fargo. Their respective URLs are

- http://www.cocacola.com/ko/

- http://www.wellsfargo.com

Chapter 11

Computer Science

COMPUTER SCIENTISTS HAVE BEEN AMONG the first groups to utilize the power of the Internet. You will find that most university computer science departments have well-established sites and that many locations have already established Web servers. Computer software and hardware vendors have established sites to hype their product, but many have added other types of information to lure potential buyers to their site. Professional computer organizations have established a presence on the Internet and have abstracts or full copies of their journals available for review.

Computer-related information on the Internet ranges from highly technical information to practical help on everyday computer software. Some of the materials you will find include

- Downloadable freeware and shareware files

- Information on a variety of programming languages

- Frequently asked questions on both hardware and software

- Computer acronyms

- Networking help

COMPUTER ORGANIZATIONS

There are numerous professional and business organizations that focus on some aspect of the computer field. A few representative organizations have been listed.

Association for Computing Machinery

```
gopher://gopher.acm.org
```

The Association for Computing Machinery (ACM) has academic computing activities as its primary emphasis. This gopher site will key you into its various activities as well as other information about the organization. Figure 11-1 shows the gopher menu that appears when you contact this site.

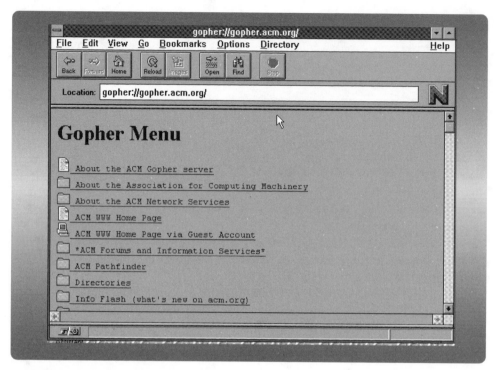

FIGURE 11-1. *ACM gopher menu*

Computing Research Association

http://cra.org

One hundred and sixty computer science departments have joined together to form this organization. This site has an excellent list of organizations conducting research in computer science.

Electronic Frontier Foundation

gopher://gopher.eff.org

The Electronic Frontier Foundation was founded to make the computer revolution available to everyone. Censorship, privacy, freedom of speech, and other policy issues are a special focus. You'll find alerts on impending issues, frequently asked questions, and publications at this site shown in Figure 11-2.

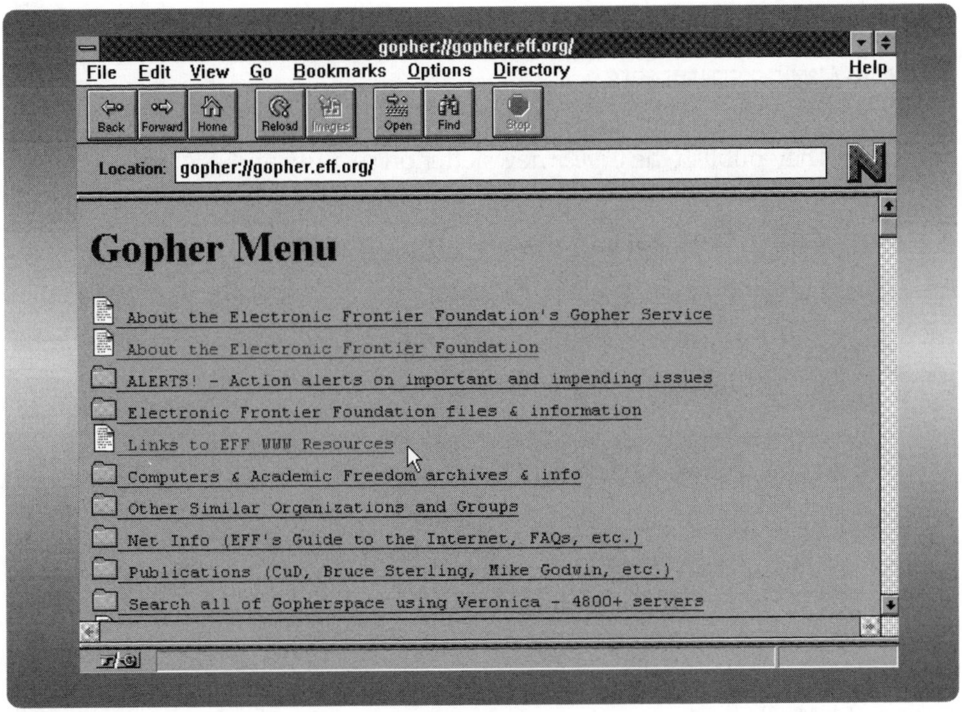

FIGURE 11-2. *Electronic Frontier Foundation gopher*

Hot Wired

`http://www.wired.com`

Hot Wired presents its computer-related resources with an interesting organizational approach. The five major channels that allow you to move through their site are

- Signal—where to go and what to see on the Net

- Renaissance—a digital gallery

- Eye Witness—bulletins from around the globe

- Piazza—information exchange

- Coin—commerce place

IEEE Computer Society

`http://www.computer.org`

You'll find articles here from IEEE publications along with other computer resources. They publish the *Cipher* newsletter on security and privacy.

National Center for Supercomputing Applications

`http://www.ncsa.uiuc.edu`

Located at the University of Illinois at Urbana–Champaign, this center focuses on performance and communications applications.

UNIVERSITY RESEARCH SITES

University computer sites represent a valuable resource to the student trying to learn about the Internet or computers in general. They are also a good source of information for more advanced students working on their own projects in computer science.

Carnegie-Mellon

`http://www.cs.cmu.edu`

One of your options after connecting is to select the SCS Local Web Home Page. You can then choose Research Projects and look at what is happening in a variety of areas such as advanced systems programming and 3D stereoscopic video.

Loughborough University of Technology, United Kingdom

`http://pipkin.lut.ac.uk`

Research related to computer-human interaction is reported at this site. Figure 11-3 shows their Web home page.

Rensselaer Polytechnic Institute

`http://www.rpi.edu`

There are all types of computer-related information here. You will find the latest computer news, how-to information, and information on network etiquette.

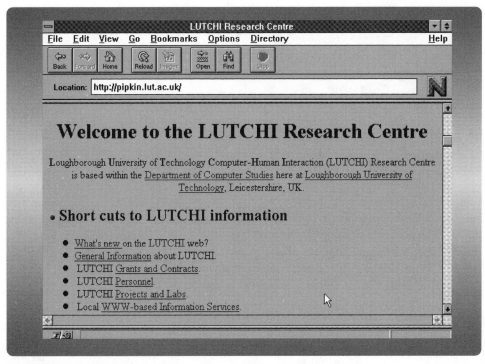

FIGURE 11-3. *Loughborough University of Technology home page*

Rice University

`http://riceinfo.rice.edu`

There are links to some interesting Internet guides at this site, including

- Internet Survival Skills 101
- Xerox PARC Video: An Overview of the Internet and the World-Wide Web
- Surfing the Internet
- Internet II
- Guide to cyberspace
- Internet index

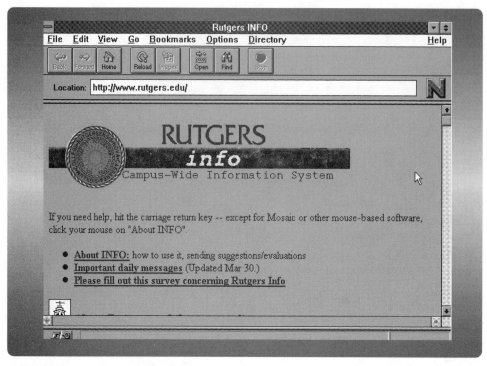

FIGURE 11-4. *Rutgers CWIS initial screen*

Rutgers University

http://www.rutgers.edu

Some of the things you will find here are software and tips for creating and using icons. You will need to select Computing Facilities, then choose RUCS Network Services and Popular Items before selecting Our Icons and Logos. Figure 11-4 shows the initial screen for Rutgers Campus Wide Information System.

Science University of Tokyo

http://SunSITE.sut.ac.jp

This Web site shown in Figure 11-5 has an easy-to-use interface to access the computer information it contains.

FIGURE 11-5. *Science University of Tokyo initial screen*

University of Aizu, Japan

`http://www.u-aizu.ac.jp`

Information with an applications orientation is located here. You will find links to information on virtual reality sound, virtual reality GUI, and image processing.

Washington University in St. Louis

`http://www.wustl.edu`

Here are just a few of your options after connecting to Washington University in St. Louis:

- Academic computing and networking

- The Software Library

- Washington University Biology Computing Facility

- School of Engineering and Applied Science
- Institute for Biomedical Computing Web Server
- CSG Visualization Laboratory
- Computer and Communications Research Center (CCRC)
- Laboratory for Pen-based Computing and Visual Languages
- Welcome to the Center for Engineering Computing (CEC)
- CEC On-Line User's Guide
- Center for the Application of Information Technology
- Information systems seminars for the St. Louis community
- Business School Computer Lab
- Information about the HyperText Mark-up Language (HTML)
- A Beginner's Guide to HTML
- HTML Quick Reference

HARDWARE GENERAL

Most of the major hardware manufacturers have gopher or Web sites that provide information on new products and make available additional documentation or drivers for their equipment. Some may share information on research topics.

PC Tuneups

```
http://pclt.cis.yale.edu/pclt/default.htm
```

A site with a cute name like PC Lube and Tune will help you remember where you got the help you needed the last time you tried to do self-maintenance on your PC. This site has lots of good information on Windows, TCP/IP, and PC hardware components such as COM ports. Some real technical information on Ethernet and other topics is here as well.

Troubleshooting Your IBM PC

```
gopher://wiretap.spies.com
```

When your system dies or seems to get a bad case of malaise, you can turn to computer doctors at local computer stores, but the repair charges may be outside your budget with a cost of around $50 an hour for service. You may be able to find the answers to fix your system or even develop a checklist for users at your site to locate problems by reviewing the information at this location. After connecting to the gopher at wiretap.spies.com, choose Technical Information, then Troubleshooting Your PC to review the material available.

HARDWARE VENDORS

You can expect to find answers to frequently asked questions, a sales pitch for new offerings, and many other related offerings including new drivers and shareware at the vendor sites. We've listed some of the major sites in this section. If yours isn't listed, search gopherspace, FTP sites, and the Web using the information provided earlier in this book to look for your manufacturer.

Amiga Resources

```
http://www.cs.cmu.edu:8001/Web/People/mjw/Computer/Amiga/
MainPage.html
```

Commodore's Amiga has an excellent site on the Web that provides all types of Amiga resources. These are some of the hypertext links you will find after connecting to the site:

- What's New
- User Support
- Hardware
- Software
- Projects
- Other Amiga Web Resources

The last option can help link you up with other Amiga users in your area.

Apple Computer

```
http://www.apple.com
```

This site contains press releases, white papers, and information on developer services. Freeware and shareware links are also part of the site.

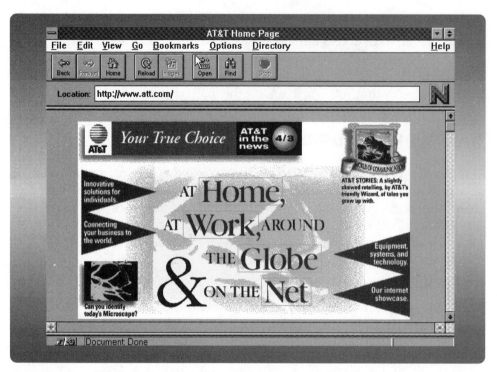

FIGURE 11-6. *AT&T's home page with an Internet showcase selection*

AT&T

```
http://www.research.com
```

This is an AT&T site with a research emphasis. You'll find a network bibliography at this site as well as papers on electronic privacy and electronic payments, and distributed systems research. For a look at AT&T's Internet showcase, check out http://www.att.com as shown in Figure 11-6. You can look at their collection of microscopic objects as shown in Figure 11-7.

Digital Equipment Corporation

```
http://www.digital.com/info/info.home.html
```

The *Digital Technical Journal* is an excellent resource to help you keep abreast of trends and research. Back issues are accessible at this site. In addition you will find these other options:

- Subject and document index searches

- Information sheets

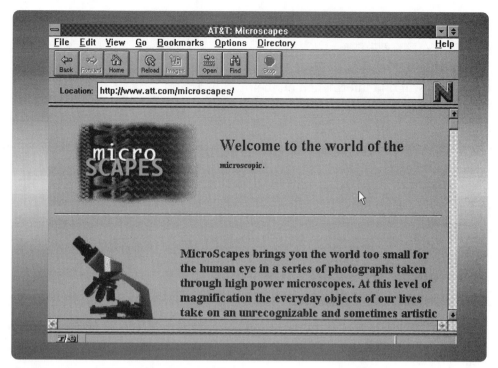

FIGURE 11-7. *AT&T's MicroScapes collection*

- Technical product overviews
- White papers

Hewlett-Packard

`http://www.hp.com`

From the folks that bring you a wide assortment of laser printers and computers, you will find a site that provides frequently asked questions and user group information.

IBM

`http://www.almaden.ibm.com`

At this IBM site you'll find all types of technical information, including a list of Redbooks and abstracts from both the *IBM Systems Journal* and the *Journal of Research and Development*.

Sun Microsystems

`http://www.sun.com`

Distributed computing products and services are the focus of Sun Microsystems. You will find information on their products and services at this site along with technical and research information.

SOFTWARE VENDORS AND RESOURCES

As software manufacturers have reduced their free customer support, they have beefed up online options that can answer many of the questions you have on their software. You can also learn about add-on products, new releases, and interesting applications as you peruse the offering at these sites.

Freeware and Shareware

`http://www.acs.oakland.edu`

The 90,000 plus files at this site can be searched by platform or description. You will find everything from help for Quicken users to patches, games, and sound files.

Microsoft Knowledge Base

`gopher://gopher.microsoft.com`

Microsoft support engineers need ready access to information on Microsoft products. You can access the same site they do for 56,000 how-to articles and answers to tech support questions. Bug lists and fixes are also available at this site. There are developer tech note files at this site that can provide the same insight needed by third-party developers constructing software products that work seamlessly with Microsoft's offerings. The 1,500 files in the software library offer patches, tools, utilities, questions and answers, and application examples.

Microsoft Research

`http://www.research.microsoft.com/research`

As one of the current industry leaders, Microsoft is working to maintain its advantage in future offerings with research stakes in current and emerging technologies. These are some of the major topical areas of research covered at this site:

- Computer graphics
- Decision theory
- Natural languages
- Operating systems
- Program analysis
- Speech recognition
- User interfaces

Reading their technical reports can help keep you abreast of the fast-paced changes in the industry.

SCO Open Systems Software

`http://www.sco.com`

With 1.5 million business and government systems installed, SCO provides this site with information on their products. Sample documentation pages, developer programs, and other interesting information can be found here.

GRAPHIC IMAGES

Many Internet users have made available graphic files and icons that they are willing to share. You can add visual interest to term papers or Web pages with a minimum of work with these images.

Computer Graphics Bibliography

`gopher://siggraph.org`

Once connected, choose Publications then Bibliography. The 15,000 entries organized by year will help you learn about the latest developments in this field.

GIF Pictures

`gopher://gopher.ccu.edu.tw`

The National Chung Cheng University collection of GIF files is impressive. Look under Miscellaneous and select one of these beauties. Images from the sea such as a sea anemone or a sports car can be selected. These files are large, averaging over 300K, so you will want to be sure you have at least a 14,400 connection before attempting to access them.

Icons Galore

http://www.di.unipi.it/iconbrowser/icons.html

Icons by the thousands can be viewed at the Web site of the Computer Science Department at the University of Pisa. Their Icon Browser will amaze you with its variety. You can download a unique set for your own use.

Images from Silicon Graphics

http://www.sgi.com/Fun/free/gallery.html

Silicon Graphics provides a lot more than information about its products at this site. Some of the other things you will find are

- Graphics contest winners

- General images

- A scientific image poster

- Stereograms

- QuickTime movie clips

COMPUTER CONCEPTS

gopher://gopher.latrobe.edu.au

Look under Information Technology then Handbook for Basic Information on Computers to learn about elementary topics such as bits and bytes and ASCII. Topics are explained so that the novice will understand.

CYBERSPACE

Cyberspace is the term often used to refer to the information highway and all its resources. The resources in this section may broaden your perspective of what is happening out there.

Communicating in Cyberspace

```
gopher://gopher.well.sf.ca.us
```

If you are still trying to get up to speed with everything happening in cyberspace, you can find some additional articles at this site. Look under Communications and Media for the articles.

Cyberspace at Wiretap

```
gopher://wiretap.spies.com
```

This gopher site has all types of computer-related information. Choose Wiretap Online Library, then Cyberspace to get in touch with a wide-ranging list of topics, all having some relationship to cyberspace. These are some of the options you will be able to choose from:

- Case for Telecommunications deregulation
- Common BBS acronyms
- Computer Underground (Meyer & Thomas)
- Concerning hackers who break into systems
- Crypto anarchist manifesto
- Cyberpunk from subculture to mainstream
- Defamation Liability of BBSs
- Electropolis (about Internet Relay Chat)
- GAO report on computer security
- Internet connectivity in Eastern Europe
- MUD as a Psychological Model
- Net & The Public Library (Jean Polly)
- Political & social implications of the net
- Soc Organiz of Comp Underground (thesis)
- The constitution in cyberspace
- Towards ethics and etiquette in e-mail
- Why are Internet resources free?

ELECTRONIC BOOKS AND MAGAZINES

Although most magazines on the network do not make the full text of current issues available, many have sample columns or selected articles as well as back issues that will provide useful information. You can tell by the samples whether the magazine has a technical orientation appropriate for your level of research. There are a number of computer-related texts on the Internet in full text form. (The computer acronyms listed might serve as a handy reference as you encounter new acronyms in your research readings.) You can also browse through sample materials to help keep yourself up-to-date with constantly changing technology.

Artificial Intelligence Journal

    gopher://gopher.cic.net

You find this journal and many others under Electronic Serials. You can get to it quickly by Choosing Alphabetic list, then A. The files are zipped, so you will need to download them before you can read them.

Computer Acronyms

    http://www.hpcc.gov

You will find fact sheets and other government reports in addition to the acronym glossary at this site. Both the National Information Infrastructure and the government's High Performance Computing project have information at this site.

Computer Music Journal

    ftp://mitpress.mit.edu

    http://mitpress.mit.edu/Computer-Music-Journal/CMJ.html

Abstract and notes for the *Computer Music Journal* are available at this site. Look at Computer-Music-Journal under the pub directory if using the FTP site.

Datamation

    http://www.datamation.com

Current and back issues of *Datamation* are available at this site. Although you need to register before accessing the information, there is no charge. Qualified users can register for a free hard copy subscription to this publication.

InfoWorld

`http://www.internet.net/stores/infoworld/index.html`

You can access archival information from this popular computer publication for information systems professionals.

MIS Quarterly

`http://www.cox.smu.edu`

In the publications listed at this site you will find the full text of award-winning articles. A table of contents of past and present issues, executive summaries of current articles, and MISQ Discovery with information on the electronic intellectual infrastructure are also available at this site.

Online Dictionary of Computing

`http://wombat.doc.ic.ac.uk/`

It is impossible to know the full vocabulary of computer jargon, so you can look up what you need here. There is a list of common and obscure programming languages as well as some other sites you will want to check out.

Ziff Davis Publishing

`http://www.ziff.com`

Selected information from *MacUser, MacWeek,* and *PC Magazine* is available at this site.

COURSES AT THE UNIVERSITY OF CALIFORNIA AT DAVIS

`http://www.cs.ucdavis.edu/online-courses.html`

The online course phenomena is growing. Even if you aren't ready to sign up for one, you will find that the homework and handouts at this site make great study guides to help you get up to speed with computers.

USENET GROUPS AND LISTSERVS OF INTEREST

Although you never know exactly what you will learn from mailing list distributions and newsgroups, it is worth following a few in your area of interest.

Listserv Sites

There are hundreds of discussion groups on computer-related topics. You might want to check out one or more of the seven listserver lists at the site listed at the end of this paragraph. They cover topics such as computer research, computer engineering research, social–political aspects of computers, computer standards and computer training. Point your gopher to this site: gopher://www.lib.ncsu.edu/cgi-bin/print_hit_bold.pl/staff/morgan/list webber.html.

Usenet Newsgroups

The following table contains some newsgroups you might want to check out if you have a news reader.

Newsgroup	Topic
comp.graphics	Computer graphics and art
comp.infosystems.gopher	Gopher search tool
comp.infosystems.wais	WAIS search tool
comp.infosystems.www	World-Wide Web
comp.lang.c	C programming language
comp.lang.c++	C++ programming language
comp.multimedia	Interactive multimedia
comp.org.eff.talk	Electronic Frontier Foundation newsletter
comp.os	Operating systems
comp.os.ms-window.apps	Windows applications
comp.os.os2.misc	OS/2 operating system
comp.security	Security issues
comp.sys.amiga	Amiga systems
comp.sys.atari	Atari systems
comp.sys.ibm.pc	IBM PC systems
comp.sys.mac	Macintosh systems
comp.unix.aix	UNIX
comp.unix.wizards	UNIX wizards

E-MAIL

Sending e-mail to a student in one of your classes is easy. You are on the same network and your Campus Wide Information Server may even provide a White Page directory. When you need to reach an individual at a different location such as Prodigy or America Online, you might find the resources in this section important.

A Gateway Guide from Oregon State

```
gopher://gopher.fsl.orst.edu
```

Not everyone you will want to contact is on the same system, let alone the same network. This document gets you started with using gateways to send mail from one network to another. Although at first glance the path to getting the guide seems longer than hand delivery, the trip down the path to get it is worth it. After connecting, select Other Sources of Information, then Hugo's Lore House, followed by Dr. Fegg's Big House of Fun. Once you choose Jeremy Smith's Guide to Gateways, you will have the document you are looking for.

Mailing Between Networks

```
file://ftp.csd.uwm.edu
```

Need to send a message to someone on Prodigy or America Online but aren't sure how to proceed? Look for Internet-mail-guide in the /pub directory for the help you need.

PROGRAMMING

Many of these university sites will have information of interest to programmers. The two resources in this section are two additional sites you might want to check.

Compilers

```
gopher://gopher.psg.com
```

The Pacific Systems Group has a wealth of different information at their site, but if you choose Programming Languages, one of the things you will find is some free compilers. They also maintain an extensive list of programming languages.

Spanky Fractal Database

`http://spanky.triumf.ca`

This is a database of fractals, fractal images, interactive fractal explorers, and programs of interest to programmers and mathematicians.

RESEARCH PAPERS

`http://manip.crhc.uiuc.edu/paper.html`

This site has links to many research papers, covering topics such as the automated design of neural networks and load balancing in distributed systems.

SECURITY AND PRIVACY

Although computers have had many positive influences on society over the last few decades, there are new problems to deal with as well. The resources in this section provide information on two of the most prominent new issues: security and privacy.

RSA Data Security

`http://www.rsa.com`

RSA, a worldwide leader in cryptography and authentication, has established the de facto standards for encryption and digital signatures. At this site you will find frequently asked questions about cryptography and many papers relating to security issues. A great place to look if you are doing writing in this area. Figure 11-8 shows a few of the options at this site.

Security Papers

`file://research.att.com/dist/internetsecurity`

The AT&T research site has links to many different security pages.

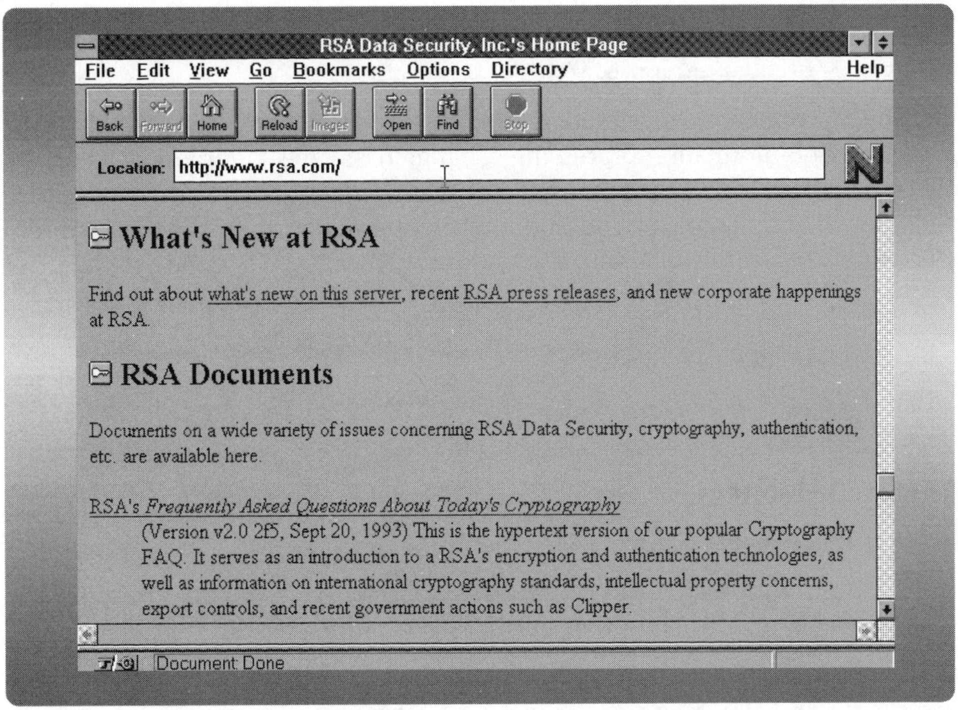

FIGURE 11-8. *RSA's home page*

Vortex Technology

`http://www.vortex.com`

You can look at their archives for the Privacy Forum (a serious discussion on privacy) and subscribe to it if you like. You will find discussion on wiretapping and employee monitoring in the workplace.

HISTORY

Much of the information relating to computers on the Internet is about new technologies and current programs, but there is some information on the fast-paced history of computers as well.

Charles Babbage Institute

http://fs1.itdean.umn.edu/cbi/cbihome.htm

The University of Minnesota maintains this site to supply information on the history of information processing. Change has come so rapidly in this area that many don't realize the magnitude of change that has occurred over the last forty years. At this site you will find recent publications on the history of information processing as well as links to these and other sites:

- Computer History Association Project

- Course materials on history

- Women and computer science

Vortex Technology

http://www.vortex.com

In addition to their privacy information, they have pointers to other resources, including the Computer History Association of California.

ROBOTICS—UNIVERSITY OF MASSACHUSETTS LABORATORY FOR PERCEPTUAL ROBOTICS

http://piglet.cs.umass.edu:4321/lpr.html

Here you will find robotics demos in MPEG format as well as other online robotics software and links to other sites.

VIRTUAL REALITY

http://guinan.gsfc.nasa.gov/WebStars/VR.html

Here you will find articles and the *Journal of Virtual Environment* as well as links to all types of resources including commercial resources, other research sites, and conferences.

Just for Fun

There are lots of places to look when you need a break from program debugging or the research you are doing on computer security. Wiretap has a collection of puns with the C language and funny manual pages. Take a look at gopher://wiretap.spies.com, then check out the Humor menu for all kinds of options. You can also find information on Hollywood plots involving computers at

```
http://fs1.itdean.umn.edu/cbi/movies.html
```

Most of the plots involve the computer in either crime or workplace manipulation and control. If a few Pentium jokes will lighten your day, take a look at

```
http://fs1.itdean.umn.edu/cbi/pentium.htm
```

Chapter 12

Education and General Reference Resources

THE INTERNET CAN PROVIDE the information you need to develop top-notch curricula and teaching materials. It can also put you in contact with teachers who have years of classroom experience and may share techniques to foster learning. These techniques can make you feel like a seasoned pro as you approach your first teaching opportunities. Whether you are in your student teaching semester or working on projects earlier in your program, you will find a wealth of education-related resources on the Internet. This chapter focuses on the ideas, methodologies, and resources that can help you develop more interesting lesson plans and projects for your classes, do better evaluations and assessments of your students' learning, and locate resources that can help you better meet the needs of all of your students. Other chapters in this book will provide reference resources for the various disciplines you might be teaching, whether they are English, accounting, chemistry, or a foreign language.

This chapter also helps you locate some online general reference resources that will be useful in your own educational pursuits. You will also find that these resources are a good way to introduce your own students to the Internet.

REFERENCE WORKS

There are numerous reference works available on the Internet. Some are available via an FTP site for downloading to your system, and others are available online whenever you need them. A few of the best are listed here.

Acronym Dictionary

```
http://dewey.lib.ncsu.edu
```

After selecting Reference Desk, you will find a wide variety of resources including the acronym dictionary, almanacs, and other directories.

CIA World Factbook

```
gopher://gopher.micro.umn.edu
```
Look at Libraries/Reference Works

```
file://ucseix.sdsu.edu
```
Look in this location: `/pub/doc/etext/world.text.Z`

```
file://ftp.cdrom.com
```
Look in this location: `/.16/gutenberg/etext94/world94.txt`

This popular reference can be found at many other sites in addition to the three listed. It provides a great classroom tool for teaching students to locate information on other countries, islands, or territories. It includes information on population, economy, trade, the political situation, climate and geography. Figure 12-1 shows a small section of one of the country reports.

Desktop References such as Almanacs, Daily Federal Register

```
http://jg.cso.uiuc.edu/pg/lists/subject2.html
```

This site contains a diverse list of references in addition to the ones listed in the heading, including

- The King James Bible
- The Bill of Rights
- The Declaration of Independence
- 1990 Census Sample
- 1994 CIA World Factbook

Dictionaries

```
gopher://gopher.uiuc.edu
```

After connecting to the University of Illinois at Champaign–Urbana you can select References/Dictionaries for a list of dictionaries including:

- American English
- Pocket Dictionary
- Computer Jargon
- Dictionary of Computing
- NASA Capitalization

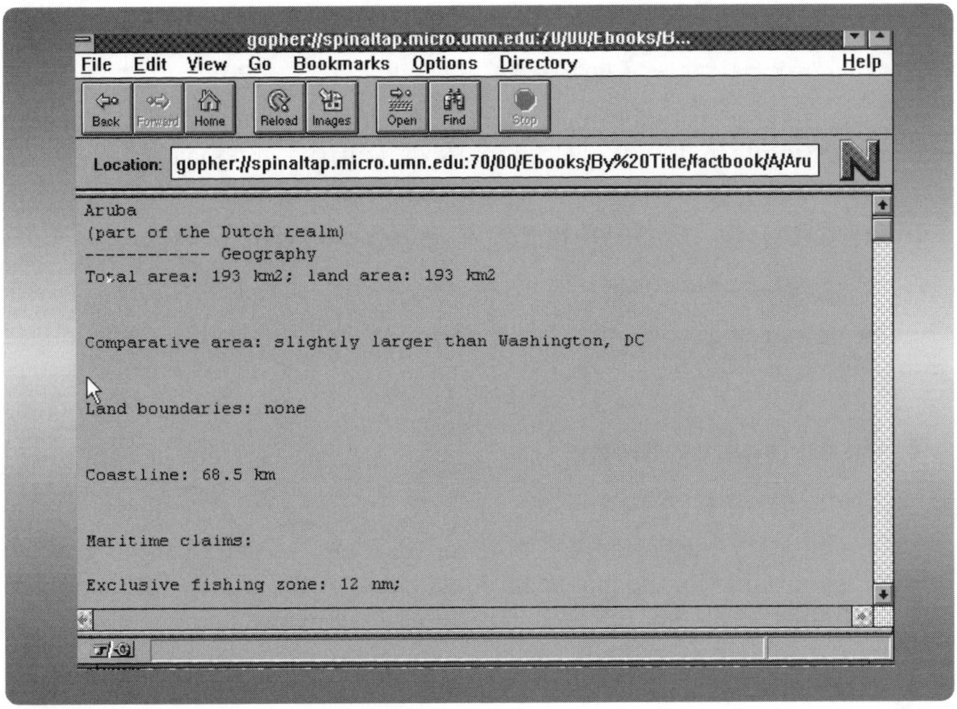

FIGURE 12-1. *A CIA Factbook country report*

- NASA Punctuation
- German–English
- French–English
- Russian–English
- Japanese–English

Electronic Books

```
gopher://vatech.lib.vt.edu
```

There are many electronic books available including classics such as *The Wizard of Oz, Little Women, The Adventures of Tom Sawyer, The Jungle Book,* and *The Complete Works of Shakespeare.*

Electronic Books and Other Online References

`http://www.cs.cmu.edu/Web/books.html`

This page is actually four pages long and contains references that will help you quickly locate hundreds of electronic texts, journals, and magazines.

Library Catalogs Worldwide You Can Access with Telnet

`gopher://libgopher.yale.edu`

Once connected, you can select the country and location to view contact instructions.

Library of Congress MARVEL

`gopher://marvel.loc.gov`

You will access the Library of Congress Machine-Assisted Realization of the Virtual Electronic Library information available at the Library of Congress. Although there is a menu option that requires a password, you will also see an option for a public connection for which you will not need a password.

Periodic Elements

`http://www.cchem.berkeley.edu/Table/index.html`

`http://www.cs.ucb.ca/elements/periodic.table`

You will find a list of elements to select from. Each element's listing provides the symbol, name, weight, boiling and melting points, specific gravity, and other key points.

Roget's Thesaurus

`gopher://odie.niaid.nih.gov`

Desktop references listed include *Roget's Thesaurus*, an area code lookup, city/zip code lookup, and nutrient data.

Weights and Measures

`gopher://gopher.uoregon.edu`

If you've ever wondered how much a quintillion is or how many square feet there are in a particular area, you will want to check out Weights and

Measures in the Desktop Reference section of this gopher. Every type of measure imaginable seems to be listed including the following:

- How many fathoms in a cable
- How many cubic feet in a cord of wood
- How many feet in a surveyor's chain
- How many gallons in a barrel
- How many grains in a troy ounce
- How many yards in a rod
- How many statute miles in a nautical mile

EDUCATION RESOURCES

The resources in this section are of interest to students and educators alike. After exploring the areas discussed for each site, you might want to look at each one a little closer as many have links to other sites containing related information.

Arizona State Educational Gopher

```
gopher://info.asu.edu
```

This wonderful link to many interesting resources for educators contains the following:

- Best of the Internet for educators
- Centers, laboratories, and clearinghouses for educators
- College and university departments of education
- Electronic journals
- Technology in education

AskERIC

```
http://eryx.syr.edu
```

This is a must-see resource for educators. There is a Toolbox of Tools for Educators including links to all types of innovative programs and reference resources. Newton's Apple provides lesson plans for science that can be used with the PBS science series with the same name. The Discovery Learning Community is designed to help teachers utilize The Discovery Channel and The Learning Channel. There are a wide assortment of lesson plans for topics such as astronomy, CNN's Newsroom daily lesson plans, science, social studies, mathematics, and many miscellaneous disciplines. AskERIC collections include many other materials for educators including links to electronic journals, ERIC digests, and educational listserv postings.

Catholic University of America Education Gopher

```
gopher://gopher.cua.edu
```

This site has a variety of educational resources. The Catholic Educational Research Exchange was recently established here.

Center for Networked Information Discovery and Retrieval

```
http://edweb.cnidr.org
```

This site serves as a clearinghouse and provides links to the following educational resources:

- National Arts and Education Information Network

- EdWeb

- Global School House Project

- Janice's K–12 Cyberspace Outpost

- Presidential Awards Internet Pilot

Chronicle of Higher Education Excerpts

```
http://chronicle.merit.edu
```

Summaries for Academe This Week are posted each Tuesday at noon. Many other resources for educators can be found here, including information on a popular academic retirement system TIAA-CREF, Jobs in Academe with 930 listings in a recent check, and Events in Academe.

College and University Links

```
gopher://marvel.loc.gov:70/11/Internet/cwis
```

```
gopher://burrow.cl.msu.edu:70/11/internet/type/cwis
```

```
http://www.clas.ufl.edu/CLAS/american-universities.html
```

You will find many links to the education departments of colleges and universities from their Web home page or gopher-based campus-wide information system. Any school with an Education Department is likely to have links to information of interest.

Community College Gophers

`gopher://gopher1.faytech.cc.nc.us`

This gopher provides links to many different community college sites.

Educational Funding and Grants

`gopher://riceinfo.rice.edu`

Look in this location for grant and funding information: Information by Subject Area/Grants, Scholarships, and Funding. You'll avoid the out-of-date nature of paper copies of this information. Some of the sources you'll find listed there are

- A Grant Getter's Guide to the Internet (U of Idaho)
- ARPA solicitations
- Biomed opportunities from Yale
- Canadian scholarships and grants from SchoolNet
- Catalog of Federal Domestic Assistance
- Commerce Business Daily
- DOE (Department of Energy)
- Division of Engineering Research (Michigan State University)
- FEDIX/MOLIS: Federal Information Exchange
- Fellowships & grants from CUNY
- National Science Foundation STIS TOPICS system

Educational Network in the United Kingdom

`gopher://news.janet.ac.uk`

The Janet Academic Network links many academic institutions in the United Kingdom. You can learn more about the network at this location.

Educational Research Resources

`gopher://gopher.cse.ucla.edu`

A broad range of educational resources can be accessed through this site, including

- National Center on Adult Literacy

- Grant and funding opportunities

- Test locator

- AskERIC

- Goals 2000

- Search ERIC

- Academic positions

Education Literature

`gopher://ericir.syr.edu`

One of the best sources for literature citations is the Education Resources Information Center (ERIC). ERIC is a network for educational literature, conference proceedings, and curriculum materials. You will find almost a million records in the ERIC database. Many gopher sites have pointers to the ERIC databases in addition to the site listed above. There are sixteen main clearinghouses located at academic institutions around the country that specialize in different areas and write the abstracts for the ERIC database. These areas include

- Adult career and vocational education

- Assessment and evaluation

- Community colleges

- Counseling and student services

- Disabilities and gifted education

- Educational management and administration

- Elementary and early childhood education

- Higher education

- Language and linguistics

- Reading and communication
- Rural education
- Science and mathematics
- Social studies
- Teacher education
- Technology
- Urban education

Education-Related USENET Groups

`file://nic.umass.edu`

After FTPing this site, look in this location for a file containing a list of usenet groups of interest to educators: pub/ednet/edusenet.gde.

Education Researchers' Guide

`http://gopher.ed.gov/pubs/ResearchersGuide/index.html`

This site contains information on the U.S Department of Education's discretionary grant programs, including eligibility requirements and contact numbers (similar information is provided for other programs as well). Services and resources offered to advance research are also covered.

Edupage—A Newsletter for Educators

`e-mail: edupage@educom.edu`

EDUCOM helps educational institutions avail themselves of what technology offers. Edupage is distributed three times weekly by e-mail. To subscribe send an e-mail message to the preceding address. You will need to send a subscribe message that includes your name, e-mail address, and school affiliation.

Elementary School Site—Hillside Elementary

`http://hillside/coled.umn.edu`

Hillside Elementary School and the University of Minnesota have a joint project to help spread the use of the Internet in teaching. At the elementary school level, students at the school have helped create the resources that are

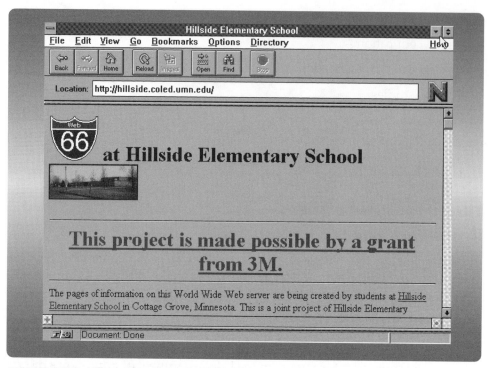

FIGURE 12-2. *Hillside Elementary's Web server*

available on this Web server. One of the things you will find is a list of many of the schools around the world that have Web servers (online.html at this site). You may be surprised to see how many are already active in your state. Figure 12-2 shows a screen from the Hillside Elementary Web server.

Experiential Learning

    http://www.princeton.edu/~rcurtis/aee.html

Learn all about wilderness programs and other adventure learning experiences at this site.

Exploratorium

    http://www.exploratorium.edu

A Web page from the San Francisco Exploratorium provides interesting and educational experiences for kids. Check out the Exploring Magazine, the Multimedia Playground, and their Digital Library. Figure 12-3 shows a screen from the Exploratorium.

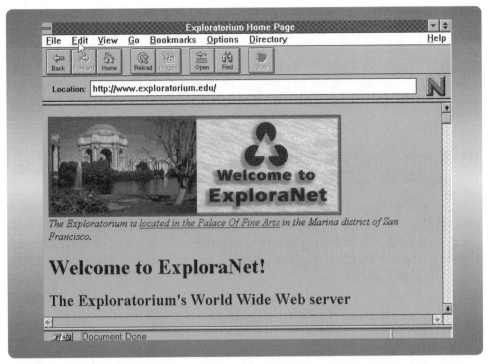

FIGURE 12-3. *The Exploratorium Museum is an interesting site for children to visit*

Federal Education Initiative

```
gopher://gopher.ed.gov

http://www.ed.gov

file://ftp.ed.gov
```

The Department of Education has an online library of materials for parents and teachers to assist in achieving high academic standards. Goals 2000 Educate America Act is the impetus behind this. You can learn more about this project, access research reports, education statistics, funding opportunities, and read full-text documents on education topics.

Globewide Network Academy

```
http://uu.gna.mit.edu:8001/uu-gna/
```

This nonprofit group is attempting to create a market for courses using the Internet. Some of these are offered by accredited schools, which is important if you are taking a course for credit.

High School Site—Claremont High School, CA

http://www.cusd.claremont.edu

This well-developed site is one of the first to be established at a California high school. There are links to all types of resources of interest to high school students or teachers. Figure 12-4 shows some of the information you can access from this site.

Home Schooling Resources

http://www.armory.com/~jon/hs/HomeSchool.html

This is an unusual site that contains many community-based resources. If you want to look at the more general offerings at this site and learn about how the Armory started, look at http:www.armory.com. You can use the Web page shown at the top for links to other home schoolers and resources that will help you with your task.

Hypermedia Instructional Materials

http://life.anu.edu.au/education.html

Australian National University Hypermedia Educational Resources is affiliated with the School of Biological Sciences. Although topics such as Bio-mathematics and Molecular Biology are covered, there are topics for general information and educational resources, including a Guide to Australia and demonstrations.

Innovation in Education

Many sites would actually qualify for listing under innovation but are included under other headings since the main focus of what they provide fits the other listing. The two sites selected for inclusion in this section are primarily focused on the generation and dissemination of innovative educational resources.

Learning Through Collaborative Visualization

http://www.covis.nwu.edu

A National Science Foundation Program sponsored a project at Northwestern University called Learning Through Collaborative Visualization. This Web site is located at Northwestern University but was developed in conjunction with research partners including The University of Illinois at

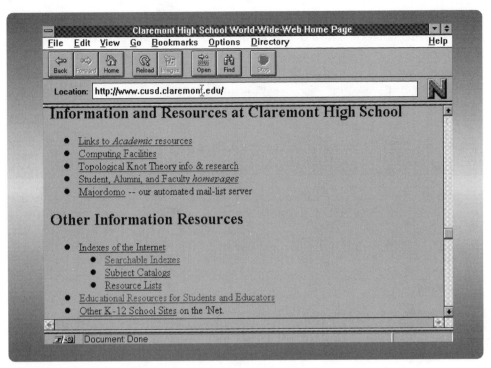

FIGURE 12-4. *Claremont High School's Web site*

Urbana–Champaign, Ameritech, Apple Computer, Bellcore, Sony, and Sun Microsystems.

Although only two Illinois high schools are participating in phase 1, there are plans to expand the current program. By 1996, fifty additional schools will be sharing collaboration tools and six schools will also use video conferencing and scientific visualization tools.

A Collaboratory Notebook Macintosh software program developed for the project allows students to collaborate on scientific projects. This software is still in the prototype stage, but proposals for its use on innovative efforts are sometimes accepted. Other software available to project members include visualizers for weather, climate, and the greenhouse effect.

Multimedia Learning Materials

```
http://unite.ukans.edu
```

This is a University of Kansas Explorer Project funded by the U.S. Department of Education to develop ways of distributing information to educators.

One of their main objectives is to develop multimedia learning resources. You will need to download the free Adobe Acrobat reader from Adobe (www.adobe.com:80/Software.html#acrordr) and integrate it into your Web browser with instructions found at the Adobe site before you can read many of the Explorer documents. The science and mathematics materials are very innovative.

International Centre for Distance Learning

gopher://rowan.open.ac.uk

Distance learning courses are offered through audio tape, e-mail, or television. The charge depends on the particular course. This is part of the Institute of Educational Technology funded by the Overseas Development Administration of the United Kingdom

Kids Web

http://www.npac.syr.edu:80/textbook/kidsweb

This is a digital library for schoolchildren. Books and other documents are available in arts, drama, music, literature, astronomy, chemistry, biology, computers, environmental science, mathematics, weather, geography, history, fun and games, sports, and other areas. There are also links to other Web digital libraries.

Learning Research and Development Center

http://www.lrdc.pitt.edu

Since 1963, the LRDC has performed research on all aspects of learning. You can look at this site to learn more about the philosophy and recent accomplishments of this group. You can also learn more about their research projects and publications, and you can search their publications by topic or author. You will also find links to other educational resources including the Center for the Neural Basis of Cognition, Cognitive and Psychological Science, and the Intelligent Systems Program at the University of Pittsburgh.

Listserv Lists

As a group, educators are very willing to share their ideas and successes. The opportunity to join listserv discussion lists abounds. You can select those that interest you most from the options that follow. You will begin getting e-mail messages broadcast to the group and can respond to the creator or the group as a whole (whichever seems most appropriate). You will find e-mailing a great way to expand your professional contact in the education field. Whether you are doing your student teaching in a small rural school or attending a major university, listserv lists can put you in touch with some of the best minds in the education business. The typical approach for subscribing to these lists is to send an e-mail message to the listserv address containing subscribe, followed by the name of the list and your e-mail address. You may be interested in reading the messages that are part of a few of these lists. Observe for a while before attempting to get involved in the discussions, and remember that you can always send a message to one of the participants in the list without sending your message to the entire list.

Topic	List
Adult Education	listserv@sumv.syr.edu
Adult Literacy	listserv@nysernet.org
Alternative Learning	listserv@sjuvm.stjohns.edu
Business School Faculty	listserv@cmuvm.csn.cmich.edu
Dead Teacher's Society	listserv@iubvm.indiana,edu
Effective Teaching	listserv@wcupa.edu
Interchange between Kids 10-15	listserv@vml.nidak.edu
Kidsphere (K-12 teachers)	kidsphere-request@vms.cis.pitt.edu
Media in the Classroom	listserv@bingvmb.cc.binghamton.edu
Reform in Education	listserv@ukcc.uky.edu
Technology in Education	listserv@gibbs.oit.unc.edu
Technology in Education	listserv@uhccvm.uhcc.hawaii.edu
Vocational Education	listserv@ucbcmsa.bitnet

NASA's K–12 Internet Initiative

```
http://quest.arc.nasa.gov/index.html
```

The purpose of this site is to help teachers and students utilize the Internet in learning. Teachers can learn about grants and put students in contact with NASA engineers and researchers. The home page for this server shown in Figure 12-5 is a familiar site for the many teachers who are already using its features.

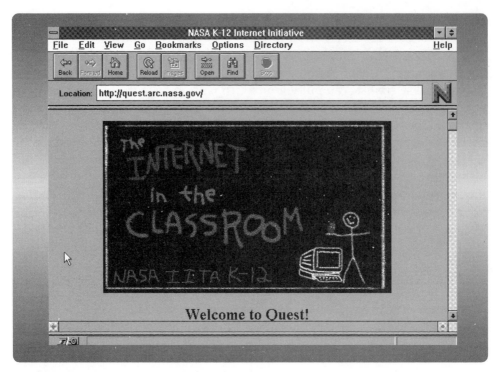

FIGURE 12-5. *NASA Internet site for education*

National Center for Research on Evaluation, Standards, and Student Testing (CRESST)

`gopher://cse.ucla.edu`

CRESST's purpose is to improve the quality of education. Projects of this group are conducted in collaboration with the faculty at the University of Colorado, the University of California at Santa Barbara, the University of Chicago, the University of Pittsburgh, the University of Southern California, and the RAND Corporation. At this site you'll find over 100 reports on assessment and evaluation, CRESST newsletters, and alternative assessments.

New York State Educational Gopher

`gopher://unix5.nysed.gov`

This gopher is similar to the gopher and Web sites being added in many states. Look in the K–12 resources for all sorts of interesting materials.

Parent Teacher Association

`http:www.prairienet.org`

`telnet prairie.org` with login of visitor with no password

Prairienet is a public service of the Graduate School of Library and Information Science at the University of Illinois at Urbana–Champaign. The Parent Teacher Association page can serve as a model if you are working with parents in a school district who would like to set up one themselves.

Penn State Site for Teachers

`telnet://psupen.psu.edu` with your state abbreviation for login

A collection of papers and other resources for educators. The CNN Newsroom Guides are available at this site.

RAND's Institute on Education and Training

`gopher://info.rand.org`

Rand Corporation sponsors a project to improve the policy and practice of education and train policy analysts. Some of the information you will find at their site is unique, including

- School-to-work and economic performance
- Social, economic, and policy context of education
- Restructuring K–12 education

Sample Multimedia Curricular Materials

`http://www.covis.nwu.edu/UIUC-modules.html`

Although these modules relate to atmospheric phenomena, there are useful studies in the development of quality instructional materials. Units are currently available for three areas: Pressure, Forces, and Wind. Additional modules are planned for topics such as weather fronts and severe weather.

Schools Online

`http://quest.arc.nasa.gov/online.html`

NASA provides a list of schools online at the Mountain K–12 site. You can use it to collaborate with other teachers and students who are already using the Internet for learning and thus make your efforts successful much more quickly.

A Teacher's Guide to the U.S. Department of Education

`http://gopher.ed.gov/#Teach`

Information and toll-free numbers for various government school programs. Some of the services and resources covered include

- GOALS 2000–National Education Goals

- GOALS 2000: Educate America Act

- The GOALS 2000 Satellite Town Meeting

- National Standards Projects

- The U.S. Department of Education Organizational Structure

- Grant and Other Programs (Grant Descriptions and Definitions)

- Office of Elementary and Secondary Education Programs

- Office of Special Education and Rehabilitative Services Programs

- Office of Postsecondary Education Programs

- Office of Vocational and Adult Education

- Office of Educational Research and Improvement

- Office of Bilingual Education and Minority Languages Affairs

- Office of Intergovernmental and Interagency Affairs

- Toll-Free Information Phone Numbers

- Electronic Access to ED Information

- U.S. Department of Education Research Library

- National Center for Education Statistics

- Regional Educational Laboratories

- Eisenhower Regional Consortia for Mathematics and Science

Technology in Education—TIES Technology and Informational Education Service

`gopher://tiesnet.ties.k12.mn.us`

TIES currently serves 400 schools with an enrollment of over 250,000 students in Minnesota. Its purpose is to help educators apply technology to both instruction and administration. It provides a fee-based teacher credentials database and could serve as a model for other school districts or state groups for disseminating information about workshops and other information.

The Virtual School

```
gopher://gopher.schoolnet.carleton.ca
```

The Canadian government funds the SchoolNet project to introduce students and teachers to the Internet. After connecting to this site, select the SchoolNet Gopher, then Virtual School. (There are many other interesting SchoolNet resources that you can explore on your own.) The Virtual School has everything from recess with Internet scavenger hunts to every academic topic for elementary and secondary schools on different floors or departments in this virtual schoolhouse. Some of them are

- Library
- Arts
- Computer Labs
- French
- Social Studies
- Staff Room

Web 66

```
http://web66.coled.umn.edu
```

This site is a catalyst for integrating the use of the Web in K–12 curricula. It provides a comprehensive list of schools already on the Web, as well as a cookbook approach for setting up a Web site, or an e-mail discussion group of educators who are Web users. Web pages are available for download in setting up your own Web pages.

Just for Fun

Being a good teacher is part showmanship. Besides learning all the latest in educational theory and techniques, you'll want to have some neat tricks up your sleeve to maintain the interest of your students. Take a look at the Schoolnet gopher for some ideas that can impress elementary school students. These are just a few of the entries if you point your gopher at gopher.schoolnet.carleton.ca and make the following choices: Schoolnet Gopher/Kindergarten to Grade 6 Corner/Neat tricks you can do. Some of the tricks that students will find to be interesting experiments are

- Floating arms
- Moving things with your mind
- Hot or cold?
- Seeing a hole in your hand

Now that you've located some fun activities for your students, check out some jokes that might interest you at this site:

```
gopher://quartz.rutgers.edu
```

Then choose Humor and School.

Chapter 13

Engineering

ENGINEERING IS THE SCIENCE of putting power and materials to work for mankind. New processes, products, materials, and systems are developed to this end. There are many different branches of engineering. This chapter focuses on some of the main branches. However, if you pursue the many links in the indexes referenced, you can also locate information on the more specialized aspects of engineering such as ceramic, biomedical, or petroleum engineering. Like the other sciences, engineering sites abound on the Internet, and many schools, organizations, and commercial sites are represented. So that the greatest amount of information can be provided within the chapter, many sites are indexes that reference as many as one hundred sites.

GENERAL ENGINEERING RESOURCES

The resources in this section are applicable to all discipline areas within the field of engineering.

American Society for Engineering Education (ASEE) Clearinghouse for Engineering Education

http://www.asee.org

Some of the resources you will find are

- ASEE engineering education in a changing world

- Engineering case program

- Engineering disciplines

- Information about the ASEE

- Universities

- Continuing education

- U.S. government projects
- Public policy
- Model rules for professional conduct

Carleton University Engineering Cases

`http://www.civeng.carleton.ca/ECL/`

A catalog of over 250 cases where you can review the abstracts and search the database to find interesting cases. Cases are reasonably priced based on the number of pages each contains.

EINet Galaxy Engineering and Technology Page

`http://galaxy.einet.net/galaxy/./Engineering-and-Technology.html`

This index addresses all areas of engineering and is quite comprehensive.

NASA Information by Subject

`http://www.nasa.gov/nasa/nasa_subjects/nasa_subjectpage.html`

This page follows the structure of NASA's Science and Technology Information Program and provides many links.

Planet Earth Index

`http://godric.nosc.mil/planet_earth/info_modern.html`

`http://teal.nosc.mil/planet_earth/info_modern.html`

Select the Science Room 1 option once you are connected, then choose Engineering. You will find a list of servers and special topics.

Society for Women Engineers

`http://www.swe.org`

You can look at the mission of the group, student services, special services, and a list of engineering links from this site.

AEROSPACE ENGINEERING

Aerospace engineering is concerned with the design and development of airplanes and spacecraft. It is also concerned with designing adequate tests for components.

Index Maintained by the Embry-Riddle Aeronautical University

`http://macwww.db.erau.edu/www_virtual_lib/aerospace.html`

This is a comprehensive aerospace index. Some of the areas covered are

- Images

- Museums

- NASA space centers

- Publications

- Research

- Rocketry resources

- Software engineering

- Universities

Aviation Education Clearinghouse of the Federal Aviation Administration

`http://web.fie.com/web/fed/faa/faamndl1.htm`

A clearinghouse of documents relating to aviation and aviation education. You can access the titles in alphabetical order, subject, grade level/audience.

U.S. Air Force Airpower Journal

`http://www.cdsar.af.mil/apje.html`

You can access current and past issues of this journal at this site. These were some of the articles in a recent issue:

- Desert Storm, The First Information War?

- Heavy Bombers Holding the Line

- Information Warfare Principles of the Third-Wave War

- Military Ethics

La Guardia Airport, N.Y. College of Aeronautics

`http://www.mordor.com/coa/links.html`

This is an index to many aviation-related resources maintained by a faculty member, including

- Aviation servers
- Aviation image archives
- Weather information
- Various airlines
- Colleges and universities
- Frequently asked questions

General Aviation Servers

`http://acro.harvard.edu/GA/ga_servers.html`

This is a very comprehensive list of aviation servers with resources in these areas:

- Aerobatics flying
- Airports
- Commercial airlines
- General aviation
- Government/research
- Publications

Aviation Usenet Newsgroups

`http://www.yahoo.com/Entertainment/Aviation/Usenet`

This page lists fifteen different Usenet newsgroups relating to aviation.

European Aviation Server

`http://www.math.ethz.ch/~zari/~zari.html`

This site has links to information such as

- Stories and reports
- Airports and airfields in Europe

- Aviation servers

- Picture archives

Johnson Space Center

`http://www.jsc.nasa.gov/jsc/Subject.html`

You can choose the Avionics Engineering Laboratory, the American Institute of Aeronautics & Astronautics, and many other resources once you connect to this site. You can also look at the biographies of astronauts or other aviation information.

Airman's Information Manual

`gopher://venus.hyperk.com:2101`

You can search for text in this manual or access it by chapter. You will learn about microwave landing systems, surveillance radar, Doppler radar, and many other topics.

CHEMICAL ENGINEERING

Chemical engineering is the study of all physical, chemical, and biological processes and elements including pharmaceuticals, minerals, plastics, and metals. Chemical engineers alter raw materials, turning them into useful products. Chemical engineers design and develop chemical plants; they also develop fertilizer, biochemicals, and pharmaceuticals.

Chemical Engineering URL Directory at Karlsruhe

`http://www.ciw.uni-karlsruhe.de/chem-eng.html`

You can spend hours looking at the vast array of chemical engineering sites through the links you'll find here.

- Academic chemical engineering institutions

- Chemical engineering organizations in Germany

- Newsgroups

- Other chemical engineering indexes

Chemical Engineering Usenet Newsgroup

`news:sci.engr.chem`

You will find everything imaginable as you read through recent postings. There are jobs offered, a list of chemical engineering graduate schools, and free subscriptions to engineering newsletters.

Listservs

`gopher://Gopher.utoledo.edu`

Since this document moved several times, the easiest way to find it is to select "Search All UT Gophers" and enter LISTSERV. You can then select listservs in chemistry and chemical engineering.

Academic Index

`http://www.che.ufl.edu:80/WWW-CHE/academic/alpha/`

This site will provide you with links to hundreds of academic chemical engineering departments.

American Institute of Chemical Engineers

`http://www.che.ufl.edu/~aiche/`

You can check the activities and publications of this organization from the site shown in Figure 13-1.

Cray Research Software for Chemical Engineering, Chemistry, and Biotechnology

`http://www.cray.com/PUBLIC/DAS/CHEMISTRY.html`

This is a repository of software programs for people using Cray computers. Take a look and you might find some things of interest, including a few games.

FTP Site for Chemistry Software at Ohio State

`ftp://infomeister.osc.edu/pub/chemistry/software/`

At this site, you will find software for all types of systems, including DEC, MAC, PC, Unix, Sun, X-Window, OS-2, and VMS.

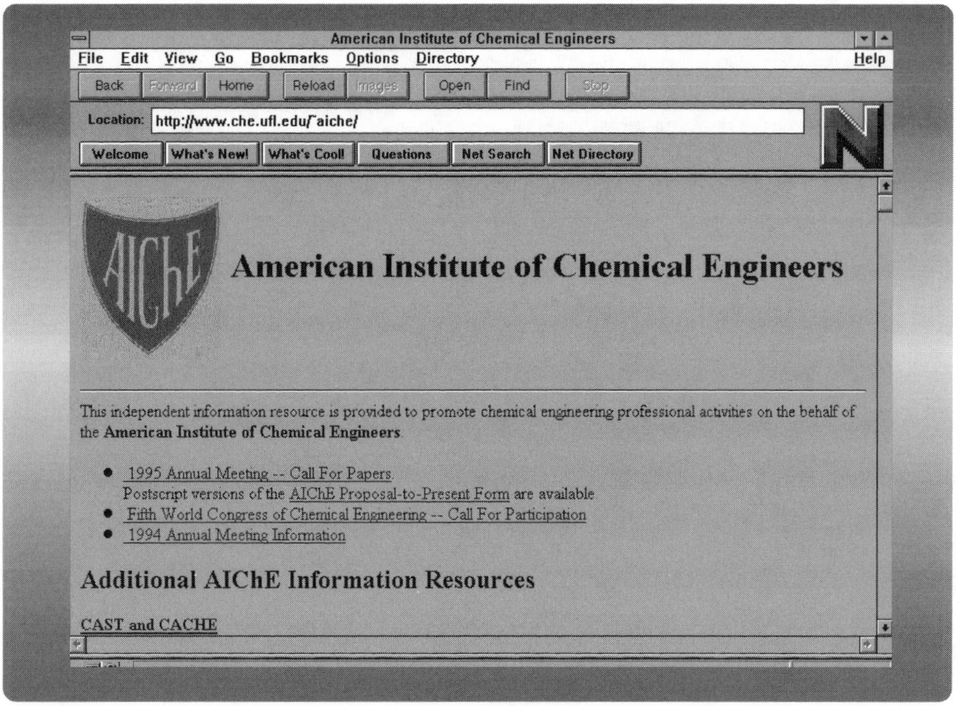

FIGURE 13-1. *American Institute of Chemical Engineers initial screen*

Electronic Membrane Information Library (EMILY)

```
ftp://aqua.ccwr.ac.za/pub/emily/emily.html
```

One of a number of databases accessible through the Internet, this is a joint project of the Water Research Commission in South Africa and the IAWQ for membrane users and researchers. Figure 13-2 shows the initial screen for this site.

Chemical Industry Institute of Toxicology

```
http://www.ciit.org./HOMEP/ciit.html
```

This group studies the potential adverse effects of chemicals, pharmaceuticals, and consumer products on human health. This site provides overviews of research programs and educational programs, copies of newsletters, CIIT Activities, and CIIT Impact. Figure 13-3 shows the initial screen for this site.

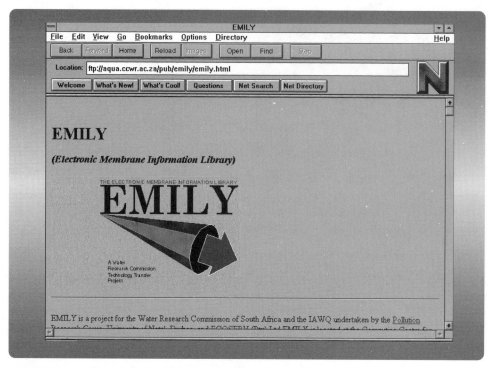

FIGURE 13-2. *Electronic Membrane Information Library initial screen*

American Chemical Society Gopher

```
gopher://acsinfo.acs.org/11/
```

You can look at pages from the *Journal of the American Chemical Society*, activities of the society, and author instructions for twenty-four peer-reviewed journals.

Chemical Engineering Catalog of Related Servers and Resources

```
http://www.che.ufl.edu/WWW-CHE/index.html
```

```
http://www.che.ufl.edu/WWW-CHE/outline.html
```

You will find pointers to the following detailed resource lists:

- Academic and research institutions
- Meeting and symposia announcements
- Professional and commercial organizations

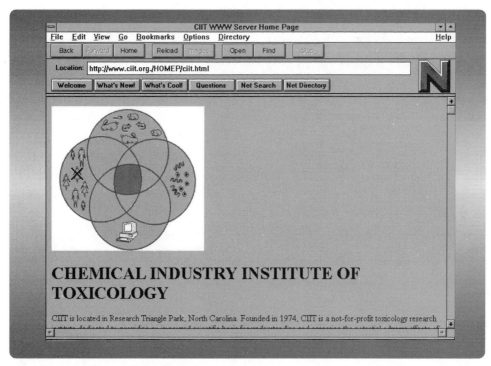

FIGURE 13-3. *Chemical Industry Institute of Toxicology initial screen*

- Chemical engineering and process engineering-related information
- Broader topics

CIVIL ENGINEERING

Civil engineering focuses on the design and construction of structures. These structures include roads, schools, bridges, and railroads as well as the framework for autos or the design of water or sewage systems.

WWW Virtual Library Civil Engineering at Georgia Tech

```
http://www.ce.gatech.edu/WWW-CE/home.html
```

From this index you can access university servers in Australia, Europe, Canada, and the United States. You can also access information about civil engineering conferences, industry servers, and related servers.

Brigham Young University

`http://www.et.byu.edu:80/~geos/`

This site will connect you to the Engineering Computer Graphics Laboratory where faculty and students in the Civil Engineering program have developed graphics and structural analysis software programs and distributed them worldwide. Some of the software available is

- Groundwater modeling system

- Watershed modeling system

- Hydrodynamic modeling system

- Automatic seepage modeling system

- Surface water modeling system

- Cquel (the next generation of computer graphics)

- Graphical User Interface Library (Owenlook)

University of Florida Civil Engineering Department

`http://www.ce.ufl.edu`

You can take a look at the eight major areas of research at this school as well as their links for cool civil engineering sites such as their concrete canoe or steel bridge competitions. Figure 13-4 shows their home page screen.

ELECTRICAL ENGINEERING

Electrical engineers have produced radar, microwaves, robots, radio, television, computers, and all the electronic devices that are such an important part of everyday life today. As electronic components and computer chips are now part of many products we buy today, the research of today will provide the products that will be commonplace tomorrow.

Electrical Engineering Index

`http://epims1.gsfc.nasa.gov/engineering/ee.html#exact`

This site provides links to all types of electrical engineering resources. You will find:

- What's New

- Announcements

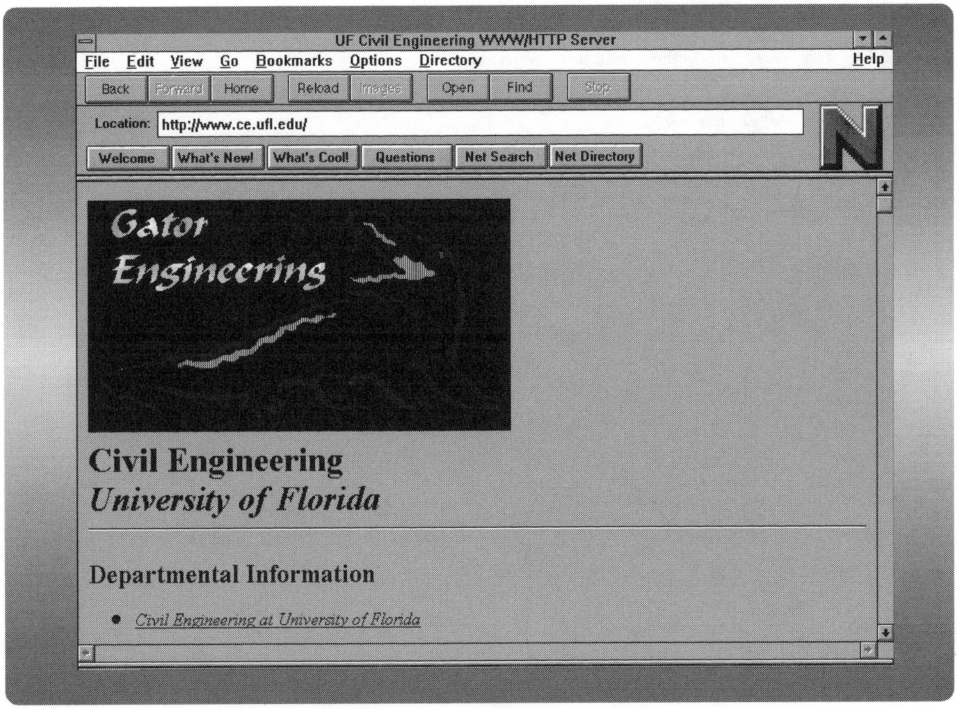

FIGURE 13-4. *Gator Engineering at the University of Florida home page*

- Information sources
- Vendors
- Academic and research institutions

Institute of Electrical and Electronics Engineers, Inc. (IEEE)

`http://www.ieee.org`

You can find out information about the activities and publications of this group, or access their student activities server. There are links to their publications preview and their gopher server. Figure 13-5 shows the home page of the IEEE.

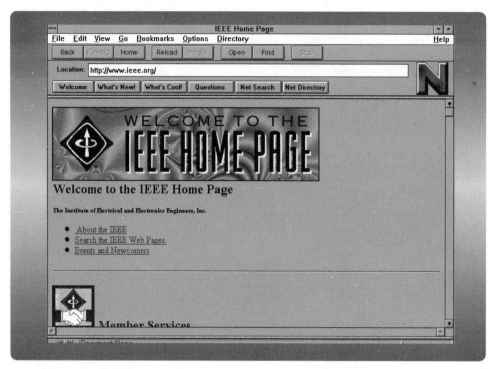

FIGURE 13-5. *IEEE home page*

Industry Net

http://www.industry.net/cgi/main/guest

You can check in as a guest or register for a free membership. Some of the areas you will find are

- Business centers
- A marketplace
- Hot new products
- Trade shows online
- Used equipment
- Industry news
- Library search

Automation and Process Control Links

`http://www.ba-karlsruhe.de/automation/home.html`

There are numerous links to these topic areas:

- Microprocessors

- Process control

- Industrial communication

- Robotics

- Commercial information

- Newsgroups

Delft University of Technology

`http://www.et.tudelft.nl`

This Dutch site has information about their research and programs, as well as links to other electrical engineering sites.

NASA Technical Reports Server

`http://techreports.larc.nasa.gov/cgi-bin/NTRS`

This server lets you select the databases you want to search using a form. Some of your choices are

- Numerical Aerodynamic Simulation Division

- Astrophysics Data System

- Goddard Institute for Space Studies

- Institute for Computer Applications in Science and Engineering

- Lewis Research Center

- Abstracts of the Stellar Project

Systems and Control Engineering Links

```
http://www-control.eng.cam.ac.uk/extras/Virtual_Library/
Control_VL.html
```

This page is housed at Cambridge University Engineering Department. These are some of the categories of links you will find:

- Control conferences
- Control groups around the world
- Control information services
- Professional and commercial organizations

Stanford University Department of Electrical Engineering

```
http://www-ee.stanford.edu/ee.html
```

You can take a look at different research projects and access many specialized servers. There is also a link to their new U.S.–Japan Technology Management Center with many links to Japanese resources in this area.

INDUSTRIAL ENGINEERING

This branch of engineering studies industrial processes, production processing, and materials handling. Students learn methods and techniques to solve problems related to production and manufacturing systems.

Industrial Engineering Index

```
http://isye.gatech.edu/www-ie/
```

The following list shows the diverse topical areas under which the links at this site are organized:

- Engineering economics and decision analysis
- Human factors
- Manufacturing systems
- Optimization
- Production distribution and material handling
- Statistics and stochastic systems

Human-Computer Interaction

http://www.cs.bgsu.edu/HCI

This site has links in these areas:

- Electronic publications
- Laboratories
- Education
- Standards
- FAQs (Frequently Asked Questions)
- Bibliographies
- Organizations

University of Illinois Research Facilities

http://www.cen.uiuc.edu/COE-Info/mie/facilities

This page allows you to link to each of the research facilities connected to the university in the industrial and mechanical engineering disciplines and look at the various projects underway in each.

Munich University of Technology: Institute for Machine Tools and Industrial Management

http://www.iwb.mw.tu-muenchen.de/welcome-e.html

This site contains the following topics:

- Teaching and technology transfer
- Product development tools
- Planning and optimizing production systems
- Machine tools and manufacturing equipment
- Robots and assembly
- Quality and availability

MECHANICAL ENGINEERING

This branch of engineering deals with mechanical power, engines, and machines. The engines that drive all of our machinery, appliances, and vehicles are the result of earlier research in this area of engineering.

National Institute of Standards and Technology (NIST)

http://www.nist.gov/welcome.html

The National Institute of Standards and Technology was established by Congress to assist industry with technology development and promote U.S. economic growth. At this site you will find information about the following:

- Mission of NIST
- Advanced technology program
- Laboratory programs
- Manufacturing extension partnerships
- Measurement services
- Quality program
- Special interest sites

Index—WWW Virtual Library at Stanford

http://CDR.stanford.edu/html/WWW-ME/home.html

You can access a variety of mechanical engineering resources from this site.

MIT

http://me.mit.edu/groups/ResearchGroups.html

Although it is still under construction, this page lists the various research groups at this institution with links to many others.

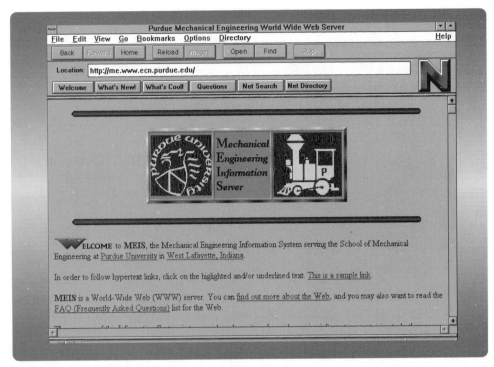

FIGURE 13-6. *Mechanical Engineering Information server at Purdue*

Purdue University Mechanical Engineering Information Server

`http://me.www.ecn.purdue.edu`

`http://me.www.ecn.purdue.edu/internet.html`

These are some of the things you will find here:

- Frequently asked questions
- Local mechanical engineering links
- Engineering computer network
- Internet services

Figure 13-6 shows the page which initially welcomes you to Purdue's Mechanical Engineering Information Server. The second URL shown above provides a direct link to the Internet site links.

Journal of Mechanical Design

`http://www-jmd.engr.ucdavis.edu/jmd/`

This site has a searchable index.

Just for Fun

The American Society for Engineering Education (ASEE) has an entire page of fun activities you will want to check out. Just enter this URL:

`http://www.asee.org/nextgen/fun/fun.html`

Some are games, and some are educational (but lighter than studying for your next EE exam). Here's what you will find:

- A tourist expedition of Antarctica
- The journey north to the Arctic
- Discovery Channel showing science and technology with a Canadian perspective
- Welcome to the planets from NASA
- Museum of Paleontology
- Chess server
- Audio clip archives
- Comics
- Food and cooking sites
- Lego
- Sports server
- Virtual pub
- Batman
- Calvin and Hobbes
- Late Show with David Letterman
- Rolling Stones
- Seinfeld
- Movies database

Chapter 14

Geography and Travel

GEOGRAPHY IS THE STUDY of the world and the people who inhabit it. Although you may not be enrolled in a geography course, you are likely to be involved in other coursework that will make the resources in this section useful. For example, you might be studying a foreign language, international business, or a discipline with an upcoming conference in an unfamiliar setting. In a much broader sense, the information in this chapter is of interest whether you are an avid armchair traveler or one who is planning to spend the summer traveling in Europe.

INDEXES AND REFERENCES

There are a number of good indexes and references that relate to geography both in the United States and the world at large. Some of the best are grouped in this section.

WWW Virtual Geography Library

```
http://hpb1.hwc.ca:10002/WWW_VL_Geography.html
```

This page provides a wide variety of geography links. Some of the options you will find are

- Canadian geographic names database

- Geographic names information system

- Frequently asked geography questions

- Geographical information about many different countries

- Department of Geography at educational institutions

Federal Geographic Data Products

`http://info.er.usgs.gov/fgdc-catalog/title.html`

This site is part of a federal government initiative to consolidate geographic information from many different federal agencies including

- Department of Agriculture
- Department of Commerce
- Department of Defense
- Department of Transportation
- Department of the Interior

The site supports access to the information of individual agencies or a key-word search.

Canadian Geographical Names

`http://www-nais.ccm.emr.ca/cgndb/geonames.html`

You can select either English or French after connecting to this site. It is the source of over 500,000 geographical names in Canada. You can enter a name and it will return a list of matches. You can click on any match for more detail such as latitude and longitude or a regional or national map with the location marked.

State Department Travel Information

`gopher://gopher.stolaf.edu:70/11/Internet%20Resources/US-State-Department-Travel-Advisories`

`gopher://kscsuna1.kennesaw.edu` then select News, Weather, and Travel Advisories

You can check for current state department advisories on any country you are studying or plan to visit. There are more countries on the list than you might expect. Just a few entries that begin with "A" are

- Albania
- Algeria
- Airline Threats
- Angola
- Antigua

Travel Guide (Fodor's World View)

`http://gnn.com/gnn/bus/wview/index.html`

This page provides a travel update for the month. You can also look at destination highlights for locations like Canada and the United States, Latin America, and Europe.

University of Edinburgh Department of Geography World-Wide Web Server

`http//www.geo.ed.ac.uk`

This is a major international resource for the field of geographical information systems. There are links to all kinds of geographic resources.

U.S. Facts

`gopher://gopher.acsu.buffalo.edu:70/00/Miscellany/American_Facts`

This document contains many facts about America including the leading exports and agricultural products and population by religion and other demographics. Although the numbers are from the late 1980s, the various breakdowns are interesting and may be as up-to-date as you need anyway.

Virtual Tourist Guide

`http://wings.buffalo.edu/world`

You select a region of the world from the map presented in Figure 14-1. You can then focus on more detailed areas to move to a list or map of Web servers in a geographic area. You can find out quite a bit about an unfamiliar area by checking out information on a few servers. The drawback is that there is not a consistent approach to information storage and organization so it provides somewhat of a hit-or-miss approach to finding what you need.

Virtual Tourist II (City Net)

`http://wings.buffalo.edu/world/vt2`

This is an extensive library of community information from all over the world. You can find out about a city's sport teams, businesses, sites, schools, and other resources.

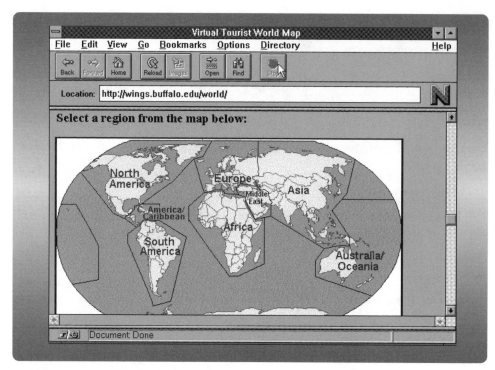

FIGURE 14-1. *Virtual Tourist World Map*

World City Maps

`http://www.lib.utexas.edu/Libs/PCL/Map_collection/Map_collection.html`

This collection is at the University of Texas at Austin. There are more than 230,000 maps in the physical collection with many available in electronic form. Some of the main menu selections are

- Maps of Africa
- Maps of America
- Maps of Asia
- Maps on the Commonwealth of Independent States (Soviet Republic)
- Maps of Europe
- Maps of islands, oceans, and poles
- Maps of the Middle East
- Maps of Texas

FOREIGN LANDS

You can access information on any country in the world on the Internet. A few countries are listed here to provide an example of the types of information you might find.

Australia

```
http://www.telstra.com.au/meta/australia.html
```

The goal of this site is to provide a complete set of links to information about Australia. You can find facts and figures, maps, guides to specific states and territories, the latest weather, and travel and culture information.

France

```
http://town.hall.org/travel/france/france.html
```

From this site you can tour the various regions of France. Some of the resources you will find are

- Learning French with Radio France

- Ministry of Culture's Painting Exhibition

- Information on various regions

Ireland

```
http://wombatix.physics.ucg.ie/irlnet
```

The Irish Online Resources page shown in Figure 14-2 is at the University College Galway. It includes

- Irish music and culture

- Foreign holiday and travel information

- Newspapers online

- Libraries

- Museums and galleries

- A separate section on Northern Ireland

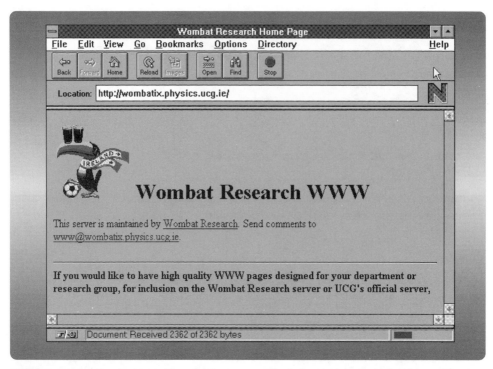

FIGURE 14-2. *Wombat provides a rich resource for information on Ireland*

Russia

    http://woodstock.hyperion.com:80/~koreth/russia/

This is an illustrated travelogue of an individual's two-week jaunt through Russia. Although it doesn't have as many links as you'll find in a country or embassy site, it provides a more intimate look at the country.

Scotland

    http://www.presence.co.uk

This Website tells you many different things about Scotland. After selecting Edinburgh Info, there are selections for Maps, How to Get There, Weather, The Big Guide, and Tourist Sites.

Thailand

`http://www.nectec.or.th`

`http://www.nectec.or.th/WWW-VL-Thailand.html (Subject Oriented)`

Some of the resources you will find are

- Tourism

- Electronic publications

- Education

- Social science

- Science and technology

- Professional organizations

When you first connect, you will see the initial screen shown in Figure 14-3. You can look further down in the display to locate the rich source of resources listed here.

UNITED STATES

Every state in the United States has sources of information available through the net. There are also sites for some cities and regions of the country. Some have a tourist orientation and others present a wide range of local resources. A few examples of the things you will find are listed in the following sections.

Alaska

`gopher://info.alaska.edu:70/11s/Alaska`

Some of the menu options are

- Alaska Bird Observatory

- Alaska Justice Resource Center

- Alaska Constitution

- Alaska weather

- Other Alaska servers

Some of the other links to Alaska-related research are the Circumpolar Expedition in 1994 and the Wolf Study Project.

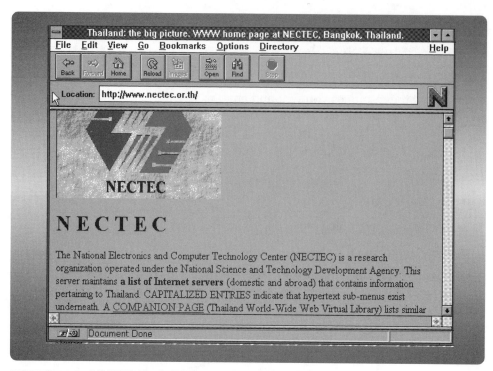

FIGURE 14-3. *NECTEC Thailand Virtual Library initial screen*

National Parks—Utah

```
http://sci.dixie.edu/NationalParks/nationalpark.html
```

The five national parks, six national monuments, and two national recreation areas in Utah are covered by this site, including

- Bryce Canyon National Park

- Dinosaur National Monument

- Flaming Gorge National Recreation Area

The screen that shows Bryce Canyon is shown in Figure 14-4.

Smoky Mountains

```
http://www.nando.net/smokies/smokies.html
```

The welcoming screen shows the map in Figure 14-5. Below this, hypertext links allow you to hear tales from the area, listen to the voices of people from the Smokies, or look at a reading list.

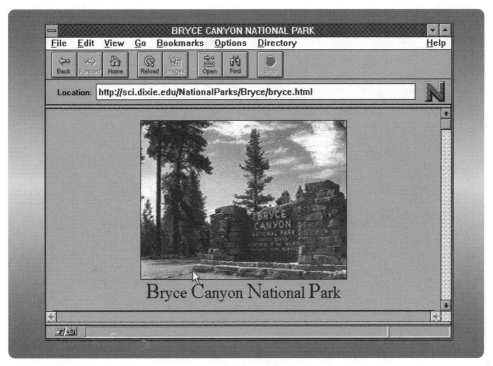

FIGURE 14-4. *Some of the information on the Utah National Parks*

South Dakota

`http://www.state.sd.us`

This resource will provide the following types of information about South Dakota:

- Cities
- Education
- Government
- South Dakota Internet resources
- Tourism information

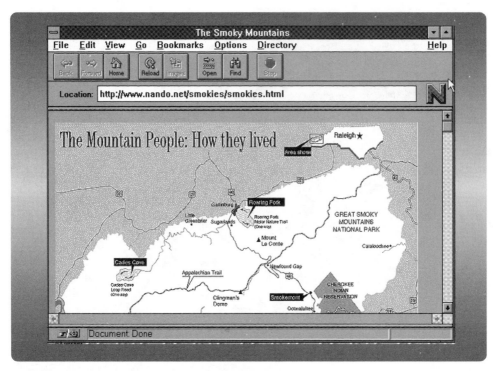

FIGURE 14-5. *Smoky Mountains welcoming screen*

States

```
gopher://marvel.loc.gov:70/11/federal/state.local
```

You will find links to agencies in each state. Since the content of each menu is determined by state, there is no consistency in what you'll find. There might be employment opportunities, tourism, small business, libraries, and any state agency.

Staunton, Virginia

```
http://www.elpress.com/staunton
```

From this site you can look at the following options:

- Take a walking tour of the historic district

- Visit Woodrow Wilson's birthplace and museum

- Visit the Museum of Frontier Culture

- Visit other local organizations and schools

MISCELLANEOUS

A few miscellaneous resources are listed in this chapter. Although they would also be appropriately listed in Chapter 19, "The Sciences and Mathematics," they are shown here because they relate to the study of the earth and indicate the wide variety of information that is available.

Aviation Weather

```
gopher://geograf1.sbs.ohio-state.edu./1/wxascii/aviation/airways
```

If you are used to reading aviation weather reports, you won't have a problem with this information. If you are a novice, you might find the abbreviations a bit cryptic. You will find the following:

- United States aviation weather (contiguous)
- Alaska
- Hawaii
- Canada aviation weather
- Caribbean aviation weather
- Mexico aviation weather
- Pilot reports

Current Weather Maps/Movies

```
http://wxweb.msu.edu/weather/
```

This site provides radar composites and infrared images for the U.S., Europe, and Africa.

Geology

```
gopher://wiretap.spies.com:70/11/Library
```

After connecting, choose Assorted Documents, then Geologic Time Table. You can follow through the period beginning almost five million years ago from Precambrian, Ordovician, and Silurian through Jurassic and Tertiary.

Polar and Marine Research Database

`http://WWW.AWI-Bremerhaven.DE`

You can access the following at this German site:

- Database of polar- and marine-related documents on the Web
- Antarctic research sites
- Ozone soundings
- Hydrographic atlas of the Southern Ocean

Research Ship Schedules

`gopher://diu.cms.udel.edu`

This database contains information on research and deep water vessels from more than 45 countries. All types of information on the ships are included: owner, weight, length, power, and range. There are even photo and deck layouts for some ships. You can access the ships in different ways including by name, country, or owner.

Transcultural Study Guide

`gopher://gopher.moon.com`

This site contains information from a book of the same title that addresses issues such as

- Men and women
- Religion and beliefs
- Economics
- Politics
- Music and art
- Communications

Volcanoes

`http://vulcan.wr.usgs.gov/home.html`

This site contains some of the most up-to-date information about volcanic eruptions and hazards. More formalized reports are also provided on specific studies and occurrences. Some of the things you will find are

- The 1991 eruptions of Mount Pinatubo, Philippines
- Volcanic emissions and global change
- Volcano monitoring
- Mass movement on and near volcanoes
- Links to volcano and geology servers

Xerox PARC Map Viewer

`http://pubweb.parc.xerox.com/map`

This site allows you to look up any location in a geographic names database, then allows you to zoom in and out for varying levels of detail. You can look at rivers, roads, railroads, and federal lands.

ORGANIZATIONS AND INSTITUTES

There are a number of organizations and institutes related to geography. Two examples are shown in this section.

Association of American Geographers Home Page

`http://www.aag.org`

You can find information about the organization as well as links to regional and specialty groups.

United States Geological Survey

`http://info.er.usgs.gov`

Some of the information you will find here includes

- National Program for Water Resources
- Monthly water conditions
- National Mapping Program for accurate cartographic data
- Teacher and student resources for cartography and geography

UNIVERSITY SITES

A number of universities have geography servers. Most of these are rich sources of links to other sites around the Internet.

SUNY/Buffalo Department of Geography

http://www.geog.buffalo.edu

This university site has links to a variety of resources including demos of geographical software packages, geographical information systems resources, and geography-related Internet sites.

University of Rhode Island

http://www.gso.uri.edu

This site is at the Graduate School of Oceanography. You will find information about these research activities:

- Marine ecosystems
- Environmental monitoring
- Global ocean ecosystem
- Coastal institute
- Physical oceanography
- Chemical oceanography

Just for Fun

If you need a few laughs as you work in this area, you might want to check the daily comics of the Avid Explorer. Check the daily comics at this site:

http:www.explore.com/E_rsrcs.html

Chapter 15

History and Political Science

HinISTORY IS A STUDY of man's activities from the past. Whether you are looking at ancient history or more recent events such as the Gulf War, you're studying history. Although the sites listed in this chapter focus primarily on American and military history, there are many Internet sites that focus on the history of foreign nations and earlier time periods. Check the departments of the university sites listed in other chapters for another large group of resources.

Political science, which covers the study of governments, public policy and administration, and international relations, is also included in this chapter. In a sense, political science is history in the making, which is why the two disciplines are combined in the same department at some colleges and universities. This chapter also provides site listings in the areas of public policy and foreign policy as well as some indexes that will make it easy for you to locate sites in other areas of political science that interest you.

HISTORY

Many important historical documents are part of Internet archives. Rather than just read about a document, you can browse through the real thing without even making a trip to the library.

American History

The sites listed here provide information about colonial times as well as the more recent events involving former presidents such as Jimmy Carter and Gerald Ford.

Historical Documents and Speeches

```
gopher://dewey.lib.ncsu.edu:70/11/library/stacks/
historical-documents-US
```

This site contains documents and speeches such as

- Mayflower Compact
- Articles of Confederation
- Annapolis Convention
- First Thanksgiving Proclamation
- Emancipation Proclamation
- German Surrender Documents
- "I have a dream" speech, Dr. Martin Luther King

American Memory from the Library of Congress

```
http://rs6.loc.gov/amhome.html
```

This site contains source and archival material relating to American history and culture. Some of the titles and topics covered by this collection are

- Early Motion Pictures 1897–1916
- Civil War photographs
- Life-history manuscripts from the Folklore Project 1936–1940
- Civil War

U.S. History Documents Archive

```
gopher://joeboy.micro.umn.edu:70/11/Ebooks/By%20Title/Histdocs
```

This University of Minnesota site contains many U.S. history documents such as

- Continental Congress Resolves
- Declaration of Arms
- Declaration of Independence
- Jefferson Inaugural
- Monroe Doctrine
- Washington Farewell

Presidential Libraries

`http://www.yahoo.com/Reference/Libraries/Presidential-Libraries`

From this site you can access the presidential libraries of recent presidents. You will find items such as oral histories, collections, bibliographies, and photographs for the following presidents:

- Reagan
- Roosevelt
- Carter
- Eisenhower
- Kennedy
- Johnson
- Nixon
- Ford

Gettysburg Address Text

`http://jefferson.village.virginia.edu/readings`

The text of the Gettysburg address can be accessed at this site.

Civil War Collection

`http://www.access.digex.net/~bdboyle/cw.html`

This site has links to many different Civil War resources including

- Civil War Archive at the U.S. Library of Congress
- Active ACW Site Preservation Groups
- Civil War documents
- Reenactment and living-history information
- Music library
- Orders of battle for major engagements
- Regimental histories
- Civil War home page at the University of Tennessee
- Civil War diaries of G. D. Molineaux

Civil War History of Virginia and Pennsylvania

```
http://jefferson.village.virginia.edu/vshadow/vshadow2.html
```

This narrative has numerous links and talks about what it was like to live in Pennsylvania or Virginia during this period. Some of the links to their archives are

- 20,000 pages of newspapers from this period
- 5,000 pages of population and agricultural censuses
- Rosters of Union and Confederate soldiers
- Official records of the War of the Rebellion
- Maps showing topography, residences, and battlefields
- Diaries

World War II Photo Album

```
http://www.webcom.com/~jbd/ww2_pictures.html
```

This site is much smaller than ones we usually recommend and it only contains a few World War II pictures. If you don't have any of the real thing stashed away in a drawer to include with your report, you might want to take a look at these. Figure 15-1 shows the list of pictures you can access.

Marshall University Byrd Historical Archives

```
ftp://byrd.mu.wvnet.edu/pub/history
```

This site has a number of files covering topics from the Civil War to more current historical events like the Korean War and the Gulf War. There are many documents in each category with things like frequently asked questions, reading lists, notes, and recollections.

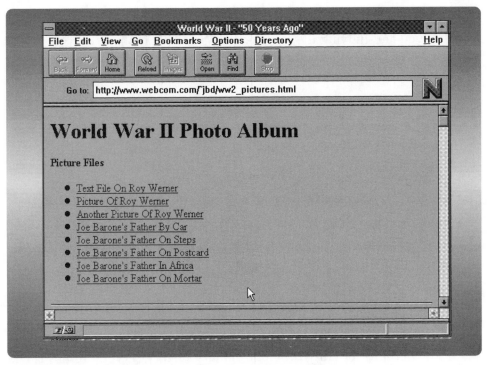

FIGURE 15-1. *An intimate look at some World War II photos*

Alphabetical History Index at the University of Kansas

`http://history.cc.ukans.edu/history/index.html`

You can use the links in this alphabetical index to connect to hundreds of sites such as

- 1492 Exhibition

- AAA: American Antiquarian Society

- ABZU: The Ancient Near East

- American Academy of Research Historians of Medieval Spain

- Ancestry, religion, death, and culture in Central Appalachia

- Ancient Egypt

- Association for History and Computing

- Clionet: Australian History

Military History

Whether you are studying the Napoleonic Wars, the Civil War, or more recent clashes, you will find information on the Internet at the sites provided below:

Library of Congress

```
http://lcweb.loc.gov
```

This site has many historical links and documents including

- Historical collections of the National Digital Library
- Descriptions of special collections of the Library of Congress
- POW/MIA database

You can see a few of the possibilities at this site in Figure 15-2 with flags on the new elements, which are added constantly.

University of Kansas Military History Resources

```
http://kuhttp.cc.ukans.edu/history/milhst
```

There are links to many different military history servers from this site including

- The Classical and Medieval Military History
- Early Modern History to Napoleonic Wars
- American Civil War
- Through 1919
- 1919–1945
- 1945–1961
- 1961–1973
- 1975–Present

Foreign History

You can check these sites as well as university libraries at schools in foreign countries for more on foreign history.

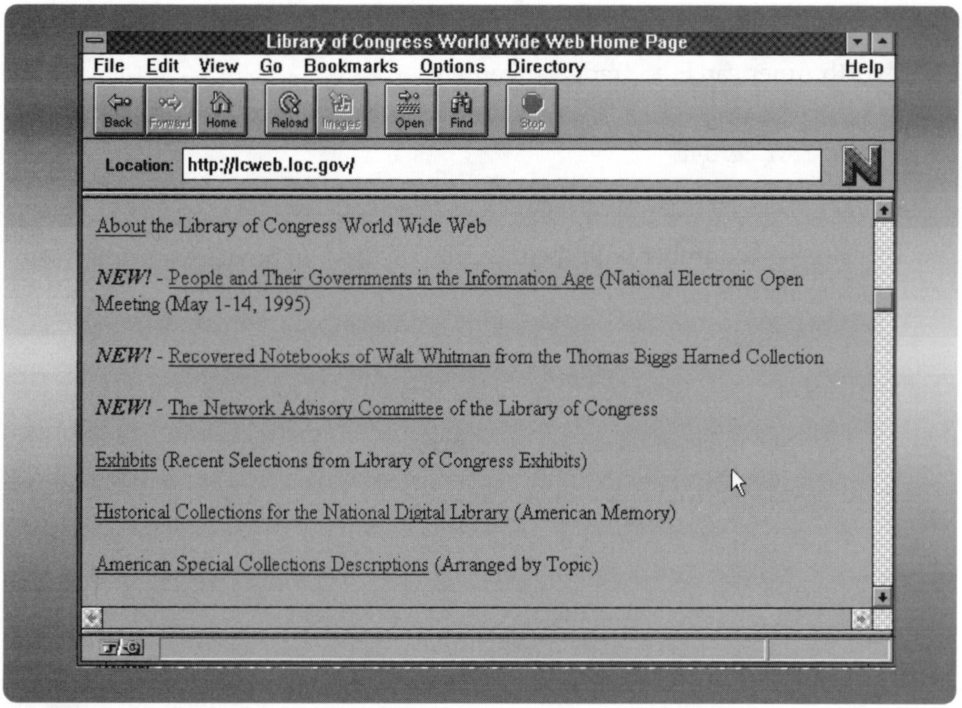

FIGURE 15-2. *Library of Congress options*

Institute of Historical Research in the United Kingdom

`http://ihr.sas.ac.uk:8080/ihr/ihr0101.html`

This is a great site if you are researching European history. Some of the menu options are

- Online resources for historians in London
- Online resources for historians in the United Kingdom
- Online resources for historians in Europe

Canadian History

`gopher://porpoise.oise.on.ca:70/11/eloise/refdesk/Documents`

Some of the historical Canadian documents you can access at this site are

- Canada Constitution Act 1867
- Canada Meech Lake Accord

- Charlottetown Constitutional Agreement
- North American Free Trade Agreement

Russia and East Europe

```
gopher://una.hh.lib.umich.edu:70/11/newstuff/exp/slavic
```

This site has a number of links primarily focused on Soviet history. Some of your options on this gopher are

- Soviet archives
- Library of Congress revelations of the Soviet archives
- East European list of electronic resources
- Authoritative Soviet E-Mail Directory
- Internet discussion groups
- Medieval

Journal—Bryn Mawr Medieval Review

```
gopher://gopher.lib.virginia.edu:70/11/alpha/bmmr
```

This journal covers all areas of medieval studies. Some titles from recent issues are

- Barbarians and Politics
- Signs of Cleopatra
- Roman Remains of South France
- Collected Works of Erasmus
- The Greek Anthology

POLITICAL SCIENCE

Whether you are studying government policy or international relations, Internet resources will make your task easier.

Voting—Project Vote Smart

gopher://chaos.dac.neu.edu:70/11/pvs-data

This site is maintained by volunteers trying to keep the electorate informed about the 2,000 candidates wanting to represent them. You will find a House and Senate Vote Key, a governor database, and a database of the current congressional session.

Index of Resources

These indices will get you started in any area of political science research.

Carnegie-Mellon

http://info.heinz.cmu.edu

This server located at the H. John Heinz School of Public Policy and Management acts as a clearinghouse for all public policy information on the Internet. You will find resources relating to crime, environment, government information, health care, and nonprofit organizations.

University of Connecticut Political Science Index

http://spirit.lib.uconn.edu/PoliSci/polisci.htm

This is an outstanding index of political science resources including college departments, research institutions, FTP sites, newsgroups, and links to resources in related fields.

University Sites

Schools and universities that have programs in political science or government can provide a vast storehouse of information no matter where you are working.

Australian National University

http://www.anu.edu.au/polsci/austpol/austpol

This site has many resources for anyone studying the Australian political scene. General categories under which links are arranged are

- Australian politics
- International and comparative politics

- Movements and theories
- Policy
- Other lists and resources

California State University at San Marcos

```
http://coyote.csusm.edu/gopher/cwis/academic_departments/
College_of_Arts_and_Sciences/Political_Science
```

This school's political science home page lets you launch your research efforts using a world map to click on areas of interest.

Kennedy School of Government–Harvard University

```
gopher://ksggopher.harvard.edu:70/11/.KSG
```

You can access the Kennedy School case studies and government sites that might support your research.

University of Wales, Aberystwyth

```
http://www.aber.ac.uk
```

Look for International Politics after selecting Academic Departments for area studies resources for the Middle East, Asia Pacific, and Africa. The Virtual Tourist World Map lets you locate resources by geographical area. Figure 15-3 shows the initial screen upon connecting to the Department of International Politics at the University of Wales.

Public Policy

There are resources available with both domestic and international scope. The sites in this section have links to many other resources.

The Carter Center

```
http://www.emory.edu/CARTER_CENTER/
```

This public policy institute has initiatives in over thirty countries to fight oppression, conflict, poverty, and hunger throughout the world. There is information about their projects as well as links to sites that relate to their projects. A few of the links from the Carter Center are shown in Figure 15-4.

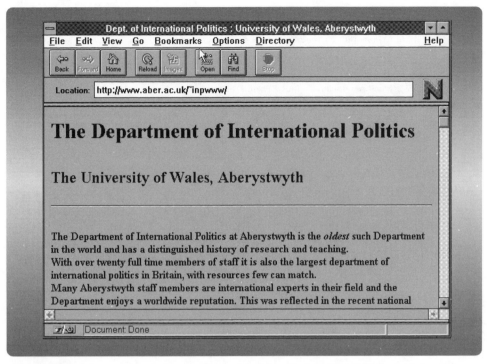

FIGURE 15-3. *Department of International Politics, University of Wales initial screen*

Hoover Institution on War, Revolution, and Peace

http://hoover.stanford.edu/www/welcome.html

This institution focuses on domestic and international affairs. You can learn about current and planned research on topics such as

- American institutions and economic performance

- Democracy and free markets

- International rivalries and global cooperation

Figure 15-5 provides some background information on the Hoover Institution.

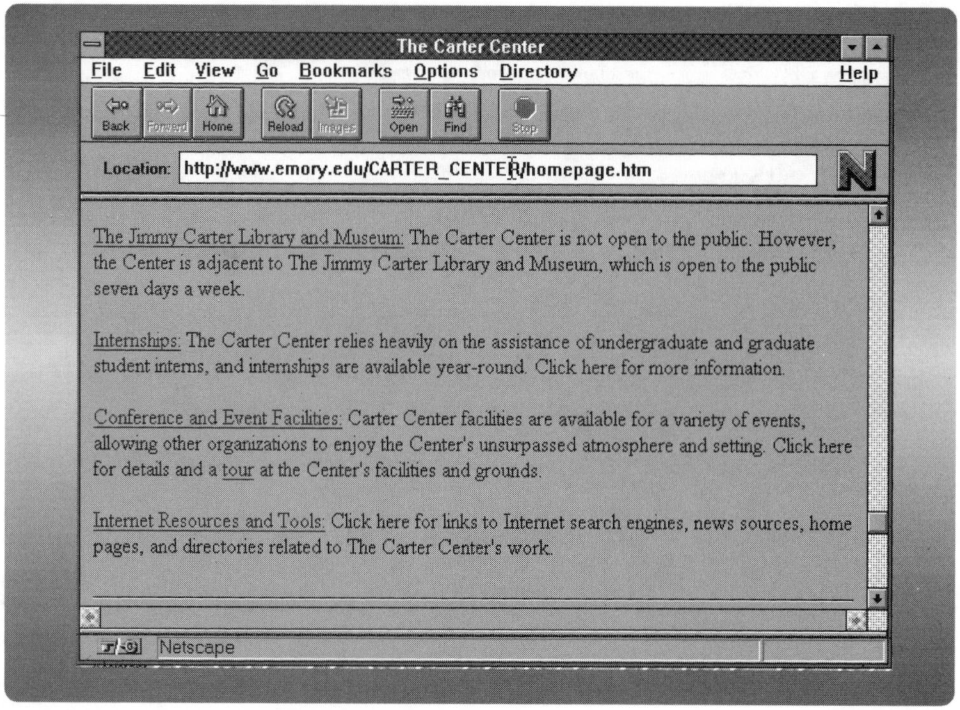

FIGURE 15-4. *The Carter Center*

Stockholm International Peace Research Institute

`http://www.sipri.se`

You can learn about the institute or read about its research in areas such as

- Arms transfers
- Arms production
- Military expenditure
- Military technology
- Chemical and biological weapons
- European security
- Peacekeeping and regional security
- Security and arms control in East Asia

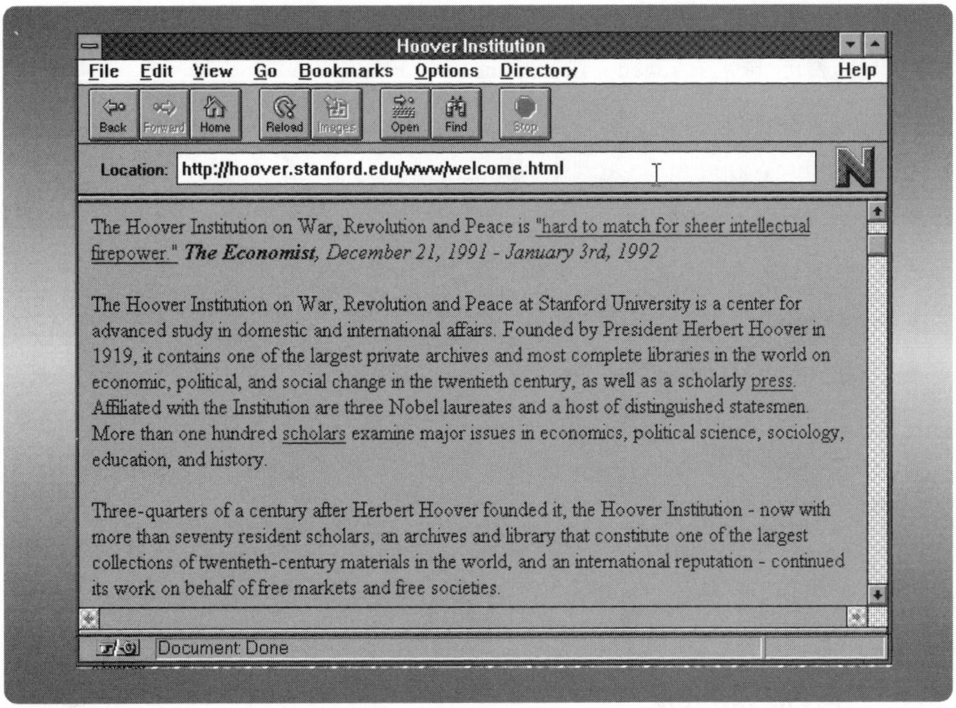

FIGURE 15-5. *The Hoover Institution initial screen*

Freedom-Related Writings

http://nw.com/jamesd

This site has links to many freedom-related documents including

- John Locke's Treatise on Civil Government
- Aristotle's Politics
- Anarcho Capitalism
- U.S. Bill of Rights

Foreign Policy

Foreign policy or international relations is a broad field that includes diplomacy as well as international law and relations.

Institute on Global Conflict and Cooperation

http://irpsbbs.ucsd.edu/igcc/igccmenu.html

Some of the links from this site are

- Economic cooperation and development
- Environment
- Middle East
- Asia Pacific
- Security and strategic issues

Gorbachev Foundation

http://www.clark.net/pub/gorbachev/home.html

This foundation addresses the challenges facing the post–Cold War world. It has information on foundation projects such as the Global Security Project and the State of the World Forum for world leaders.

North American Institute

http://sol.uvic.ca:70/0h/nami/HOMEPAGE.html

This organization is designed to promote dialogue between the citizens of Mexico, Canada, and the United States. There are links relating to NAFTA, environmental cooperation, and transborder citizens.

Just for Fun

Even if you can't afford the time or money to travel to Washington, D.C., you can visit the White House when you are finished with your studies tonight. We are not suggesting a Star Trek beaming device to get you there either—all you have to do is connect with http://www/whitehouse.gov. Once connected, you will see the display in Figure 15-6. You can take a tour or visit with the First Family. If you choose the visit, one option is family life at the White House. You will find pictures of President Clinton with his saxophone, horseback riding, and sharing a leisure moment with Socks, the cat.

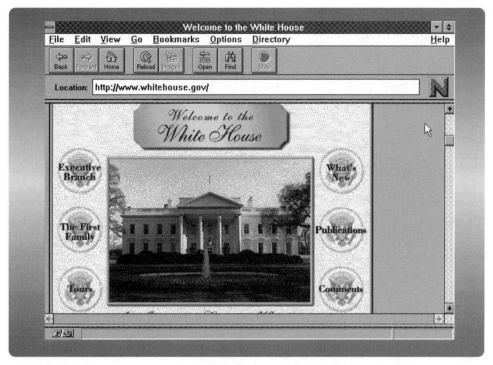

FIGURE 15-6. *You can take a tour or visit with the First Family from the White House site*

Chapter 16

Legal Resources

ALTHOUGH THE BEST-KNOWN online legal resources are fee-based databases like Lexis and Nexis, there are plenty of Internet legal sources that won't cost you a cent to use. If you are an accounting major, you will find that the tax code available online is a lot easier to search than your textbook. There are also law school sites of interest to law students or someone studying cases for a business law or policy class. The legal resources available through the Internet can help you in many areas of your studies. You can monitor current legislative issues, such as privacy and electronic surveillance. The foreign law resources will help you get a better picture of politics and economies of foreign lands. Although the sites selected are listed under only one category, most of them have been chosen because they have resource links to several areas of the law. After exploring the ones of immediate interest, you will want to check out some of the others.

FOREIGN LAW

You can find links to legal information all around the globe. At many foreign sites the legal information is in the language of the country rather than English.

Canadian Legal and Government Resources

`http://www.io.org/~agahtan/canada.htm`

This site has links to the following locations:

- Supreme Court of Canada
- Quebec Law—University of Montreal
- Canadian Constitution Act
- Master index to Internet resources
- North American Free Trade Agreement
- Canadian law schools

- Canadian citizenship and immigration information
- Canadian heritage information network
- Canadian Open Government Project
- Health Canada
- Industry Canada Web Server

Bentham Archive of British Law

```
http://www-server.bcc.ac.uk/~uctlxjh/Bentham.html
```

This site is at University College in London. Among the many resources you can access:

- Just Mooting Law Index
- English criminal law
- Property law cases
- Legal humour

Bracton Law Society

```
http://www.ex.ac.uk/~mpradfor/societies/bls_page/bls.html
```

The home page for this British association provides links to back issues of their journal as well as historical documents and sites like the European Commission and German Law at Humboldt University.

Russian Legal Server

```
http://solar.rtd.utk.edu/~nikforov/main.html
```

This server's information is in English and provides some information on news, listservs, and legal digests. There is also a link that provides an overview of the Russian legal structure, a tutorial on legal research, legal and business documents, and classifieds. The main menu options are shown in Figure 16-1.

Mexican Constitution

```
http://info.ic.gc.ca/~will/Other/Legal/Constitutions/Mexico/
constitution-mex.html
```

This is the complete constitution in Spanish. It is 250K in length, so it will take a while to retrieve on a slow-speed modem.

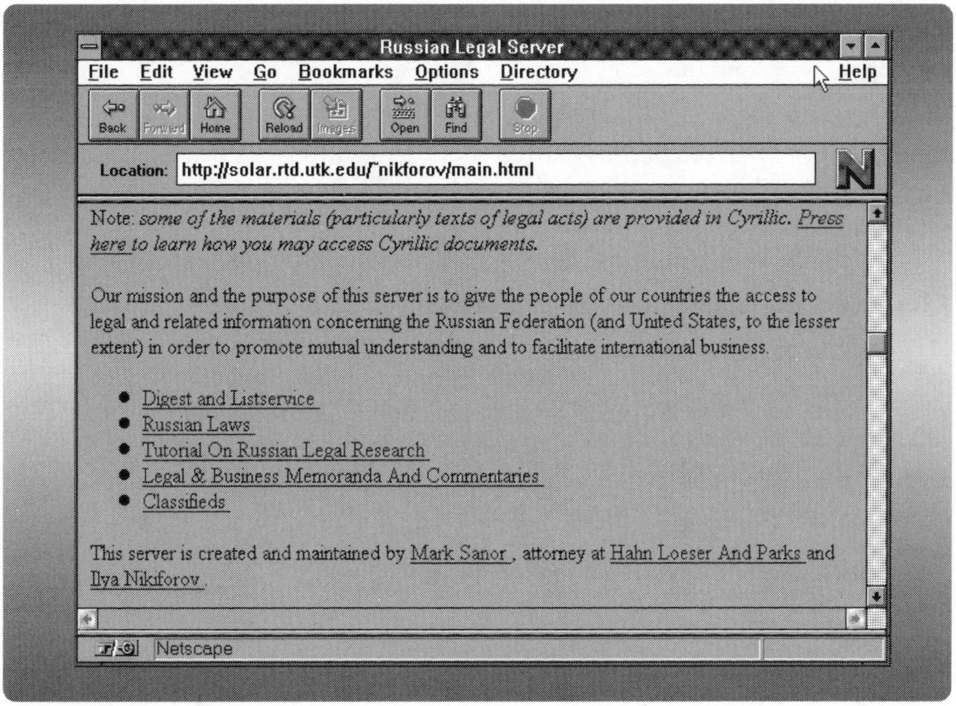

FIGURE 16-1. *Russian Legal Server*

LAW FIRMS AND SCHOOLS ON THE WEB

```
http://akebono.stanford.edu/yahoo/Law
```

This site provides a list of law schools and law firms with sites on the Web. You will also find links to many other legal resources at this site.

LAW SCHOOLS

The leading law schools are a good place to shop for sites you will want to visit. Although some schools specialize in specific areas of the law for their site, most have references to a wide variety of resources.

Chicago–Kent College of Law

`http://www.kentlaw.edu`

Access the Legal Domain Network at this law school for read-only access to many USENET discussion groups, including: law.aba, law.legaldomain, law.cyber, law.library, law-listserv, law.school, alt.dear.whitehouse, alt-politics, alt-inventors, and alt-law-enforcement.

Cleveland Marshall College of Law Library

`http://www.law.csuohio.edu`

This site focuses on legal education, law, and the law library. It provides links that allow you to access many libraries within Ohio as well as a list of Internet legal links such as

- The 1990 Computer Misuse Act

- Information on subscribing to legal listservs

- Legal Internet resources by site

- FEDIX–Federal Opportunities Information BBS Service

- LEGI-SLATE containing the Congressional Record and the Federal Register

Cornell Law School

`http://www.law.cornell.edu`

From this site you can access Cornell's Legal Information Institute's hypertext files of Supreme Court decisions.

Emory Law School

`http://law.emory.edu/LAW/law.html`

This site lists case information from the Eleventh Circuit Court of Appeals. Other links include Federal Agencies and Organizations, Federal Laws and Bases, International Resources, Public Interest, and Human Rights. There are also links to Georgia Legal materials stored in the Emory Law Library. Figure 16-2 shows a partial list of resources at this site.

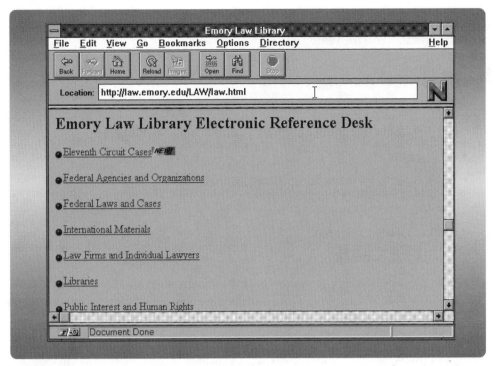

FIGURE 16-2. *Emory Law School Web server*

Indiana Law School

http://www.law.indiana.edu

Hypertext versions of the Global Legal Studies Journal and the Federal Communications Law Journal. LawTalk, which is authored by the school's faculty, provides segments on various law or legal studies topics. There is also a variety of other interesting links.

Vanderbilt University Owen Graduate School of Management

http://www.vanderbilt.edu/Owen/froeb/mgt352/mgt352.html

This site is designed for students in the Economic, Social, and Legal Environment of Business course at the school and provides the following resources to students:

- Lecture notes
- Term paper topics

- Sample term paper
- Information on the network

Washington and Lee Law Library

```
gopher://liberty.uc.wlu.edu:70/11/library/law
```

You can access many links from this gopher site, including

- Law gophers
- Netlink server's international law resources
- Adoption laws
- Canadian legal research
- Disability information
- FTP files containing programs and other documents such as treaties

INTELLECTUAL PROPERTY

Intellectual property such as software and written materials is difficult to protect, even though laws do exist. In certain parts of the world, rights to intellectual properties are disregarded, thereby making protection of intellectual property a major issue in our global economy. If you are looking for copyright or trademark information, let the Internet sources be the first place you check.

Copyright Act of 1976

```
http://www.law.cornell.edu/usc/17/overview.html
```

This site has all the detail of this act, organized under these chapter headings:

Chapter 1. Subject matter and scope of copyright

Chapter 2. Copyright ownership and transfer

Chapter 3. Duration of copyright

Chapter 4. Copyright notice, deposit, and registration

Chapter 5. Copyright infringement and remedies

Chapter 6. Manufacturing requirements and importation

Copyright Resources on the Web

`http://www.io.org/~agahtan/copyrite.htm`

Some of the topics covered at this site are

- Copies of Copyright Office records and deposits
- Audio Home Recording Act of 1992
- Books, manuscripts, and speeches
- Cartoons and comic strips
- Computer programs
- Investigating the copyright status of a work
- International copyright
- Musical compositions
- Photographs

Also check the World Guide to Copyright at http://www.theworld.com/LAW/copyrigh/subject.htm

Databases

`http://tarlton.law.utexas.edu/library/netref/intellprop.html`

Through this site you can access the U.S. Patent Database, the U.S. Patent Act, the Copyright Act of 1976, and Copyright Basics.

U.S. Patents Database

`http://town.hall.org/patent/patent.html`

This site allows you to use WAIS search techniques on the data archives of the U.S. Patent Office for all the patents issued in 1994 and 1995.

PRIVACY

As we move further and further into the electronic age, it seems as though every detail of our existence winds up in some database. These sites deal with research and current cases involving privacy legislation.

Privacy Forum

http://www.vortex.com/privacy.html

You can access current and back issues of this moderated digest as well as a collection of papers on the topic.

Privacy Rights Clearinghouse

http://emma.manymedia.com/prc

Some of the topics covered are

- Privacy debate
- Educating consumers
- Clearinghouse services

SPECIAL TOPICS

The topics in this section are a conglomeration of topics in the legal forefront today. These are just a sampling of the Internet legal resources.

Antitrust Law

http://www.vanderbilt.edu/Owen/froeb/antitrust/antitrust.html

This online journal provides information on mergers, price fixing, and vertical markets. Cross-disciplinary issues relating to economics, public policy, and law are discussed. Figure 16-3 shows the initial screen after connecting.

Bankruptcy Law

http://www.kentlaw.edu/cgi-bin/ldn_news/-T+law.listserv.bankrlaw

You'll find an archive of current transmissions from their mailing list. Dialog from several previous months is also available.

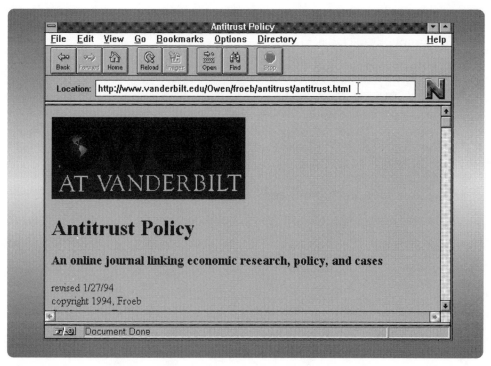

FIGURE 16-3. *Vanderbilt's Antitrust Policy journal initial screen*

CyberLaw and CyberLex

    http://www.portal.com/~cyberlaw

These two online publications provide information on the law and the computer industry.

Environmental Law Sites

    http://www.law.indiana.edu/law/intenvlaw.html

This is a great list with Web and gopher sites for both international and environmental law. There is also a list of Usenet groups dealing with these issues.

Federal Rules of Evidence

    http://www.law.cornell.edu/rules/fre/overview.html

Cornell's Legal Information Institute provides access to the full text of the Federal Rules of Evidence. The following topics are covered:

- Judicial notice

- Presumptions in civil actions

- Relevancy and its limits

- Privileges

- Witnesses

- Opinions and expert testimony

- Hearsay

- Authentication and identification

- Contents of writings, recordings, and photographs

- Miscellaneous rules

Labor Issues

http://venable.com/wlu/wlu3.htm

This site is maintained by the law firm of Venable, Baetjer, and Howard and publishes quarterly articles relating to labor issues such as

- Violence in the Workplace

- Retroactivity of the Civil Rights Act of 1991

- County Not Required to Accommodate Asthmatic Firefighter

Law and Cyberspace

http://www.law.indiana.edu/lawlib/iclu.html

For a look at all kinds of cases affecting cyberspace, check out this site. These are some of the highlights:

- An Almost Complete Privacy Toolkit

- Citizen's Guide to the Net

- Internet Libel

- Civil Liberties in Cyberspace

- A Civil Liberties Ride on the Information Superhighway

- Intellectual Property and the National Information Infrastructure

Securities Law Index

`http://www.law.uc.edu:80/CCL`

This site provides access to the federal securities laws, their rules, and forms. Figure 16-4 shows the screen after connecting.

State Government Information Servers

`http://www.law.indiana.edu/law/states.html`

There are links to many state resources. Although availability varies by state, this is a list of what is offered for the state of Oregon:

- Oregon Legislative Administration Committee Information Systems

- Oregon Online

- State Archives

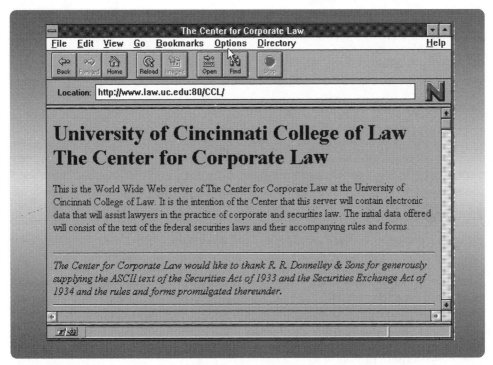

FIGURE 16-4. *University of Cincinnati College of Law site, which allows you to access the Securities Law Index*

- Department of Administrative Services Printing Division

- Department of Agriculture

- Department of Fish and Wildlife

- Department of Transportation

Technology Law Resource

`http://www.kuesterlaw.com`

This site was created by an intellectual property attorney in Atlanta. It provides information on copyright law and answers questions about these topics:

- Type of patent needed

- When to file a patent

- What is needed for a good trademark

- Determining patentability

- How to register a trademark

There are also links to relevant cases, intellectual property law resources, and many other resources.

Technology and Law Bibliography

`http://web.mit.edu/org/c/ctpid/www/tl/TL-pub.html`

This bibliography is current and would be a great help for any research paper you are doing on issues relating to technology and the law.

Trade Law

`http://ananse.irv.uit.no/trade_law/nav/trade.html`

This site is maintained by the University of Tromso in Norway. This is a great site for all sorts of trade-related information. You will find links to trade organizations such as WTO/GATT, the United Nations, and the ICC. Various trade treaties, conventions, laws, and rules can also be accessed including information on topics like these:

- Procurement of goods

- Carriage of goods

- Electronic data interchange

- Protection of intellectual property

- Arbitration

- Treaties related to greater freedom of trade

- Trade law libraries

Uniform Commercial Code

`http://www.law.cornell.edu/ucc/ucc.table.html`

Articles 1–9 of the Uniform Commercial Code are available in hypertext format. This includes sales, leases, negotiable instruments, bank deposits and collections, fund transfers, bulk transfers, warehouse receipts, investment securities, and secured transactions.

Women's Legal Resources

`http://asa.ugl.lib.umich.edu/chdocs/womenpolicy/womenlawpolicy.html`

The issues covered by this site include

- Health care/reproductive issues

- Lesbian women

- Mothers and children

- Violence against women

- Women and development

- Women in the military

- Women of color

- Women with disabilities

- Work issues

CONSUMER LEGAL ISSUES

Organizations, law firms, and even software companies that provide legal services to consumers have provided some self-help legal information that is available through the Internet.

LEGAL.NET

http://www.legal.net

This site is called "legal dot net" and is of primary interest to consumers. There are articles from magazines such as *Esquire* and *Legal Tech*. You can access a list of attorneys or use their links to jump to a variety of other locations.

Law.Net

http://law.net/

This site, which is designed for one-stop shopping for the consumer and business, is a joint venture between Volant Corporation and United Reporting, Inc. Figure 16-5 shows the Law Net logo that will become familiar if you are researching consumer legal issues. Some of the resources you will find are

- Links to the top 25 law schools

- The Consortium for Optical Imaging in law libraries

- LSAT information

- An index of legal indexes

There are also sections of this server for newsletters and contests.

UNITED STATES GOVERNMENT

Government agencies all have gopher or Web sites that you can access for information on Congressional activities, IRS forms, and vast databases of government information. Check out these sites as well as links they provide to other government entities.

CIA Server

http://www.ic.gov

This server provides access to the CIA's World Factbook and the Factbook on Intelligence.

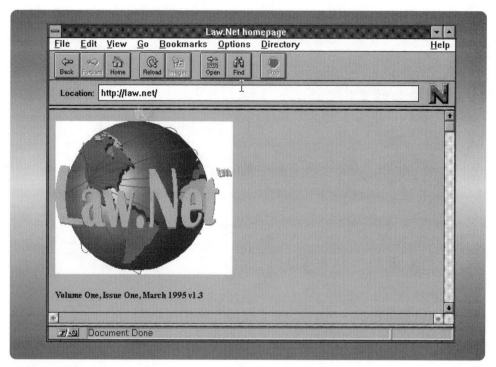

FIGURE 16-5. *Law Net site*

Congress

    http://thomas.loc.gov

This site of the U.S. Library of Congress provides documents explaining how laws are made and provides access to the House of Representatives gopher, constituent e-mail, and the Senate gopher, with frequently asked questions about the Senate's Internet services for constituents. Figure 16-6 shows the initial screen for the Thomas Legislative Information.

Federal Bureau of Investigation

    http://naic.nasa.gov/fbi/

This site provides information in these areas:

- Criminal law enforcement
- Foreign counterintelligence

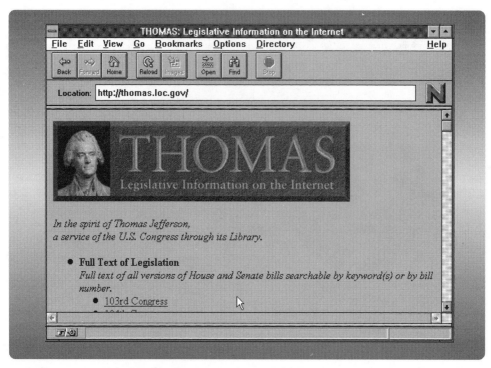

FIGURE 16-6. *Legislative information made available by the U.S. Congress*

- Investigative and operational support
- Law enforcement services
- Direction, control, and administration
- FBI UNABOM Case

Supreme Court Justices

`http://www.law.cornell.edu/supct/justices/fullcourt.html`

You can access a picture of the justices and a bio on each of them.

U.S. House of Representatives Internet Law Library

`http://www.pls.com:8001/d2/kelli/httpd/htdocs/his/115.GBM`

Resources at this site include the following:

- WAIS access to West Publishing's Legal Directory
- Cornell's Directory of Legal Academia
- Addresses for the top legal journals based on the number of citations

ASSOCIATIONS AND ORGANIZATIONS

Organizations in the legal area provide information about their activities but are also a rich source of links to other sites.

American Bar Association

`http://www.abanet.org/ABA/aba.html`

This site provides general information about the ABA and provides abstracts of articles in recent issues of the *ABA Journal*. Check out Chapter 10 for more detail on the resources available at this site.

ACLU American Civil Liberties Union

`gopher://aclu.org:6601/1`

This site allows you to look at the Civil Liberties newsletter as well as some state-affiliated newsletters. The newsroom feature lets you look at a synopsis of recent cases. Speeches, letters, issues and answers, and current legislation are all covered. You can also find out how to join the group or seek help from it.

United Nations

`http://www.undcp.org/unlinks.html`

This site provides links to development banks and all of the UN's WWW and gopher servers including the International Atomic Energy Agency, the United Nations Children's Fund, and the United Nations Crime Prevention and Criminal Justice Branch.

IMMIGRATION AND CITIZENSHIP

You can look to the Internet for information about immigration forms and procedures as well as what is involved with dual citizenship.

Dual Citizenship

`http://www/mks.com/~richw/dualcit.html`

This site provides answers to frequently asked questions about dual citizenship and the U.S. law. These questions relate to the following topics:

- Possibility of dual citizenship
- U.S. laws regarding dual citizenship
- U.S. citizenship and moving abroad
- U.S. Constitution and dual citizenship
- Renunciation in U.S. naturalization oath
- Special U.S./Israeli dual citizenship deal
- Foreign military service
- Going back to visit one's native country

Immigration

`http://www.fred.net/mahesh/immigration.html`

Frequently asked questions from the alt.visa.us newsgroup including information on F, H, J, K, and L visas, green cards, and citizenship. There are also links to other home pages, including one on dual citizenship. Figure 16-7 shows a page put together by an individual to share research on immigration forms and procedures.

HUMAN RIGHTS

If you are studying current human rights issues, you will want to check out the Amnesty International site listed here as well as the report of conditions in various foreign countries.

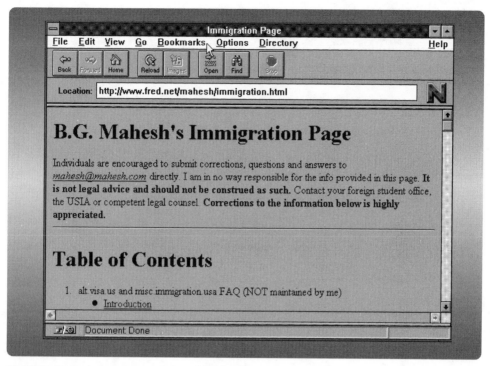

FIGURE 16-7. *Information on immigration page*

Amnesty International Online

http://www.io.org/amnesty/overview.html

This site contains links to other human rights organizations. It also contains information on the latest Amnesty International Campaigns. In April 1995 these were

- Tears of Orphans–Sudan Campaign
- Indonesian Electronic Publishing Project

Human Rights Country Report

gopher://cyfer.esusda.gov/11/ace/state/hrcr

This U.S. State Department report covers human rights conditions in many countries including Algeria, Andorra, Angola, Antigua, Austria, Australia, Azerbaijan, Afghanistan, and Albania. These reports address women, children, workers' rights, respect for human rights, and respect for civil liberties.

LEGAL RESEARCH

Although all the sites in this chapter can be used for some type of legal research, the main purpose of the sites in this section is research.

Legal Indexes

`http://tarlton.law.utexas.edu/library/netref/law_search.html`

This site provides links that allow you to search many legal indexes, including

- U.S. Supreme Court Syllabi
- U.S. Code at the U.S. House of Representatives
- Full text legislation of the 103rd and 104th Congress
- West's Legal Directory
- Directory of Legal Academia
- Back Issues of the Federal Communications Law Journal
- Law-Related Usenet newsgroups
- Chicago–Kent's Law Links

Law and Regulations

`http://galaxy.einet.net/galaxy/Government/Laws-and-Regulations.html`

This site is organized with many links in each of these areas:

- Foreign laws and regulations
- International laws and regulations
- Local, county, municipal laws, and regulations
- State laws and regulations
- U.S. laws and regulations

There are also links to collections, law schools, and several publications.

Law Topical Index

`http://www.io.org/~agahtan/lawindx.htm`

This index to legal resources is organized by these general areas:

- Administrative
- Commercial
- Constitutional
- Criminal
- Environmental
- Intellectual property
- Legal profession
- Military
- Personal finance
- Societal
- Tax

JOURNALS

There are many electronic law journals on the Internet. Some are research oriented and are published by the major law schools. Others are published by associations and are of interest to attorney members. Lately, a new source of journals or newsletters comes from law firms who are using these online vehicles to establish the expertise of their firm in a particular area of law. Their hope is that clients will think of their firm when they need to retain an attorney for a case in this area.

Canadian Law Notes

`http://www-bprc.mps.ohio-state.edu/cgi-bin/hpp?MurCo.html`

This site provides access to the bimonthly newsletter of a Canadian law firm but also provides a link to many legal resources in Canada.

Journal—Rules and Regulations in Russia

`http://www.spb.su/rulesreg/index.html`

Government controls, export duties, and tariffs are some of the topics covered by articles in the current issue at this St. Petersburg site.

Indiana Journal of Global Legal Studies

`http://www.law.indiana.edu/glsj/glsj.html`

Recent issues of the *Journal of Global Legal Studies* are available at this site. Some of the articles in the current issue focused on these topics:

- Migration and globalization

- Immigration in a global context

- Democracy and demography

- European and U.S. perspectives on civic republicanism

- Immigration policy

TAX LAW

Whether you want to look at proposed tax changes or get copies of tax forms, there are sites on the Internet to help you get what you need to complete your project.

Bipartisan Committee on Entitlement and Tax Reform

`http://www.charm.net/dcarolco`

You can monitor commission meetings and activities or try your hand at reform at this site.

Canadian Tax Information

`http://tax.ey.ca/ey`

Ernst & Young's Canadian office provides a variety of tax resources on Canadian tax law. You will be able to access E&Y's Tax News Releases and some of their other tax publications.

Government Tax Publications—FedWorld

You will find links to over 500 tax forms as well as information about the Commerce Information Locator Service, government information servers, and recent government reports.

IRS

http://www.ustreas.gov/treasury/bureaus/irs/irs.html

You will find tax forms, frequently asked questions, and information on how to get help with your tax filings at this site.

Public Domain Tax Software

ftp://ftp.scubed.com/pub/proffer/tax

You will find some tax software programs for Macintosh and PCs at this site.

Taxing Times

http://inept.scubed.com:8001/tax/tax.html

This site contains links to all types of tax information including federal tax forms, Revenue Canada, several states' tax forms, the Federal Tax Code, and abstracts of *Tax Digest* articles. Main options at this site are shown in Figure 16-8.

Tax Planning and Other Personal Finance Tools

http://plaza.xor.com:80/resources

This site provides online calculators and a great deal of information to the consumer. The tax planning site is currently under development but the fully operational home loan site provides answers to questions on rate quotes, loan descriptions, prequalification, and other topics. It also provides calculators to answer questions relating to comparing loans, deciding whether to rent or buy, combining first and second mortgages, refinancing nondeductible consumer loans, estimating the amount for which you qualify, and calculating the key elements of a loan.

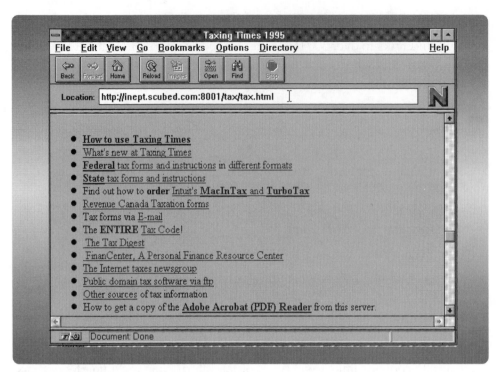

FIGURE 16-8. *Taxing Times main options*

Just for Fun

If law research has you blurry-eyed, take a short break and look at some of the great lawyer jokes at the Nolo Press site. Although the main focus of the site is providing self-help information for consumers, you'll find quite a few lawyer jokes relating to all sorts of things such as ticks, reptiles, Santa Claus, bills, whining, barn animals, airplanes, computers, and avocado. Use your Web browser to connect to:

```
http://nearnet.gnn.com/gnn/bus/nolo/jokes.html
```

Chapter 17

Literature

IN THE BROADEST SENSE, literature is everything that has ever been written from the classical novel or sonnet to a soap opera script or comic book. The two broadest classifications for literature are fiction and nonfiction.

There is a large body of quality literature available on the Internet through projects such as Project Gutenberg, which aims to make the cost of online books so low that an entire library of 10,000 books would only cost $100. Although Project Gutenberg and similar undertakings have not yet reached their goals, there is at this time a large body of both English and foreign literature online.

CATALOGS, INDEXES, AND LARGE COLLECTIONS

The sites in this section can all be classified as super sites, since each makes available a vast literature repository or provides an index or catalog to tell you where to look for a particular book or the writings of an individual author.

Alex Catalog

http://www.lib.ncsu.edu/stacks/alex-index.html

There are 1,800 electronic texts cataloged in this index. You can search the catalog by a specific entry or browse by author, date, host, language, subject, or title. When browsing the authors with a last name beginning with B, for example, Baum's *Wonderful Wizard of Oz* and Bronte's *Wuthering Heights* are two of the options.

ARTFL Project

http://tuna.uchicago.edu/

If you are studying French literature, you will want to take a look at this site with its many resources and links.

Bibliography of English Literature

`http://www.hull.ac.uk/Hull/FR_Web/abell.html`

This index covers scholarly articles, doctoral dissertations, books, and reviews relating to English literature. It is currently available free for a trial period. Figure 17-1 shows the introductory screen for the ABELL Bibliography of English Language and Literature.

Carnegie-Mellon English Server

`http://english-www.hss.cmu.edu`

This server is located at Carnegie-Mellon and is a major resource for all types of writing in the humanities. Cultural studies, drama, fiction, and poetry are just a few of the main categories available.

Classics - Electronic Works

`http://www.wonderland.org/works`

This is a major resource for electronic literature. Although the site is still under construction, there are lots of great classics available now:

- *Through the Looking Glass*
- *The Pit and the Pendulum*
- *Tom Sawyer*
- *Wuthering Heights*
- *The Time Machine*
- *Around the World in 80 Days*
- *Jungle Book*
- *The Wizard of Oz*
- *The Adventures of Huckleberry Finn*
- *Canterbury Tales*
- *A Christmas Carol*
- *Great Expectations*
- *Alice's Adventures in Wonderland*

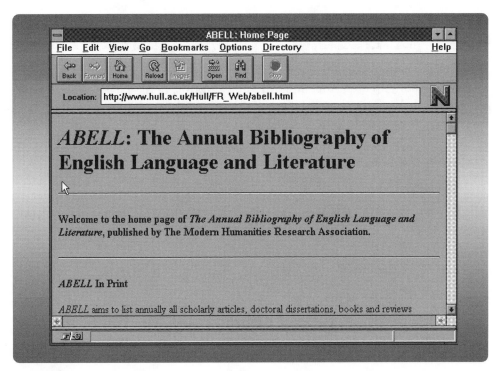

FIGURE 17-1. *Abell: The Annual Bibliography of English Literature and Language*

Eris Project Books

```
gopher://gopher.vt.edu:10010/10/33
```

This site contains a large collection of online books accessible from an alphabetical list of author names.

Great Etext Links

```
http://www.cs.rmit.edu.au/etext/links.html
```

This site provides links to all sorts of electronic repositories including

- The Online Book Initiative
- The Etext Archives
- GNA Meta Library

Index of Literary Servers

```
http://www.cs.fsu.edu/projects/group4/litpage.html
```

This is a comprehensive index of literature sources. It includes online books, listservs relating to literature, literature newsgroups, home pages relating to literature, and WAIS databases. Figure 17-2 is symbolic of the Rosetta Stone linking literature and the Internet.

Online Book Initiative

```
http://www.std.com
```

This site has a large collection of electronic books that can be redistributed freely.

Oxford Text Archive

```
ftp://ota.ox.ac.uk/pub/ota
```

This site contains literary works in English and more than a dozen other languages. Although only registered users at the Oxford Computing Center can access the full range of material, public domain text is accessible by all.

Project Gutenberg Index

```
http://www.w3.org/hypertext/DataSources/bySubject/Literature
/Gutenberg/Overview.html
```

This site provides an easy access to an unofficial list of the Project Gutenberg electronic texts. You can access the Gutenberg works from an alphabetical list or by author.

Project Gutenberg

```
http://jg.cso.uiuc.edu/PG/welcome.html
```

This aggressive project hopes to have over 10,000 books in ASCII text format available in a few years. This page provides links to worldwide FTP sites where the texts and indexes are stored.

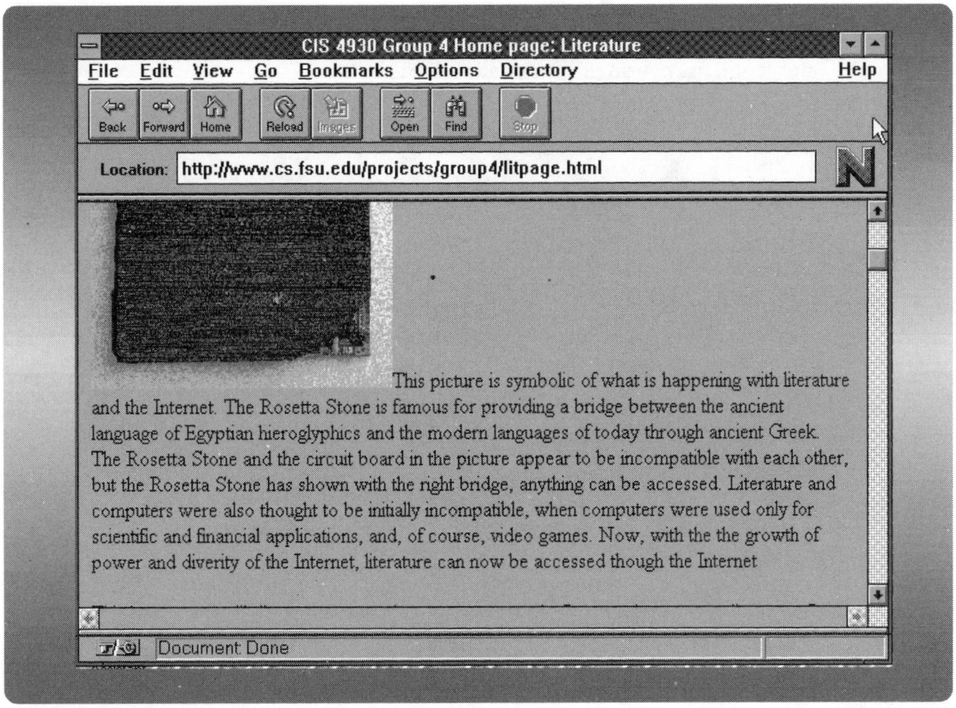

FIGURE 17-2. *Accessing an index of literary services*

Project Bartleby at Columbia

http://www.cc.columbia.edu/~svl2/index.html

Some of the works of the following authors are available at this public Internet library:

- John Keats
- Oscar Wilde
- Walt Whitman
- Percy Shelley
- Herman Melville
- Emily Dickinson
- John Bartlett
- George Chapman
- William Wordsworth

Shakespeare

`http://the-tech.mit.edu/Shakespeare/works.html`

This site provides access to the complete works of Shakespeare, including the following:

- *As You Like It*
- *Hamlet*
- *Julius Caesar*
- *Macbeth*
- *The Merchant of Venice*
- *The Taming of the Shrew*
- *The Sonnets*
- *Venus and Adonis*

Text Project at MIT

`http://sturgeon.mit.edu:8001/uu-gna/text/index.html`

This site at MIT is designed to provide textbooks in hypertext format online. One example is on Greek mythology, but more resources are being added.

University of Michigan—Middle English Collection Bibliography

`http://asa.uge.lib.umich.edu:80/libtext/english`

This is a good bibliography of Middle English literature including the writings of Chaucer.

University of Virginia Electronic Text Center

`http:/www.lib.virginia.edu/etext/ETC.html`

This site contains thousands of electronic texts in English and other languages including French, German, and Latin.

World-Wide Web Virtual Library

`http://sunsite.unc.edu/ibic/IBIC-homepage.html`

This site is very busy and may be hard to reach, but it contains pointers to libraries and electronic text worldwide. It's a good site to try if you are up late cramming for a test. Some of the links they have are categorized like this:

- Authors
- Virtual Review of Books
- Libraries
- Online Books and Magazines
- Reference Shelf
- Newsgroups relating to books
- World Literature

SPECIAL AREAS

There are many specialized areas of literature accessible through the Internet. College campuses around the world have electronic literature resources available. We have noticed that some sites restrict full access, more than in other disciplines, to their literature collections to students on their campus or regional area.

Banned Books

`http://www.cs.cmu.edu/Web/People/spok/banned-books.html`

Carnegie-Mellon maintains a page for books that were banned by legal authorities at some time in the past. These include:

- *Ulysses*
- *Candide*
- *Fanny Hill*
- *Canterbury Tales*
- *Leaves of Grass*
- *Lady Chatterley's Lover*
- *The Adventures of Tom Sawyer and Huckleberry Finn*

The initial screen for this site of banned book links is shown in Figure 17-3.

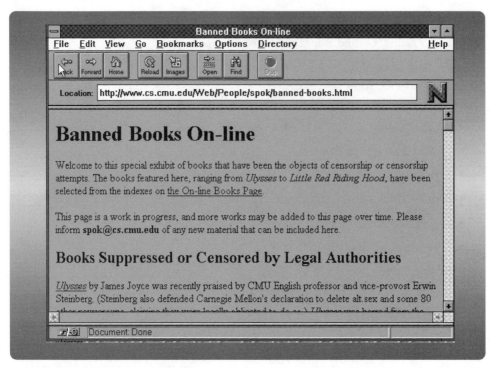

FIGURE 17-3. *Accessing via the Internet books that were once banned*

A Celebration of Women Writers

```
http://www.cs.cmu.edu/afs/cs.cmu.edu/user/mmbt/www/women/
celebration.html
```

This site focuses on plays, poetry, and novels written by women. Many of the titles are linked to online copies of the texts.

Nordic Literature

```
http://www.lysator.liu.se/runeberg/
```

This site provides free access to many Nordic literature titles. Some of the menu options at this site are shown in Figure 17-4.

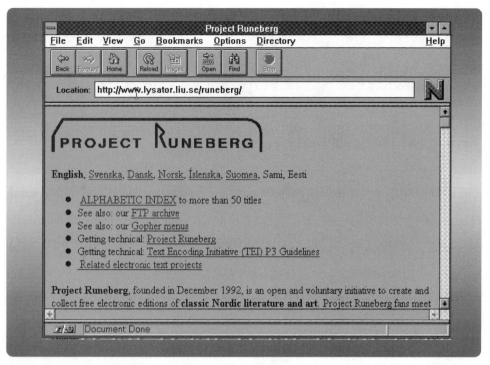

FIGURE 17-4. *Project Runeberg for Nordic literature*

Russian and East European Studies

http://www.pitt.edu/~cjp/rslang.html

This site provides links to Russian and East European literature, including the following:

- *Slavic Review*

- *Brothers Karamazov*

- *Anna Karenina*

- *War and Peace*

- Collection of Bulgarian poetry

- Estonian language and literature

- Romanian poetry

- 40,000-volume collection of Polish literature

JOURNALS

Although literature has lagged behind the sciences in getting journals in an electronic format, there is a move in this direction. Many English departments at major universities are beginning to publish their journals of quarterly poems or literary reviews on the Internet.

Bryn Mawr Medieval Review

`gopher://gopher.lib.virginia.edu:70/11/alpha/bmnr`

This journal provides reviews of work in medieval studies, including medieval literature.

Bryn Mawr Classics Review

`gopher://gopher.lib.virginia.edu:70/11/alpha/bmcr`

This journal views classical topics including literature and poetry.

Electronic Journals

`gopher://gopher.cic.net`

This site provides a listing of electronic journals on the Internet. Although they include literature, there are many other disciplines covered as well. Some of the links are shown in Figure 17-5.

Stanford Humanities Review

`http://symbol.stanford.edu/SEHR/homepage.html`

This journal covers humanities topics including literary criticism.

POETRY

Poetry appeals more strongly to the imagination than novels and other written works. Typically words are arranged by sound or thought patterns, and vivid pictures are painted with words in verses. The sites on the Internet represent a diverse set of poetry forms including both lyric and narrative forms.

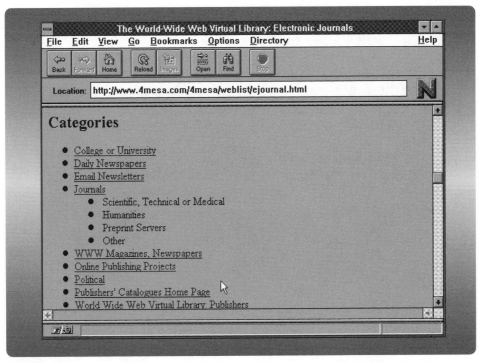

FIGURE 17-5. *Accessing electronic journals for literature and other areas*

British Poetry

`http://www.lib.virginia.edu/etext/britpo/britpo.html`

This archive is designed to make poetry available for classroom study. Some of the poets whose works are represented here:

- Lewis Carroll

- Alfred Lord Tennyson

- William Wordsworth

- John Milton

Contemporary Poetry Archive

`http://sunsite.unc.edu/dykki/poetry/home.html`

This site is located at the University of North Carolina and makes available the work of contemporary poets. The initial unit covers the work of eight poets including the Nobel prize winner in poetry, Czeslaw Milosz, shown in Figure 17-6.

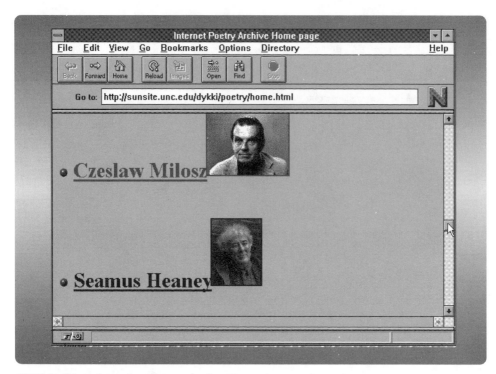

FIGURE 17-6. *Accessing the work of some contemporary poets*

Electronic Poetry Center at the University of Buffalo

`http://wings.buffalo.edu/internet/library/e-journals/ub/rift/`

This site provides an electronic poetry journal and links to other poetry resources.

English Server Poetry Archives

`http://english-www.hss.cmu.edu/Poetry.html`

This server provides access to the works of popular poets such as Whitman, Tennyson, Virgil, Sandburg, Shakespeare, Longfellow, Cummings, and Byron, as well as lesser known writers.

Poetry

Just for Fun

Tired of reading poetry or other literature assignments? If so, you might want to see if you can write something you think is better than what you've been reading. You can even have an outside judge evaluate your work if you write a poem. You will want to take a look at the contest sponsored by the National Library of Poetry for amateur poets. In 1995, their contest awarded 250 prizes totaling $24,000. You can connect to this site and submit your entries: http:www.kiosk.net/poetry/. Although your prize winnings couldn't possibly cover your tuition, it may pay for the books for your next English lit class.

Chapter 18

Medicine and Health

THERE ARE MANY MEDICAL RESOURCES on the Internet that are available at no charge. This may surprise you since most of the medical research databases you have heard about are probably available through Dialog or MEAD Data Services. These databases are great but may not be practical for students unless they are affiliated with a medical school or other location that makes these available to faculty and students. The Internet resources that will be of interest, whether you are researching for a course or your own health care needs, are commonly available through university health centers, medical schools, and government agencies. The selections presented represent a wide cross section of the type of material available. Many of the sites listed also have links to a wide variety of other sites expanding the potential for you to locate the information you need.

EDUCATIONAL RESOURCES

These sites have information of interest to students and educators as well as links to many other sites.

Cleveland Clinic Foundation Educational Server

    http://www.anes.ccf.org:8080

This site contains educational materials and links to many Internet locations.

Medical Education

    http://www.primenet.com/~gwa/med.ed

You will find frequently asked questions, FTP sites for medical software, a list of Web and gopher sites, and a list of Internet medical indexes. There are also links to many medical schools, a list of medical newsgroups, and the 1995 rankings of medical schools.

Software for Medical Education

```
gopher://orion.oac.uci.edu:1071/11/med-ed
```

This site contains a number of programs that are useful in medical education. You will want to read the readme text available from this menu for more information.

Visible Human Project

```
http://www.nlm.nih.gov/factsheets.dir/visible_human.html
```

At this site you'll find digital imaging research with sample MRI and CAT scan images.

DISEASES

There are Internet sources for most of the major diseases. Later in the chapter you will find listings for other diseases such as cancer, AIDS, and tuberculosis.

Allergies—Allergy Immunology Medical College of Georgia

```
gopher://lab.allergy.mcg.edu:70/1
```

You will find links to the following at this location:

- Asthma Online

- Journals in Allergy–Immunology

- Allergens, Molecular Biology

- American College of Allergy, Asthma, and Immunology

Diabetes

```
gopher://drinet.med.miami.edu:70/1
```

There is information on current research projects, symposia, and links to many other related resources here.

Lyme Disease

`gopher://gopher.lymenet.org`

Learn about lyme disease, associated court cases, and public opinion relating to the disease.

Tropical Diseases

`gopher://info.med.yale.edu`

This site has papers on a variety of diseases with information on tropical disease statistics on a country-by-country basis.

GENERAL HEALTH INFORMATION

These sites can provide ideas of current topics for research projects. They can also give you the information you need to stay healthy.

Boston University School of Public Health

`http://www-busph.bu.edu/`

You can look at some of the current research being conducted or connect to the Boston University Medical School server. The medical school server provides interesting medical links, including the following:

- Hippocratic oath

- Admissions offices to all U.S. medical schools

- Software archives

- Links to miscellaneous medical resources

HEALTHLINE

`gopher://healthline.umt.edu:700`

This site provides all types of information on everything from diseases to sexuality to drug and alcohol information. It's a great resource for information at the consumer level.

New York State Department of Health

```
gopher://gopher.health.state.ny.us
```

You will find a variety of information of interest to the public on this server. Every communicable disease from chicken pox to botulism and anthrax seems to be listed. There is a wide variety of other consumer health information and newsletters. You will find information about heart disease and cancer at this location as well. Figure 18-1 shows the initial gopher menu at this location.

Student Health Issues

```
gopher://nuinfo.nwu.edu:70/11/service/health
```

This Northwestern University gopher has information on sexuality issues such as condoms and contraceptive foam as well as information on alcohol and substance abuse.

University of Chicago Health Service

```
gopher://bio-1.bsd.uchicago.edu
```

After connecting, select the University Health Service Infoline for a wide variety of general health information, including an excellent section on women's health issues. There are also special sections on preventive health care and reproductive health.

University of Montana HEALTHLINE

```
gopher://healthline.umt.edu:700
```

Some of the main menu options are Sexuality, General Health, Health Care Reform in Montana, and Internet Health-Related Resources. The General Health selection has a wide variety of interesting papers, as shown by this partial list of selections:

- Dietary Information

- Dental Information

- Sports Medicine

- Anorexia and Bulimia

- Antidepressants and Sleep Disorders

- Antioxidants: Why Do I Need Them?

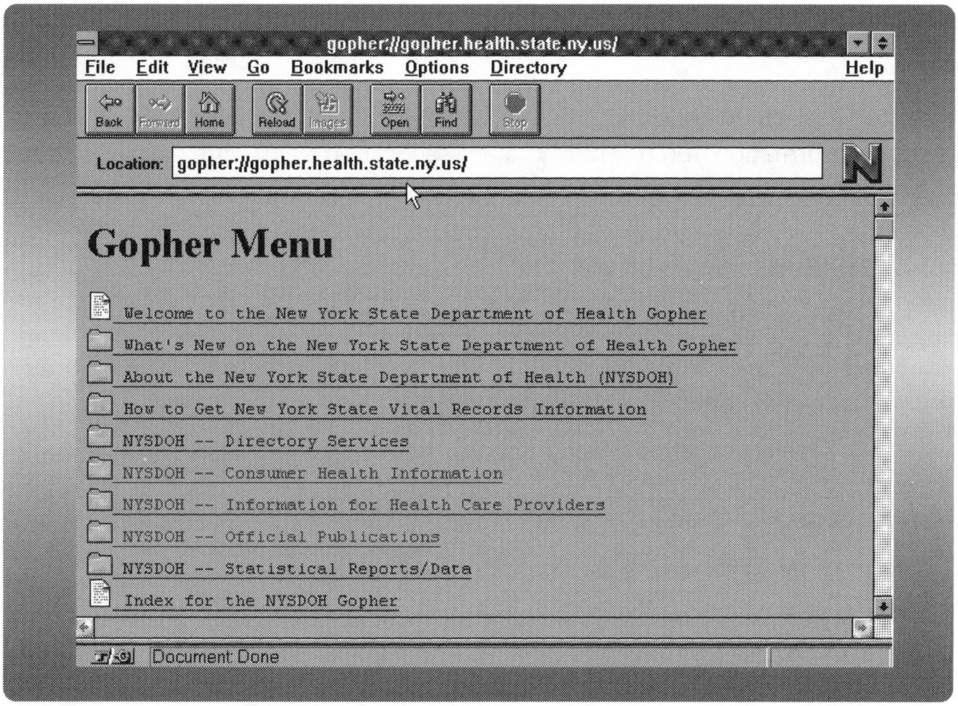

FIGURE 18-1. *New York State Department of Health gopher*

- Asthma

- Back Pain Questionnaire

- Chondromalacia (Abnormal Mechanical Wear of Kneecap Area)

- Hay Fever (Allergenic Rhinitis)

- Health Information for International Travel

- How Do Your Eyes Work?

- Information About Measles, Mumps, and Rubella

- Migraine Headaches

- The "Common" Cold

- The Darker Side of Tanning

- When Your Diagnosis Is Cystitis

MEDICAL SCHOOLS

There are Web or gopher sites for most of the medical schools in the United States and many in other countries. The sites listed are representative of the types of information you might find at these locations, although each one has a slightly different emphasis depending on the research projects at the school.

Johns Hopkins University

    http://www.welsh.jhu.edu

You can access Johns Hopkins University's Welsh Medical Library Resources as well as other information at their gopher or Web servers with these links.

Mayo Medical School

    http://www.mayo.edu/education/rst/mms.html

You will find information about the medical school as well as medical information of interest to physicians and patients at this site. The logo at the top of the screen in Figure 18-2 indicates that you are linked to the prestigious Mayo Clinic.

Monash University

    gopher://gopher.vifp.monash.edu.au

This Australian gopher site has a handicap news archive and information on forensic medicine.

ORGANIZATIONS

There are medical organizations with physician, patient, and research orientations. A few organizations are represented by the entries in this list, but a search with Veronica or the World-Wide Web Worm for the organization you are looking for is likely to turn up a site.

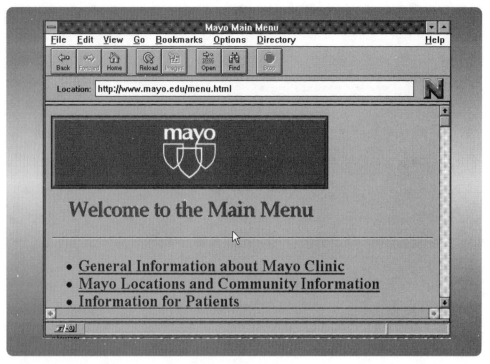

FIGURE 18-2. *Making the connection with the Mayo Clinic*

American Heart Association

`gopher://gopher.amhrt.org:70`

Information on research projects and even some recipes for a healthy heart can be found here.

American Medical Association—Medical Student Section

`http://www2.umdnj.edu/~ama/ama.html`

You will find the following fact sheets at the American Medical Association Student Section home page shown in Figure 18-3:

- AMA Guide on Breast Cancer

- AMA Position on Tobacco

- AMA & Medical Education

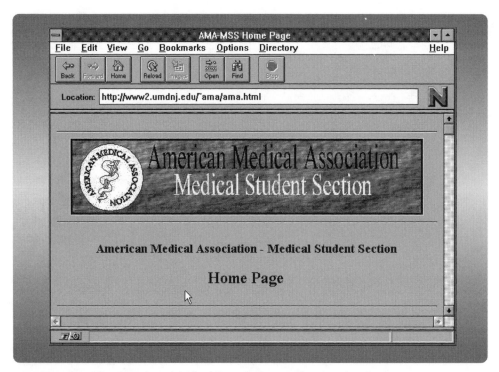

FIGURE 18-3. *The American Medical Association student section home page*

- AMA Fights for Student Loans
- AMA-MSS Workforce Analysis
- Information on Primary Care Internships

National Heart, Lung, and Blood Gopher

`gopher://gopher.nhlbi.nih.gov:70/1`

You will find biennial reports, press releases, and scientific reports from task forces. There are also a number of papers with topics such as "The Use of Hydroxyurea for Sickle Cell" and "Calcium Channel Blockers for Hypertension."

World Health Organization

```
http://www.who.ch
```

If you want to learn more about the World Health Organization, this is the site to check out. You will find copies of press releases and newsletters and a write-up on major programs. You can also get vaccination requirements and health advice if you are planning to travel to a foreign country. The WHOSIS system provides access to databases on a wide variety of topics like these:

- Health-for-all global indicators

- The mortality database

- Malaria information

- AIDS reporting by region

- Veterinary public health information

- Demographic and health surveys

RESEARCH SITES

Although you can find research information at any of the sites in this chapter, the ones in this section are oriented toward research needs for specific projects.

Health Care Outlook

```
gopher://msa1.medsearch.com:70/11/hio
```

Want to know the outlook for the health care industry? You can check it out at this location while posting your resume at the same site.

MEDLINE

```
http://atlas.nlm.nih.gov:5700/entrezFORMSmquery.html
```

If you are using a browser that can handle forms, you can query the resources at the National Library of Medicine using the form shown in Figure 18-4.

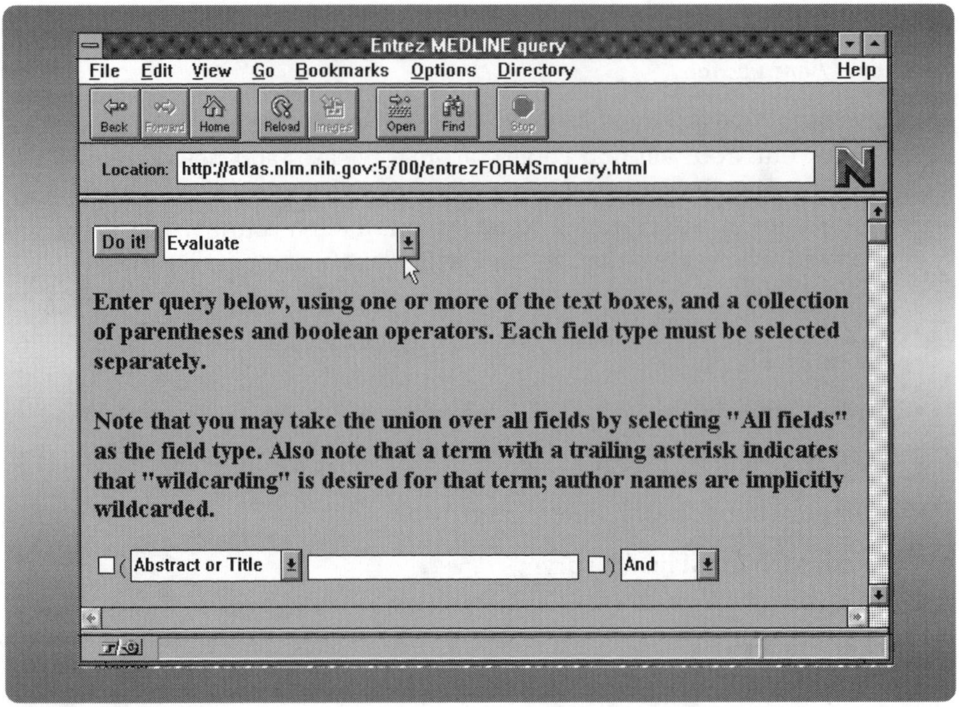

FIGURE 18-4. *Query form for the National Library of Medicine*

Morbidity and Mortality Report

gopher://cwis.usc.edu/11/The_Health_Sciences_Campus/Periodicals/mmwr

If you are doing research on life expectancies or causes of death, you'll want to check out this resource.

National Library of Medicine

gopher://gopher.nlm.nih.gov:70/1

You will find a wealth of research data at this site including the following:

- Fact sheets
- AIDS information
- Health service/technical assessment text
- Clinical alerts
- Resource and bibliography lists
- Toxicology and environmental health information program

Online Medical Resources

`file://ftp2.cc.ukans.edu/pub/hmatrix`

This list of resources has information on clinical medicine, health, disease, and therapies. It was created by Dr. Gary Malet and Lee Hancock. It is stored at the location specified as medlist94.txt or medlist94.zip.

Research and Computing Resource

`gopher://mchip00.med.nyu.edu`

This gopher provides a few helpful hints for utilizing the Internet for your research in medicine or biology under the Research Computing Resource selection. There is also a database at this location relating to medical humanities.

SPECIALTY AREAS

There are links for almost every specialty area within the field of medicine. We've listed a few to give you an idea of what's available.

Anesthesiology

`gopher://eja.anes.hscsyr.edu:70/1`

You will find lecture notes, book reviews, anesthesia videos and journals, a critical care discussion group, and an Anest-L archive at this site.

Anesthesiology Server at New York University

`http://gasnet.med.nyu.edu/`

You will find a great list of links to other anesthesiology sites worldwide including

- Ehime University School of Medicine Department of Anesthesiology
- Erasmus University Department of Anesthesia
- State University at New York at Syracuse Department of Anesthesiology
- GASNET Anesthesiology Home Page
- Stanford University Department of Anesthesia

- The Swiss Anesthesia Server

- UCLA Department of Anesthesiology WWW Server

- University of Florida Department of Anesthesiology

- University of Ottawa Department of Anesthesia

- University of Pittsburgh Department of Anesthesiology

Bioethics

`gopher://gopher.mcw.edu`

This gopher site is home to the University of Wisconsin's Bioethics Online Service. Here you will find information on bioethics texts, news alerts, and other bioethics resources. You can browse their online database for information that meets your needs. Figure 18-5 shows the initial gopher menu.

Bio-Gophers

`http://biocsever.bioc.cwru.edu:70/1s/biogoph`

This biology-oriented gopher provides links of interest to biologists, medical professionals, and researchers. Some of the options you will find in the initial menu are

- Bio-newsgroups

- Bio-databases

- Biological WAIS searches

- Human genome data base

- Other bio gophers

Medical Physiology

`gopher://mphywww.tamu.edu:70/`

Texas A &M University's Department of Medical Physiology's gopher provides information about their program and research as well as some .GIF images from their research projects.

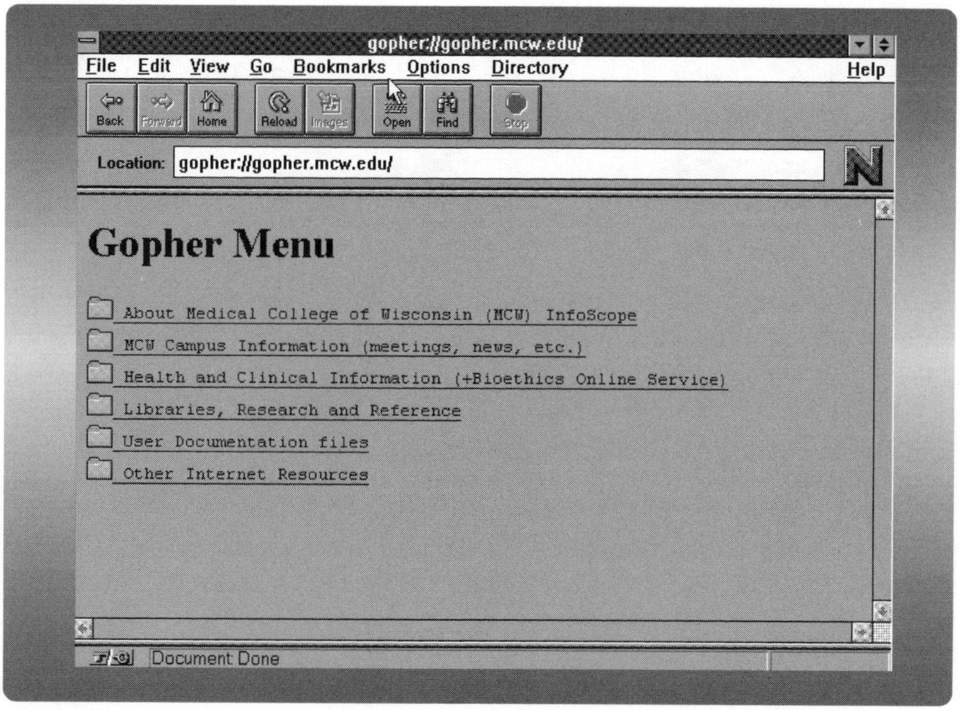

```
                    gopher://gopher.mcw.edu/
 File   Edit   View   Go   Bookmarks   Options   Directory              Help

 [Back] [Forward] [Home]  [Reload] [Images]   [Open] [Find]  [Stop]

 Location:  gopher://gopher.mcw.edu/                                      N
```

Gopher Menu

📁 About Medical College of Wisconsin (MCW) InfoScope
📁 MCW Campus Information (meetings, news, etc.)
📁 Health and Clinical Information (+Bioethics Online Service)
📁 Libraries, Research and Reference
📁 User Documentation files
📁 Other Internet Resources

```
 Document Done
```

FIGURE 18-5. *Medical College of Wisconsin gopher with a number of bioethics resources*

Radiology

    http://www.xray.hmc.psu.edu

This site at the Milton Hershey Department of Radiology provides access to a radiology database. There are also medical image databases and radiology journals at this site.

Toxicology

    gopher://gopher.niehs.nih.gov/11/ntp

The National Toxicology Program at this site offers a WAIS search of their studies, abstracts of reports, and an annual report on carcinogens.

ALTERNATIVE MEDICINE

In addition to the disciplines of traditional medicines, the Internet provides a wealth of information on alternative healing practices.

Alternative Therapies

```
http://sunsite.sut.ac.jp
```

This site is rich in all types of information about alternative medicine. You can explore information about herbs, massage therapy, aromatherapy, homeopathy, nutrition, and many other techniques.

Complementary Medicine Home Page

```
http://galen.med.virginia.edu/~pjb3s/ComplementaryHomePage
```

If you want more information on alternative therapies and practitioners, this is the place to visit. Here is just a little of what you will find:

- Complementary practices
    - Acupuncture
    - Osteopathy
    - Neural tissue testing
    - Ayurvedic medicine
    - Reiki
    - Herbal medicine
    - Shiatsu
    - Flower remedies
    - Oigong
    - Traditional Chinese medicine
    - Yoga
- Current research topics
- Complementary practitioners
- The Dogwood Institute, Body-Mind Medicine
- Other Internet links

Homeopathy

http://www.dungeon.com/~cam/homeo.html

This Internet service provider has an interesting set of homeopathy links. You can download a copy of Internet resources on homeopathy from this site, view frequently asked questions, see what books are available, or get a list of addresses in the United States or the United Kingdom that can help you locate a homeopathic physician.

AIDS

There are many different sites relating to AIDS. Some have a support orientation, others are designed to share information or current research about the disease.

AIDS Information Newsletter

http://www.cmpharm.ucsf.edu/~troyer/safesex/vanews

The U.S Department of Veterans Affairs issues this biweekly AIDS newsletter. You can get back copies at gopher://gopher.niaid.nih.gov.

NIH AIDS Materials

gopher://odie.niaid.nih.gov:70/11/aids

These selections in the first menu indicate what a rich source of information can be found through the links to other locations at this site and other servers:

- Search glossary of AIDS-related terminology
- Study recruitment information
- NIAID AIDS-related press releases
- Nursing HIV/AIDS
- CDC daily summaries
- More general AIDS information
- CDC National AIDS Clearinghouse (this entry going away soon)
- Morbidity and Mortality Weekly Report
- National Commission on AIDS

- VA AIDS Information Newsletter
- U.S. Community AIDS Resources
- CDC National AIDS Clearinghouse
- International AIDS Resources
- CDC HIV Surveillance Reports
- National Library of Medicine AIDS Information
- NIAID-Provided Pamphlets on Sexually Transmitted Diseases

HIV-Net

```
http://www.hivnet.org/aidres.html
```

This site allows you to reference a number of AIDS/HIV resources such as Project Inform and magazines, periodicals, and libraries.

Safe Sex

```
http://www.cmpharm.ucsf.edu/~troyer/safesex.html
```

Some of the information you will find here includes

- HIV testing and counseling
- Playing the AIDS odds
- Sex myths
- Women and AIDS
- How to use a condom

Safe Sex at the University of Canberra

```
gopher://services.canberra.edu.au:70/11/Services/Student/Women/
SAFE_SEX
```

There are a number of papers worth checking at this Australian resource:

- Contraception A–Z
- Sexually transmitted diseases
- Women and AIDS

- Chlamydia

- Gonorrhea

AIDS Information on the University of Louisville Nursing Gopher

`gopher://ULKYVM.LOUISVILLE.EDU:70/11/schools/nursing`

This site has a number of links to sites with AIDS information. Figure 18-6 shows the initial gopher menu with its emphasis on AIDS information.

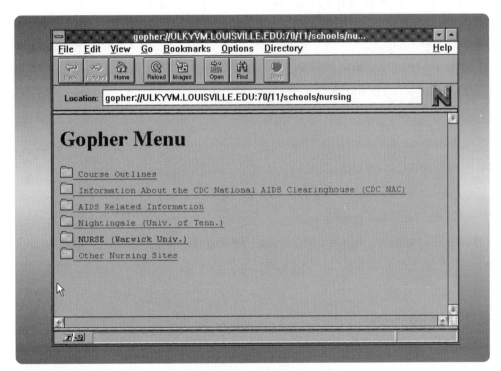

FIGURE 18-6. *University of Louisville Nursing gopher*

CANCER

Since a significant number of research dollars are spent on cancer research each year, it is not surprising to find many different cancer sites. A few of them are listed in this section.

Breast Cancer Information Clearinghouse

http://nypernet.org/bcic

All types of information about breast cancer can be found at this site.

Cancernet

gopher://gopher.nih.gov:70/11/clin/cancernet

Here are some of the things you will find at this site:

- News about PDQ and Cancernet
- National Cancer Institute bulletins
- Bulletins related to the NSABP
- Publication ordering information
- Limited full-text publications

PDQ information consists of cancer information, research protocols for patient referrals, and organizations and physicians who are care providers for cancer patients.

Multiple Myeloma

http://www.comed.com/IMF/imf.html

You will find all types of information about multiple myeloma at this site. Selected articles from *Myeloma Today* are available in full text. There is information about their other publications, their patient-to-patient network, clinical meetings, and scientific advisors.

National Cancer Institute

`gopher://gopher.nci.nih.gov:70/1`

You can learn about legislation and congressional activities related to cancer research at this site.

OncoLink

`http://cancer.med.upenn.edu`

This is a great resource for all types of cancer research. These are just a few of the areas you can look through once connected:

- What's new
- Cancer news
- Meetings
- Disease-oriented information
- Specialty-oriented information
- Advanced search
- Support groups

CHILDREN'S HEALTH

`gopher://mchnet.ichp.ufl.edu:70/1`

This site provides information on the following:

- Adolescent issues
- Child health data
- Grants
- Disability issues
- Early childhood
- Infant topics
- HIV
- Nutrition
- Technology issues

DENTAL RESOURCES

Dentists are beginning to use the Internet to provide information to their patients. At a basic level this may be of interest, although you can look into higher-level materials through the second reference, which will link you to all the major dental schools in the country.

DentalNet

`http://www.pencom.com:80/dentalweb`

Two Austin dentists have created this online network. You will find information on Dental Health Options and Dental Tips as well as links to other online health resources.

Dental Links

`http://www.nyu.edu/Dental`

For a list of links to major dental schools and many related dental resources, check this site.

DISABILITIES

`gopher://val-dor.cc.buffalo.edu:70/11/`

This site is called the "Cornucopia of Disability Information." There is information on what's new, New York state and local information, college services, a digest of data on persons with disabilities, a directory of independent living centers, bibliographic information, and a variety of other options.

HISTORY OF MEDICINE

`http://indy.radiology.uiowa.edu/HistOfMedHP.html`

Reading about medical history gives you a real picture of how much technology has changed the course of today's medicine.

NEWSGROUPS

There are hundreds of newsgroups that provide information on some aspect of health or medicine. Here are just a few:

Newsgroup	Topic
alt.med.cfs	Chronic fatigue syndrome
misc-health-alternative	Alternative health
misc.health.diabetes	Diabetes management
sci.med-aids	AIDS treatment
sci.meds.dentistry	Dentistry topics
sci.meds.nursing	Nursing topics
sci.meds.pharmacy	Pharmacy topics

NURSING—THE VIRTUAL NURSING CENTER

```
http://www-sci.lib.uci.edu/~martindale/nursing.html
```

This site has links to some interesting resources. You will find main menu selections for nursing schools, nursing courses, and other nursing resources.

NUTRITION

```
gopher://bluehen.ags.udel.edu:70/11/.extbull/.nutrition/.cholesterol
```

The University of Delaware extension service publishes all types of bulletins. The document shown in Figure 18-7 tells about saturated and unsaturated fats and the number of grams in some common foods.

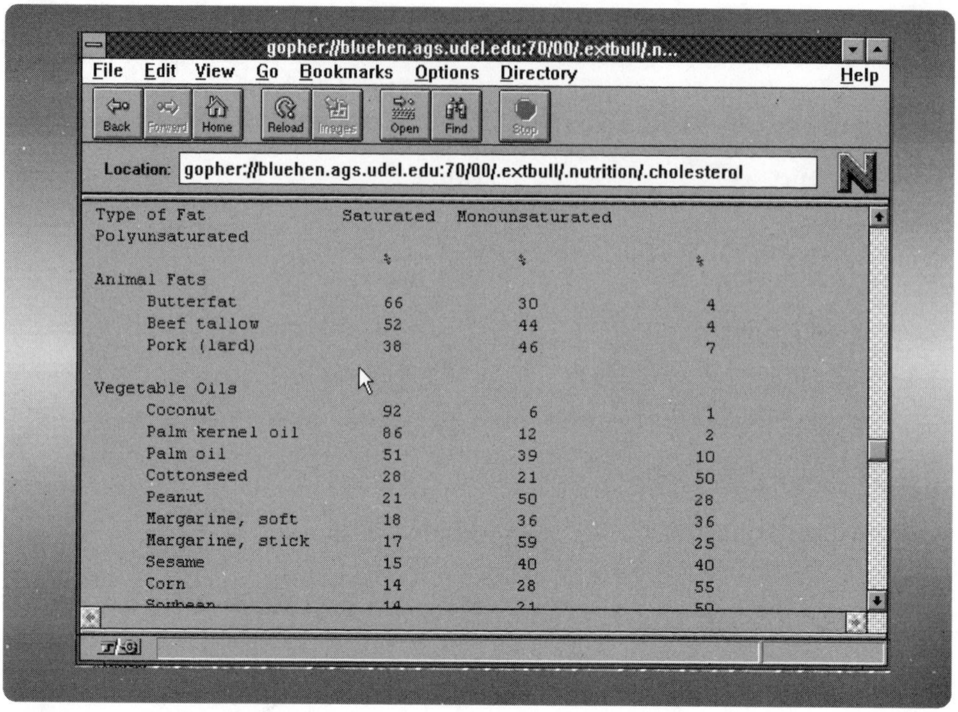

FIGURE 18-7. *Learning about fat grams through the Internet*

RURAL HEALTH CARE

http://ruralnet.mu.wvnet.edu

This server is maintained by the Marshall University School of Medicine to help improve health care in rural areas. Some of the options you will find are

- What's new
- Rural health care and community resources
- Student resources for health care education
- WWW home pages for Marshall University School of Medicine
- Heath care Internet resources
- Nursing

TUBERCULOSIS

Although tuberculosis seemed to be a disease in permanent decline, the advent of AIDS has brought about an increase in the disease. These two sites will key you into some of the current research in the area.

Brown University Tuberculosis Information

http://www.brown.edu/Research/TB-HIV_Lab

This site explores TB/HIV. Some of the topic areas covered are

- The development of TB vaccines
- Algorithms used to design novel vaccines
- Epidemiology of TB and HIV
- Prevention of HIV

Tuberculosis Research Center at Stanford

http://molepi.stanford.edu

Links to other TB Web sites, Experts Online, and the DNA fingerprints of the San Francisco tuberculosis cases can be found here.

VETERINARY MEDICINE

Most veterinary schools have Web or Gopher servers. You can use the two sites listed for links to other veterinary resources.

Washington University in St. Louis–Veterinary Medicine

gopher://vetinfo.wustl.edu

Whether you are researching colleges of veterinary medicine or are further along with your studies, this site has it all. Here are some of the options in the first menu if you choose NETVET.

- College of Veterinary Medicine
- Veterinary journals
- Veterinary and animal legislation

- Veterinary and animal mailing list and Usenet groups

- Veterinary and animal organizations

- Animal resources

- The Electronic Zoo

University of California Davis–Veterinary Medicine

`gopher://vmgopher.ucdavis.edu:70`

The School of Veterinary Medicine's newsletters, research news, information about the Equine Research Laboratory, and other resources are at this site. Figure 18-8 shows the initial menu at this site.

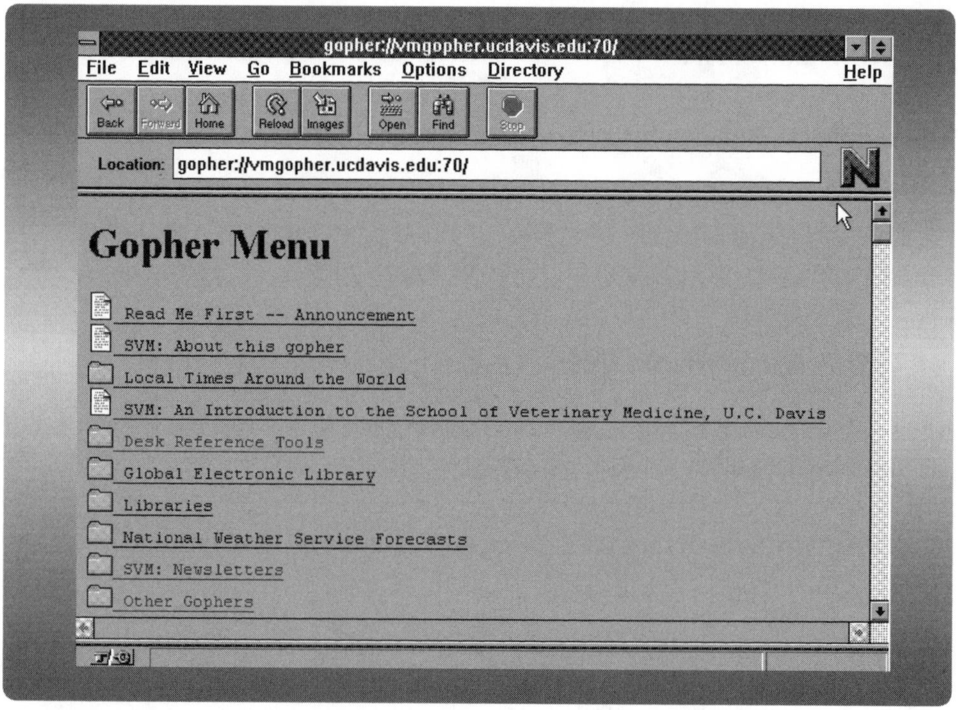

FIGURE 18-8. *The Veterinary Medicine gopher at the University of California, Davis*

Just for Fun

Want to check out a site that has the medical information you are looking for, yet need a break? The Albert Einstein College of Medicine has a recipe database you can search. Connect to the gopher at gopher.aecom.yu.edu, then look under Miscellaneous.

Chapter 19

The Sciences
and Mathematics

MATHEMATICS AND THE SCIENCES serve as foundation requirements for degrees offered across various academic disciplines such as business, engineering, and the physical and natural sciences. While the references in this chapter are designed to assist those who are conducting in-depth research in the sciences and mathematics, you may find the materials useful to you in related fields of study (for example, an operations management course in management programs or an electronic circuit design course in electrical engineering).

GENERAL SCIENCE RESOURCE

There are a number of good indices and other links that are related to the sciences. They are classified in this section because they present links across science disciplines or are a lower-level reference appropriate for reference in a general science course. Some interesting sites worth exploring follow.

Fed World Math

http://www.fedworld.gov/math.htm

You will find links to topics such as chemistry, mathematical sciences, biomedical technology, and physics at this site.

History of Science

http://www.physics.mcgill.ca/physics-services/physics_history.html

Although the URL seems to indicate that this site provides the history of physics, it is much more comprehensive. You will find links to the history of many science disciplines and to science museums.

Science Links

`http://www.eskimo.com/~billb/`

The individual who put together these science links is Bill Beaty. They are diverse and might provide some links you don't find at other locations. Some of the link categories are

- Weird

- Education

- Demos

- Home Schooling

Scientific Web Servers Index from Queens University, Belfast

`http://boris.qub.ac.uk/edward/GeneralSci.html`

You can access a wide range of links. A few of the entries are

- Toxic chemicals

- Japanese National Cancer Research Center

- Organ transplantation and donation Web

- BioMolecular Engineering Research Center

- United States Geological Survey home page

- Weights and measures

- Evolution etc.

- RAND organization

- Scientific movies

ASTRONOMY

Astronomy is the study of the universe: the stars, sun, planets, galaxies, and so on. Given the scope of study in this area, we have selected sites with many links to a broad range of organizations and academic sites that should provide an excellent start to your research in this area.

Astronomy Observatories

```
http://www.w3.org/hypertext/DataSources/bySubject/astro/
observatories.html
```

You can select from the various types of observatories listed here:

- Radio

- Optical

- Space

- Solar

- Cosmic rays, gamma rays, and neutrines

There are hundreds of possible links from this page.

EINet Galaxy Astronomy Resources

```
http://www.einet.net/galaxy/Science/Astronomy.html
```

Resource links are organized into these categories:

- Amateur astronomy

- Astronautics

- Astrophysics

- Observatories

- Space physics

Index of Astronomical Resources

```
gopher://stsci.edu/11/net-resources
```

This is a great list of resources including gophers, FTP sites, WAIS databases, and Telnet connections.

Lake Afton Public Observatory

```
http://www.twsu.edu/o0.html
```

You can access information about the observatory, astronomical images, links to other interesting Web sites, and access an "ask an astronomer" service. Figure 19-1 shows the initial screen.

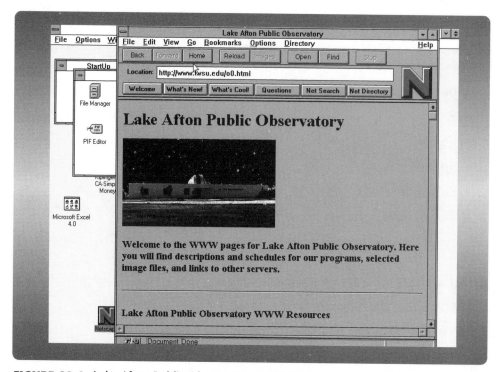

FIGURE 19-1. *Lake Afton Public Observatory Site initial screen*

Lawrence Livermore National Laboratory for Physics and Space Technology

`http://www-phys.llnl.gov`

This site has many links, including the following:

- Clementine moon photographs
- 1994 Physics and Space Technology in Review
- Astrophysics and space science and technology research
- Institute for Geophysics and Planetary Physics

Library of Congress Astronomy Collection

`gopher://marvel.loc.gov/11/global/sci/astro`

You can link to many resources, including the following:

- Space Telescope Electronic Information System

- Lunar/Planetary Institute

- Case Western Reserve University

- Center for Extreme Ultraviolet Astrophysics

Planetary Data System Archives

`http://stardust.jpl.nasa.gov`

You can access organizations, research, and information relating to such topics as atmospheres, central node, geosciences, and planetary imaging node. There are also numerous catalogs related to the research areas.

Planetary Society

`http://planetary.org/tps`

This group has 100,000 members in 100 countries. You can find out about their activities at this site.

BIOLOGY

Biology in this section actually encompasses many different fields including zoology, botany, entomology, and microbiology. Because the resources are so widely available and diverse, many indexes have been included to present the largest number of links possible.

Biologists Resources Cambridge, England

`http://www.bio.cam.ac.uk`

This is an excellent list of resources for biologists. It has more of an emphasis on databases than other sites, but also includes journals, molecular biology facilities and services, and many wide-ranging biology links.

Botany Gophers

gopher://genome-gopher.Stanford.EDU/11/topic/botanical

This list is maintained at Stanford University. A few of the many links are

- Australian National Botanic Gardens and University BioInfomatics
- National Plant Germplasm System
- Poplar Molecular Network
- Plant Gene Register
- USDA Extension Service

Centers for Disease Control

http://www.cdc.gov

After connecting, you should look around a bit. You can move to a menu option for brochures on numerous infectious diseases. You will find entries for cholera, hanta virus, hepatitis, hookworm, lyme disease, and salmonella.

Entomology Index

http://www.public.iastate.edu/~entomology/ResourceList.html

This list is a virtual treasure trove for the entomologists. Some of the links listed are

- Smithsonian Institute National Museum of Natural History
- Ohio State University Insect Collection
- Beekeeper's home page
- Mosquito genomics
- Pest alert from the USDA
- Malaria database
- Images of books on insects
- Listservs and Usenet groups

Fish Information Service

`http://www.actwin.com:80/fish/index.html`

At this site you will find a glossary of terms, frequently asked questions, catalog of marine and freshwater fish, and archives of discussions. There are also many links to related areas.

Human Genome Project Information

`http://www.ornl.gov/TechResources/Human_Genome/home.html`

This site will put you in touch with newsletters and other information on the Human Genome Project.

Molecular Virology at the University of Wisconsin

`http://www.bocklabs.wisc.edu:80/`

Here are some of the categories of information and links you can access from this server:

- Virology-related news and articles
- Computer visualizations of viruses
- Topographical maps of viruses
- Virus sequences
- ICTV classification of viruses
- Course notes and tutorials
- Virologists on the Internet

Oxford University Molecular Biology Data Center

`gopher://gopher.molbiol.ox.ac.uk/`

This site is the Oxford University Molecular Biology Data Center. It has links to resources outside of Oxford as well as within.

Scripps Institution of Oceanography

`http://sio.ucsd.edu/loc_services`

Some of the links from this well-known institute are

- Oceanographic data
- Weather FTP server
- Library and archives
- Links to other oceanographic servers

World Guide to Biology

`http://www.theworld.com/SCIENCE/BIOLOGY/SUBJECT.HTM`

This list of resources provides links to biology servers at many different universities as well as other biology resources. Some of the links you will find, in addition to the many university links, are

- Biological aging
- Bio tool box
- Molecular biology network
- BioWWW server
- Animal Genome database–Japan
- Marine Biological Laboratory

Woods Hole Oceanographic Institution

`http://www.whoi.edu`

This site has links to their many servers. There are links to education programs, science departments, and gopher server links. Figure 19-2 shows the initial screen for Woods Hole.

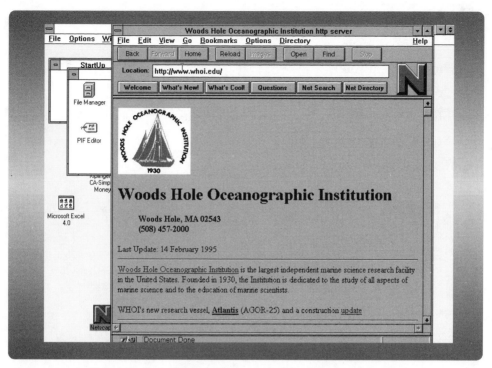

FIGURE 19-2. *Woods Hole Oceanographic Institution initial screen*

WWW Sites of Biological Interest

`http://www.abc.hu/biosites.html`

Some of the links accessible from this site are

- Bio-catalogs, tutorials, conferences, and some online documentation
- Biological databases online
- Utilities, homology searches
- Servers at companies, biological research institutes, and departments

WWW Virtual Library for Plant Biology

`http://golgi.harvard.edu:80/biopages/botany.html`

This index covers a wide range of topical groups, including

- Agriculture
- Forestry

- Genetics
- Biological journals
- Biological software
- Botanical glossaries
- BEST North America—a database of scientists and projects
- British Society for Plant Pathology

Figure 19-3 shows a partial list of links

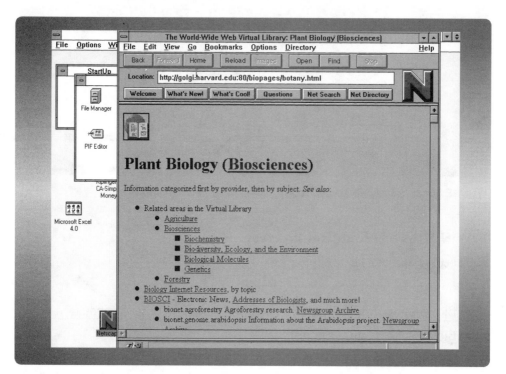

FIGURE 19-3. *Plant Biology index*

CHEMISTRY

Chemistry is a field that has links across various disciplines and professions such as engineering, medicine, and industrial management. In addition, chemical research spans the realm of basic or applied investigations. With this in mind, we have provided site references that include indexes, and resource links of broad interest to jump-start your research in particular fields in this area.

American Chemical Society

`http://www.acs.org`

This server is for the American Chemical Society, which has 150,000 chemists and chemical engineers. You can learn about membership, products, and services from this server shown in Figure 19-4.

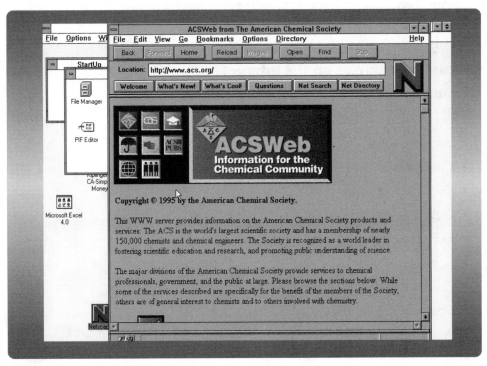

FIGURE 19-4. *American Chemical Society server*

Chemistry Education Resources

`http://www.halcyon.com/cairns/chemistry.html`

Some of the resources you can access from this site are

- Instructional software for chemistry
- ChemPrime project
- Resources for chemistry teachers
- Chemistry hypermedia project
- Science Education Programs Office Curriculum Materials
- Hyperactive molecules database
- History of chemistry

Chemistry Index

`http://www.chemie.fu-berlin.de/index-e.html`

This general chemistry index is in Berlin, Germany.

Chemistry Resources on the Internet

`http://www.rpi.edu/dept/chem/cheminfo/chemres.html`

This index is categorized as follows:

- Book catalogs
- Databases
- Document delivery
- E-mail servers
- FTP resources
- Gophers
- Guides to Internet resources
- Online search services
- Periodicals and conference proceedings
- Software
- Teaching resources
- World-Wide Web resources

Crystallography Index

http:/www.unige.ch:80/crystal/crystal_index.html

This index includes many entries on databases and journals in crystallography.

National Institute of Standards and Technology

http://www.nist.gov

This government group attempts to encourage economic growth by exploring the commercial potential of various technologies. Some of the main options at this site are

- Standards and analysis

- Advanced technology

- Manufacturing extension

NIH Molecules R US

http://www.nih.gov:80/htbin/pdb

This site allows a full text search of the PDB database.

Organic Chemistry

http://www.chem.vt.edu/chem-ed/org-home.html

This is a great introductory site for organic chemistry resources. Topics include computer graphics, atomic orbitals, molecular modeling, stereochemistry, and laboratory techniques.

Periodic Table of Elements

http://hydrogen.cchem.berkeley.edu/Table

This table provides complete information on the periodic table of elements. In addition to general information, the following items are provided:

- Radii/pmValence shell orbital Rmax

- Ionic radii

- Electronegativities

- Effective nuclear charge

- Bond enthalpies
- Temperatures
- Enthalpies/ kJ per mol
- Ionization enthalpies
- Isotropic abundances

Polymer and Plastics Resources

`http://www.iii.net/biz/phoenix/polylink.html`

In this index you will find the following:

- Commercial polymer sites
- Business tools
- Polymer academia
- Polymer toxicity
- Chemistry and polymer Internet lists
- Plastics engineering resources
- Polymer chemistry resources
- Scientific and engineering resources

Stanford Yahoo Chemistry Index

`http://akebono.stanford.edu/yahoo/Science/Chemistry`

You will find information on conferences, all branches of chemistry, indices, and other resources.

WWW Virtual Library Chemistry

`http://www.chem.ucla.edu/chempointers.html`

This index provides a host of direct links to campus chemistry servers around the world, FTP sites, chemistry sites at commercial organizations, chemistry sites at nonprofit organizations, and USENET newsgroups. Figure 19-5 shows the main topic list in the Chemistry Index.

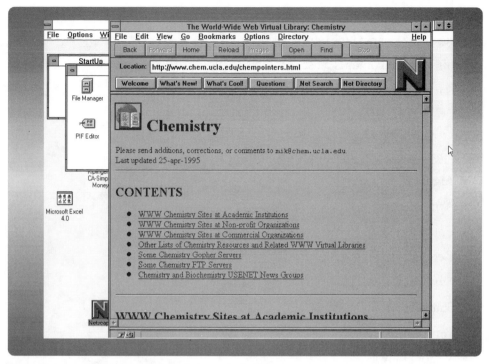

FIGURE 19-5. *Chemistry Index main topic list*

MATHEMATICS

Mathematics provides a foundation for study across numerous disciplines. In addition, applied mathematicians play important roles in industry and government. The sites presented next reflect the diverse aspects of mathematics and provide an array of resources to help start your research adventure.

American Mathematical Society

`http://e-math.ams.org`

This site provides information on the organization as well as extensive electronic publications and many links to related resources.

Computational Fluid Dynamics Codes

`http://www.mpa-garching.mpg.de/~tomek/CFD/CFD_codes.html`

You can access codes and mirror sites from this Web page.

CSC Top Math

`http://www.csc.fi/cgi-bin/math-top`

This location contains a list of math sites you can select to visit.

ElNet Math Guide

`http://galaxy.einet.net/galaxy/Science/Mathematics.html`

Topics in this popular index include

- Algebra
- Applied math
- Calculus
- Geometry
- Number theory
- Statistics
- Topology
- Vector analysis

Fractal Images

`http://www.cnam.fr/fractals.html`

Some of the fractal resources and material you will find are

- Mandlebrot pictures and animation
- Fractal FAQ
- Links to the Spanky fractal database
- Fractal images and programs

GAMS (Guide to Available Math Software)

`http://gams.cam.nist.gov`

You can locate math and statistics packages using search criteria for the problem to be solved, the package name, or the module name. Figure 19-6 shows the initial screen from the GAMS Guide.

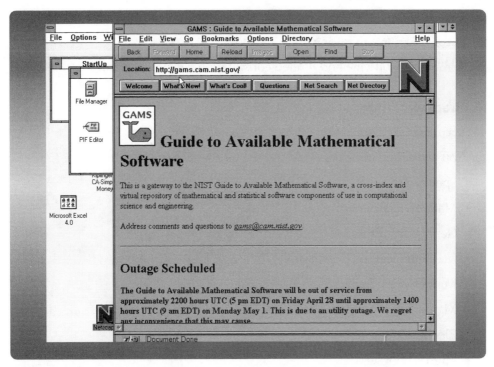

FIGURE 19-6. *Guide to Available Mathematical Software initial screen*

IMA Institute for Math and Its Applications

http://www.ima.umn.edu

You can access the newsletter for this group as well as an industrial math archive, preprints, and links to other math resources.

Indiana Statistics/Math Center

http://www.statmath.indiana.edu/

There are links to all kinds of resources from this site including:

- Latest news

- Statistics

- Stat/Math computing

- Electronic journals

- Stat/Math newsgroups

Jet Propulsion Lab

http://www.jpl.nasa.gov

Some math software and limited consultation are available through this site.

Mathematics Index

http://euclid.math.fsu.edu/Science/math.html

You can access information under the following headers:

- Specialized fields
- Mathematics departments Web servers
- General resources
- Mathematical software index
- Mathematics gophers
- Mathematics newsgroups
- Electronic journals
- High school servers
- Bibliographies

Math Bulletin Boards

http://www.cs.colorado.edu/homes/mcbryan/public_html/bb/37/summa-ry.html

Some of the resource categories you will find are

- Applied and numerical mathematics
- Geometry
- Math departments
- Network resources

Math History

`http://aleph0.clarku.edu/~djoyce/mathhist/mathhist.html`

Some of the topics you will find listed are

- History of numbers and counting
- History of mathematical Analysis
- History of geometry
- History of arithmetic and number theory
- History of probability and statistics
- Bibliographies

Math Resources

`http://www.math.psu.edu/OtherMath.html`

This is a really extensive list of resources. You will find Web site by country, math journals, preprints, and software.

Math Topics

`http://www.math.ufl.edu/math/math-web.html`

You will find these links among your many options at this site:

- Publications
- Software archive links
- Math departments and organizations

Mentor Project

`http://www.strath.ac.uk/Departments/MgtSci/mentor.html`

This is the site for a three-year project to develop operations research modules for seventeen topics commonly taught in operations research. Some of the modules already available are

- Linear programming
- Simulation
- Stock control
- Forecasting

Netlib Numerical Packages

`http://netlib2.cs.utk.edu/master/`

Here are just a few of the things you will find here:

- Approximation algorithms
- Bessel functions
- Linear and non-linear programming
- C & C++ modules
- Eigenvalues and eigenvectors

New York Journal of Math

`http://nyjm.albany.edu:8000/nyjm.html`

The site for the first electronic math journal allows you to access articles or link to other math resources.

Northwestern Math Guide

`http://gopher.math.nwu.edu:70/1/mathgopher`

Math servers listed at this site are organized by Web servers, gophers, and FTP sites.

Problem of the Month

`http://indy1.hamline.edu/depts/math/aguetter/pom/prob_of_month.html`

Each month a new problem tests your logic and problem-solving abilities. One month, the problem was to figure out the number of games needed in an elimination tournament to determine a winner.

Rice University

`gopher://riceinfo.rice.edu/11/Subject/Math`

Some of the links you will find at Rice include

- Fuzzy logic tutorial
- Algebraic geometry—University of Chicago

- Cornell Theory Center
- Euromath Gopher–Denmark
- Applied and computational math
- Archive for mathematics
- Argonne National Laboratory

SIAM—Society for Industrial and Applied Math

`http://www.siam.org`

This group is concerned with the advanced application of math and science to industry.

Statistics Library Index

`http://lib.stat.cmu.edu`

This site is designed to help promote the distribution of free statistical software and datasets. Some of the things you will find here are

- Selected applied statistics
- Macros and fixes for the BLSS Statistical Package
- Data from case studies in biometry
- General statistical software
- P-stat functions and software

University of Florida Department of Statistics

`http://www.stat.ufl.edu/vlib/statistics.html`

You can access journals, statistics archives, university departments, and journals from this site. Figure 19-7 shows a section of the Statistics Index.

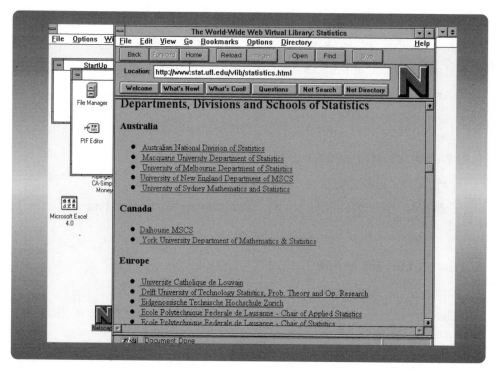

FIGURE 19-7. *A section of the Statistics Index*

WWW Math Guide

`http://euclid.math.fsu.edu/Science/math.html`

Some of the main categories of index entries here are

- Specialized fields
- Math Department Web servers
- Journals
- High school servers
- Preprints
- Newsgroups
- Bibliographies

GEOLOGY

This science involves the study of the forces (physical, chemical, and biological) that influence the earth and its inhabitants. We have selected site listings that should provide a solid base to expand your research into various areas of interest within this field.

Earth Science and Geology Links

```
http://jacobson.isgs.uiuc.edu/earthsci_links.html
```

You will find information on geochemistry, geology departments and schools, geological survey data, geophysics links, paleontology sites, meteorology information, and volcanology links at this site.

Environmental Index on the Internet

```
http://www.lib.kth.se/lg.html
```

You will find links to earth science sites, biodiversity and ecology sites, and environmental law.

United States Geological Survey

```
http://www.yahoo.com/Government/Agencies/Department_of_the_
Interior/Geological Survey
```

You'll find a number of unique links from this site.

PHYSICS

This discipline relates to the study of the basic laws of nature that deal with matter, energy, motion, and force. We have selected sites that provide links to a number of organizations and library links to help research the breadth of this field.

Geophysics Virtual Library

```
http://www-crewes.geo.ucalgary.ca/VL/html/gp-gp-orgs-by-
location.html
```

Resources at this site include libraries and free online geophysics books.

National Nuclear Data Center

```
http://datwww.dne.bnl.gov/html/nndc.html
```

```
http://datwww.dne.bnl.gov/html/dathome.html
```

If your research project involves low-and medium-energy physics, check out this site. You will find the following links among the options available:

- Programs, data, files, and manuals

- Tables and displays of nuclear decay data

- Mirror of the Table of Nuclides at the Korean Atomic Energy Research Institute

The second URL provides a direct link to their Department of Advanced Technology.

Physics FAQs

```
http://www.physics.mcgill.ca/physics-services/physics_faqs.html
```

You will find frequently asked questions in areas ranging from general physics to a variety of specialized topics.

Physics News

```
http://www.het.brown.edu/news/index.html
```

This site contains tidbits of physics news from all over. These are some of the newslinks you can access:

- American Institute of Physics News Update

- What's New from the American Physical Society

- Hot Topics from NASA

- Science news from wire services

- News headlines

Figure 19-8 shows a section of the Physics Index.

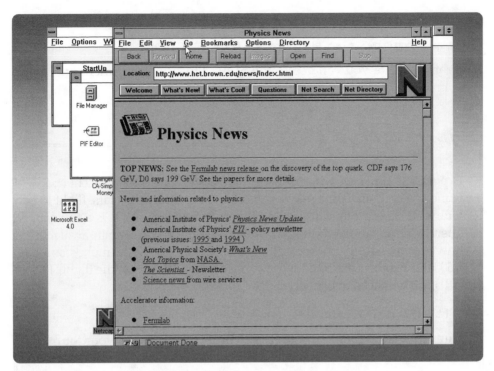

FIGURE 19-8. *A section of the Physics Index*

Physics Societies and Space Agencies Around the World

`http://www.physics.mcgill.ca/physics-services/physics_soc.html`

In any discipline, the professional societies tend to be dissemination points for the latest information. This page of links puts you in contact with sites around the world. Here are a few of the links:

- American Physical Society
- Biophysical Society
- European Physical Society
- New England Fiber Optic Council
- American Association of Physics Teachers

Stanford Linear Accelerator Center

`http://heplibw3.slac.stanford.edu/FIND/SLAC.HTML`

From this site you can access the SLAC Physics Department and many other links.

Just for Fun

Explore the universe with NASA's Astro 2 site set up for a recent space launch. With QuickTime movies, instruments to view the stars, flight log information, and other interesting tidbits from the flight, it is a fun site. There is no guarantee how long after the flight it will remain available; however, no doubt there will be new sites for new launches since 2,600,000 people from 59 countries visited in the 16 days of the flight. The URL you will need to connect is

`http://astro-2.msfc.nasa.gov`

You can see the initial screen from which to embark on your journey in Figure 19-9.

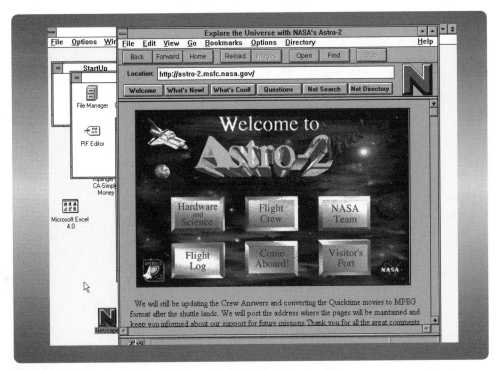

FIGURE 19-9. *Astro-2 from NASA initial screen*

Appendix

Beyond School

ONCE YOU FINISH WITH SCHOOL, your use of the Internet doesn't have to stop. Undoubtedly you will find many opportunities for tapping the resources of the Internet as you take your first job. If you don't have that first elusive offer for a job, you can even use the Internet to scour for opportunities. There are numerous newsgroups as well as head-hunting firms that will allow you to browse through their job listings, or even post a copy of your resume on the net. Although we did encounter a few that were fee-based, the majority operated with no cost at all for the job applicant and all fees were employer-paid. You find a few sites to get you started in the table that follows.

<u>Site</u>	<u>URL</u>
Business Job Finder	http://www.cob.ohio-state.edu/dept/fin/osujobs.htm
Career Related Newsgroups	http://www.teleport.com/~pcllgn/newsgrps.html
Career Taxi	http://www.iquest.net/Career_Taxi/taxi.html
Contract Employment Weekly	http://www.ceweekly.wa.com
Employment Edge	http://sensemedia.net/employment.edge
Get a Job	http://www.teleport.com/~pcllgn/gaj.html
Internet Employment Network	http://garnet.msen.com:70/1/vendor/napa
Jobs	http://www.drake.edu/stulife/caremp.html
Monster Board	http://www0.monster.com:81/home.html

Site	URL
Online Job Services	http://www.netline.com/Career/career.html
Papyrus International Employment Opportunities	http://www.britain.eu.net/~idea
TKP Personnel, Inc.— Jobs in Japan and Asia	http://www.internet-is.com/tko
Virtual Contractor	http://www.iquest.net/cw/VC/VC.html

Index